Discussions of

Shakespeare's Roman Plays

Discussions of
SHAKESPEARE'S
ROMAN PLAYS

Edited with an Introduction by
MAURICE CHARNEY
Rutgers University

D. C. HEATH AND COMPANY
BOSTON

CONTENTS

INTRODUCTION

Do Shakespeare's Roman plays form a distinct group like the "problem" plays, the English history plays, or the late romantic comedies? There are strong arguments against such an assumption; most obvious is the chronological one: *Julius Caesar* was written before the series of major tragedies, while *Antony and Cleopatra* and *Coriolanus* were written after. Nor is there a "Roman" style common to all three plays. In *Julius Caesar* Shakespeare does seem to be experimenting in a deliberately limited and simple style, best expressed in the analogy form of similes and a greatly restricted vocabulary. If he attempted there to create a "Roman" style, he did not continue the experiment in *Antony and Cleopatra* and *Coriolanus*. *Antony and Cleopatra* is elaborately metaphoric, its characteristic figure is the hyperbole, and its imaginative world is far from the disciplined perfection of *Julius Caesar*. The tight and objective public style of *Coriolanus*, with its emphasis on the dramatic function of imagery, represents a third possibility different from both *Antony and Cleopatra* and *Julius Caesar*. In the Roman plays, then, we have to deal with three distinctive styles.

On the other hand, it is clear that all three plays do convey a sense of Rome as an historical, geographical, and moral entity. We know that Shakespeare read carefully Sir Thomas North's version of Plutarch's *Lives of the Noble Grecians and Romans,* first published in 1579. Shakespeare's Roman plays all follow North's translation closely, if not literally in some places, and by sharing a common source these plays also share a common sense of the Roman world and Roman virtue. Other elements of unity are the fancy-dress Roman costume used in these plays and their special moral attitudes, particularly the favorable attitude toward suicide:

> By your leave, gods. This is a Roman's part.
> Come, Cassius' sword, and find Titinius' heart.
>   (*Julius Caesar* V, iii, 89–90)

The essay by T. J. B. Spencer argues strongly for the importance of Roman history in these plays and for the remarkably authentic picture of the ancient world that they convey. In *Coriolanus* Spencer sees one of the great feats of the historical imagination in Renaissance Europe. This essay should set us thinking about the Roman plays as history plays: how are they like or unlike Shakespeare's English history plays? And how shall we take account of the extent to which, as Spencer reminds us, our own image of ancient Rome has been formed by reading and seeing Shakespeare's Roman plays?

The selections on *Julius Caesar* all agree that this is not a simple play. The issues are so evenly balanced between the party of Caesar and the party of the conspirators that it is difficult to come to definite conclusions about the nature of guilt, evil, and tragic error in the play. If Antony is indeed the savior of Rome and the avenger of Caesar, we still do not have a very favorable view of him right after his oration when, in the proscription scene (IV, i), he is deciding whose heads will roll. On the other hand, the arguments of Cassius and Brutus about the supposed or potential tryranny of Caesar are sometimes petty, sometimes high-minded, and sometimes specious. We are not quite sure where our sympathies should lie, and this dramatic ambivalence helps to make Brutus an interesting tragic protagonist. He is afflicted with a tragic blindness that seals his doom, and his own excess of virtue is his undoing. In this sense he looks ahead to Hamlet—but not the brooding, meditative scholar so dear to Romantic critics, for both Brutus and Hamlet are full of the illusions and self-deceptions of men active in public life.

Julius Caesar may be the Roman play of which "discussion" is most inevitable. The remarks of Dowden on Caesar focus the political issues of the play with great skill. Caesar has become so institutionalized that he has put himself out of touch with reality: "The real man Caesar disappears for himself under the greatness of the Caesar myth." This is one of the seeds of the tragedy, but the conspirators on their side have been unwillingly caught up in the blood and guilt and butchery of their deeds. It is on this basis that both Wilson and Schanzer insist on the ironic complexity and detachment of the play, its impartial view of history. The stages in the development of the tragedy are vividly traced by Moulton, one of the most astute critics of the structure of a Shakespearean play.

Antony and Cleopatra has attracted at one and the same time confirmed misogynists and idolaters of the fair sex: Cleopatra's magic is either a perfect example of how a woman can annihilate a man against his better judgment—poor Antony!—or of how a woman can intensify and make transcendent the otherwise humdrum existence of a Roman general. Is it properly tragic to give "All for Love" and to think the

"World Well Lost" (as Dryden translated the title for his Restoration audience)? Or should one play it straight, open, sane, moral, and sober as Octavius Caesar and all winners do? Shakespeare obviously saw Cleopatra for what she was: a courtesan and a trull, deceitful and histrionic, and being past her prime, a woman who needed to put into play all the arts of allurement. The sexual attraction is there, and it is even a bit forced; yet there is something else, too, a splendor and energy and imaginative fulfillment of the possibilities of life. Otherwise, it would be pure blasphemy for the "holy priests," even those of the goddess Isis, to bless Cleopatra "when she is riggish." As Knights argues, there is a "moral realism" in the play that forces us to abandon any simple solutions and to accept Antony and Cleopatra as dramatic characters. They are certainly not under any illusions about themselves, and their acute self-awareness gives a sense of deliberateness and high sophistication to the tragedy.

All of the essays in this section owe a strong debt to Coleridge's extraordinary remarks on *Antony and Cleopatra.* He felt vividly the "happy valiancy" of its style, but he also felt the dramatic sense of boredom, of "voluntary stimulus and sought-for associations" in place of "spontaneous emotion." Some of his points about Cleopatra are translated into the demands of Elizabethan dramaturgy by Granville-Barker. In his Cleopatra one is conscious above all of the boy actor playing the part in the Globe Theater; one realizes why the torrid sexuality of the play has to be so much a matter of words. Both Traversi and Knights try to define more closely the double perspective of the play that Coleridge first pointed out. Is there always something self-deceiving and unreal in *Antony and Cleopatra,* as Knights says? Is the play somber in its realism and little comforting to the Romantic imagination? Or, as Traversi argues, does the poetic quality of the play "redeem" its rottenness and disintegration? One is led to the larger esthetic question: what is the relation between poetry and morality?

Despite T. S. Eliot's remark that *Coriolanus* is, with *Antony and Cleopatra,* "Shakespeare's most assured artistic success," the play has not attracted a great deal of interest in modern times and it is rarely performed. As a Shakespearean tragedy it lacks just those elements that seem to us most characteristic: self-awareness, inner torment and doubt, an agonizing process of recognition, and a calm and self-willed reconciliation with the forces of one's destiny. Coriolanus himself is the least inward of Shakespeare's tragic protagonists, he is literally isolated and uncomfortable in soliloquy, and he does not have the rich and pregnant consciousness of what he is doing and of what is happening to him. As A. C. Bradley has said, "If Lear's thunderstorm had beat upon his head, he would merely have set his teeth." But with all of these shortcomings—if they are indeed shortcomings—*Coriolanus* is a remarkable play. It has a dramatic economy, a conciseness and brilliance of speech and structure that are difficult to match anywhere else in Shakespeare. A central difficulty in the discussion of this play is to determine just where its merits lie: they are obviously neither in the protagonist as a tragic hero nor in the metaphoric texture of the verse. If we are to appreciate *Coriolanus*, we are forced to study it primarily as a dramatic work presented in a theater; we need to exercise what Francis Fergusson calls our "histrionic imagination."

Perhaps Dr. Johnson was right when he said that this play is "one of the most amusing of our author's performances." "Amusing" in what sense? One possibility is that *Coriolanus* is "amusing" because of its "very pleasing and interesting variety"; that is, it depicts a variety of persons and manners as in high comedy. Does this element detract from the tragedy? It is, for a tragedy, notably objective, public, and cere-monial in tone. Is the play a "magnificent failure," as Farnham calls it, because the paradox of the deeply flawed noble hero is pushed too far, and Coriolanus shows himself so monstrously deficient as a human being that he alienates our sympathy? Jorgensen makes allowances for Corio-lanus as "the noble soldier who fails as a citizen." His essay helps us to understand the unbridgeable gap between "the casque and the cushion," the military life and the life of civil society. Coriolanus' splendid virtues as a warrior work against him when he stands for consul; he is isolated, insolent, acridly insistent on his own worth, but his refusal to be "politic" is both a virtue and a defect. His harsh integrity is, in fact, his only attractive quality, but we know from the beginning, by the dictum from Aristotle's *Politics*, that he is doomed: "He that is incapable of living in a society is a god or a beast. . . ." Enright thinks that because Coriolanus cannot evoke the full measure of our tragic sympathy the play has the qualities of an intellectual debate rather than a tragedy. There is no true tragic conflict; each side understands the other, but neither under-stands itself. One may wonder whether it is fair for Enright to criticize *Coriolanus* for not being like *Macbeth*. Isn't the problem rather, by care-ful and sympathetic study, to find out just what sort of tragedy *Corio-lanus* is? Does it, like *Antony and Cleopatra*, look toward the objective and detached mood of the last plays?

All of the questions raised in this introduction—and many others too complex to be stated in a sentence or two—may be found in the essays that follow. Their chief merit as a group is that they coerce us or pro-voke us or sting us (like Socrates' gadfly) into discussion, and even if they do not accomplish the triumphant act of convincing us, they force us to read the plays again and to think about their meanings and dramatic effectiveness.

Notes and Suggestions for Further Reading

Of general books on Shakespeare's Roman plays, M. W. MacCallum's thorough study, *Shakespeare's Roman Plays and their Background* (1910), is still useful. G. Wilson Knight's *The Imperial Theme* (1931) is a stimulating if occasionally extravagant discussion of the symbolic structure of the Roman plays. A more recent book on these plays, *Shakespeare's Roman Plays: The Function of Imagery in the Drama* (1961) by Maurice Charney, puts special emphasis on their presentation in the Elizabethan theater.

Among other books with substantial sections devoted to the Roman plays, *The State in Shakespeare's Greek and Roman Plays* (1940), by James Emerson Phillips, Jr., has interesting comments on politics. John Palmer's *Political Characters of Shakespeare* (1945) contributes notably to this theme, as does Brents Stirling in his *The Populace in Shakespeare* (1949). Harley Granville-Barker has an essay on each of the Roman plays in his *Prefaces to Shakespeare* (1946–47). One of the best essays on the contemporary background of the Roman plays is by J. Leeds Barroll, "Shakespeare and Roman History," *Modern Language Review*, LIII (1958), 327–43.

Of older studies of *Julius Caesar*, one of the best is by W. Warde Fowler, "The Tragic Element in Shakespeare's *Julius Caesar*," collected in his *Roman Essays and Interpretations* (1920). Another solid and full study is Sir Mark Hunter's "Politics and Character in Shakespeare's 'Julius Caesar,' " in *Transactions of the Royal Society of Literature*, N. S., X (1931), 109–40. The student should also consult the suggestions in R. A. Foakes, "An Approach to *Julius Caesar*," *Shakespeare Quarterly*, V (1954), 259–70, and in Brents Stirling, *Unity in Shakespearian Tragedy* (1956), especially Chapter IV. Another essay by Ernest Schanzer, "The Problem of *Julius Caesar*," *Shakespeare Quarterly*, VI (1955), 297–308, completes the selection in the present volume.

Of the extensive literature on *Antony and Cleopatra*, only a few titles can be given here. The article by Benjamin T. Spencer, "*Antony and Cleopatra* and the Paradoxical Metaphor," *Shakespeare Quarterly*, IX (1958), 373–78, has a good analysis of the style of the play. The symbolic contrast of Egypt and Rome is developed in two essays: John F. Danby's "The Shakespearean Dialectic: An Aspect of 'Antony & Cleopatra,' " *Scrutiny*, XVI (1949), 196–213, and S. L. Bethell's *Shakespeare & The Popular Dramatic Tradition* (1944), pp. 116–31. More special studies are by F. R. Leavis, " 'Antony and Cleopatra' and 'All for Love' " (*Scrutiny*, V [1936], 158–69) and Elkin Calhoun Wilson, "Shakespeare's Enobarbus," (in *Joseph Quincy Adams Memorial Studies* [1948], pp. 391–408).

Coriolanus has not attracted a great deal of critical attention. A. C. Bradley's essay, "Coriolanus," in *Proceedings of the British Academy: 1911–12*, pp. 457–73, still has interest for the modern reader. Oscar James Campbell presents, in *Shakespeare's Satire* (1943), what seems an untenable theory about *Coriolanus* as a "tragical satire," but makes a number of acute observations on the tone of the play. Two special studies of details of imagery are worth consulting: Leonard F. Dean, "Voice and Deed in *Coriolanus*," *University of Kansas City Review*, XXI (1955), 177–84, and J. C. Maxwell, "Animal Imagery in 'Coriolanus,'" *Modern Language Review*, XLII (1947), 417–21.

Maurice Charney

notes on the

CONTRIBUTORS

Maurice Charney is Professor of English at Rutgers. He is the author of *Shakespeare's Roman Plays: The Function of Imagery in the Drama* (1961) and of various essays on Shakespeare and on American literature.

Samuel Taylor Coleridge (1772–1834), the poet, was also, in *Biographia Literaria* (1817), the *Lectures,* and other writings the originator of some of the most important concerns of modern criticism.

Edward Dowden (1843–1913), known as editor, critic, biographer, and poet, was Professor of English at Trinity College, Dublin. His critical studies include *Shakspere: A Critical Study of His Mind and Art* (1875) and *Shakspere: Scenes and Characters* (1876).

D. J. Enright, English poet and critic, is Professor of English at the University of Singapore. His wide-ranging interests are partially indicated by his *Commentary on Goethe's Faust* (1949) and *The World of Dew: Aspects of Living Japan* (1955).

Willard Farnham, Professor of English, Emeritus, at the University of California (Berkeley), is the author of *The Medieval Heritage of Elizabethan Tragedy* (1936) and *Shakespeare's Tragic Frontier: The World of His Final Tragedies* (1950).

Harley Granville-Barker (1877–1946) was playwright, actor, theatrical manager, and producer. He helped introduce the plays of Ibsen and Shaw to England, and the revolution he worked in Shakespearean productions is reflected in his *Prefaces to Shakespeare,* which began to appear in 1923.

Samuel Johnson (1709–1784) needs no introduction to students of English literature. His edition of Shakespeare (1765) with its long Preface was of great historical and critical importance.

Paul A. Jorgensen, Professor of English at the University of California (Los Angeles), is author of *Shakespeare's Military World* (1956) and *Redeeming Shakespeare's Words* (1962).

L. C. Knights, Professor of English at the University of Bristol, is one of the leading English critics. His publications include *Drama and Society in the Age of Jonson* (1937), *Some Shakespearean Themes* (1959), and *An Approach to Hamlet* (1960).

Richard G. Moulton (1849–1924) was Professor at the University of Chicago from 1892 until 1919. Among his most important books are *The Literary Study of the Bible* (1896) and *The Moral System of Shakespeare* (1903).

Ernest Schanzer, Lecturer at the University of Liverpool, is the author of *Shakespeare's Problem Plays* (1963) and editor of *Shakespeare's Appian* (1956).

T. J. B. Spencer, Professor at the University of Birmingham, is also Director of the Shakespeare Institute (Stratford-upon-Avon), Honorary Secretary of the Shakespeare Association, and General Editor of the *Modern Language Review*. Among his publications are *Fair Greece, Sad Relic: Literary Panhellenism from Shakespeare to Byron* (1954) and *The Tyranny of Shakespeare* (1959).

D. A. Traversi came to critical prominence as a contributor to *Scrutiny*. His publications include *An Approach to Shakespeare* (1938), *Shakespeare: The Last Phase* (1954), and *Shakespeare: The Roman Plays* (1963).

Harold S. Wilson (1904–1959) was Professor of English at the University of Toronto. His *On the Design of Shakespearian Tragedy* appeared in 1957.

Discussions of
Shakespeare's Roman Plays

T. J. B. SPENCER

Shakespeare and
the Elizabethan Romans[1]

SHAKESPEARE has, at various times, received some very handsome compliments for his ancient Romans; for his picture of the Roman world,
its institutions, and the causation of events; for his representation of the
Roman people at three critical stages of their development: the turbu-
lent republic with its conflict of the classes; the transition from an
oligarchic to a monarchic government which was vainly delayed by the
assassination of Julius Caesar; and the final stages by which the rule of
the civilized world came to lie in the hands of Octavius Caesar. These
are quite often praised as veracious or penetrating or plausible. Moreover, the compliments begin early, and they begin at a time when no
high opinion was held of Shakespeare's learning. The name of Nahum
Tate, for example, is not a revered one in the history of Shakespeare
studies; yet in 1680 he wrote:

> I confess I cou'd never yet get a true account of his Learning, and am
> apt to think it more than Common Report allows him. I am sure he never
> touches on a Roman Story, but the Persons, the Passages, the Manners, the
> Circumstances, the Ceremonies, all are Roman.[2]

And Dryden, too, in conversation said "that there was something in this
very tragedy of *Coriolanus,* as it was writ by Shakespeare, that is truly
great and truly Roman."[3] And Pope (for all his comparison of Shakespeare to "an ancient majestick piece of *Gothick* Architecture") declared
in his Preface that he found him

From *Shakespeare Survey 10,* 1957, pp. 27–38. Reprinted by permission of Cambridge
University Press and the author. Footnote 13 added by the author for this edition.
[1] A lecture delivered to the Shakespeare Conference at Stratford-upon-Avon, 6 September
1955.
[2] Letter before *The Loyal General, A Tragedy* (1680); *The Shakspere Allusion Book . . .
1591 to 1700* (Oxford, 1932), II, 266.
[3] Reported by Dennis; see D. Nichol Smith, *Eighteenth Century Essays on Shakespeare*
(Glasgow, 1903), p. 309.

very knowing in the customs, rites, and manners of Antiquity. In *Coriolanus* and *Julius Caesar*, not only the Spirit, but Manners, of the *Romans* are exactly drawn; and still a nicer distinction is shewn, between the manners of the *Romans* in the time of the former and of the latter.[4]

The odd thing is that this veracity or authenticity was approved at a time when Shakespeare's educational background was suspect; when the word "learning" practically meant a knowledge of the Greek and Roman writers; when the usual description of Shakespeare was "wild"; when he was regarded as a member of what Thomas Rymer called "the gang of the strolling fraternity."

There were, of course, one or two exceptions; Rymer wrote, towards the end of the seventeenth century, in his most cutting way about *Julius Caesar*:

> *Caesar* and *Brutus* were above his conversation. To put them in Fools Coats, and make them Jackpuddens in the *Shakespear* dress, is a *Sacriledge*. . . . The Truth is, this authors head was full of villainous, unnatural images, and history has only furnish'd him with great names, thereby to recommend them to the World.[5]

There was, too, the problem of Shakespeare's undignified Roman mobs. It was obvious that Cleopatra's vision of a Rome where

> mechanic slaves
> With greasy aprons, rules, and hammers, shall
> Uplift us to the view

was derived from Shakespeare's own London. And Casca's description: "The rabblement hooted and clapped their chopped hands and threw up their sweaty night-caps . . ."—this was the English populace and not the Roman *plebs*. Dennis thought that the introduction of the mob by Shakespeare "offends not only against the Dignity of Tragedy, but against the Truth of History likewise, and the Customs of Ancient *Rome*, and the majesty of the *Roman* People."[6] But the opinions of Rymer and Dennis were eccentric; the worst they could say against Shakespeare's Romans was that they were not sufficiently dignified; and this counted for very little beside the usual opinion of better minds that Shakespeare got his Romans right.

More surprising, therefore, was Shakespeare's frequent neglect of details; and it was just at *this* time that the scholars and critics (if not the theatrical and reading publics) were becoming sensitive to Shakespeare's anachronisms, his aberrations from good sense and common

4 D. Nichol Smith, *op. cit.* pp. 53, 62.
5 *A Short View of Tragedy* (1693), p. 148.
6 D. Nichol Smith, *op. cit.* p. 26.

knowledge about the ancients, and were carefully scrutinizing his text for mistakes. It was apparent that, when it came to details, Shakespeare's Romans often belonged to the time of Queen Elizabeth and King James. And the industrious commentators of the eighteenth century collected a formidable array of nonsense from his plays on classical antiquity: how clocks strike in ancient Rome; how Cleopatra has lace in her stays and plays at billiards; how Titus Lartius compares Coriolanus's *hm* to the sound of a battery; and so on. Above all, it could be observed that Shakespeare was occasionally careless or forgetful about ancient costume. Coriolanus stood in the Forum waving his hat. The very idea of a Roman candidate for the consulship standing waving his hat was enough to make a whole form of schoolboys break into irrepressible mirth. Pope softened the horror by emending *hat* to *cap;* and Coriolanus was permitted to wave his cap, not his hat, in the texts of Theobald, Hanmer, Warburton, and Dr Johnson, and perhaps even later. What seemed remarkable and what made the eighteenth-century editors so fussy about these anachronisms was Shakespeare's inconsistency in his historical reconstructions: his care and scrupulosity over preserving Roman manners, alongside occasional carelessness or indifference. The very reason they noticed the blunders was that they jarred against the pervading sense of authenticity everywhere else in the Roman plays.

I take it that Dryden and Pope were right; that Shakespeare knew what he was doing in writing Roman plays; that part of his intention was a serious effort at representing the Roman scene as genuinely as he could. He was not telling a fairy tale with Duke Theseus on St Valentine's Day, nor dramatizing a novelette about Kings of Sicilia and Bohemia, but producing a *mimesis* of the veritable history of the most important people (humanly speaking) who ever lived, the concern of every educated man in Europe and not merely something of local, national, patriotic interest; and he was conscious of all this while he was building up his dramatic situations and expositions of characters for the players to fulfil. It can, therefore, hardly fail to be relevant to our interpretations of the plays to explore the views of Roman history in Shakespeare's time. It is at least important to make sure that we do not unthinkingly take it for granted that they were the same as our own in the twentieth century to which we belong or the nineteenth century from which we derive. It is worth while tracing to what extent Shakespeare was in step with ideas about ancient Rome among his contemporaries and to what extent (and why) he diverged from them.

"Histories make men wise." Ancient, and in particular Roman, history was explored as the material of political lessons, because it was one of the few bodies of consistent and continuous historical material available. Modern national history (in spite of patriotism) could not be regarded as so central, nor were the writers so good; and the narratives in the scriptures were already overworked by the parson. Roman history was written and interpreted tendentiously in Europe in the sixteenth century, as has happened at other times. In writing his Roman plays Shakespeare was touching upon the gravest and most exciting as well as the most pedantic of Renaissance studies, of European scholarship. Although Shakespeare himself turned to Roman history after he had been occupied with English history for some years, nevertheless it was Roman history which usually had the primacy for the study of political morality. Yet in spite of the widespread interest in ancient culture among educated persons, the actual writing of the history of the Greeks and Romans was not very successful in England in the sixteenth century. There was no history of the Romans in Shakespeare's lifetime comparable (for example) to the *History of Great Britain* by John Speed or the *Generall Historie of the Turkes* by Richard Knolles. Sir Walter Raleigh did not get very far in his *History of the World* and dealt only with the earlier and duller centuries of Rome. Probably the reason for the scarcity of books of Roman history and their undistinguished nature was that the sense of the supremacy of the ancients and of the impudence of endeavouring to provide a substitute for Livy and Tacitus, was too strong.[7] So explained William Fulbecke, who published a book called *An Historicall Collection of the Continuall Factions, Tumults, and Massacres of the Romans* in 1601 and dedicated it to Sackville, Lord Buckhurst (the primary author of *A Mirror for Magistrates*). "I do not despaire" (wrote Fulbecke) "to follow these Romanes, though I do not aspire to their exquisite and industrious perfection: for that were to climbe above the climates: but to imitate any man, is every mans talent." His book is a poor thing. And so is Richard Reynoldes' *Chronicle of all the Noble Emperours of the Romaines* (1571). And the translations of the Roman historians, apart from North's Plutarch, before the seventeenth century are not particularly distinguished. But for this very reason the books on Roman history are useful evidence for the normal attitude to the Romans and their story in Shakespeare's lifetime. For it is not so much what we can find in Plutarch, but what Shakespeare noticed in Plutarch that we need to know; not merely Plutarch's narrative, but the preconceptions with which his biographies could be read by a lively modern mind about the turn of the seventeenth century; for

---

[7] Cf. A. Momigliano, *Contributo alla storia degli studi classici* (Rome, 1955), pp. 75–6: "To the best of my knowledge, the idea that one could write a history of Rome which should replace Livy and Tacitus was not yet born in the early seventeenth century. The first Camden Praelector of history in the University of Oxford had the statutory duty of commenting on Florus and other ancient historians (1622). . . . Both in Oxford and Cambridge Ancient History was taught in the form of a commentary on ancient historians."

> men may construe things after their fashion
> Clean from the purpose of the things themselves.

It is by no means certain that we, by the unaided light of reason and mid-twentieth-century assumptions, will always be able to notice the things to which Shakespeare was sensitive.

First then, the title of William Fulbecke's book is worth attention: *An Historicall Collection of the Continuall Factions, Tumults, and Massacres of the Romans and Italians during the space of one hundred and twentie yeares next before the peaceable Empire of Augustus Caesar.* There is not much of the majesty of the Roman People (which Dennis desiderated) in these continual factions, tumults and massacres. In his preface Fulbecke writes:

> The use of this historie is threefold; first the revealing of the mischiefes of discord and civill discention. . . . Secondly the opening of the cause hereof, which is nothing else but ambition, for out of this seed groweth a whole harvest of evils. Thirdly the declaring of the remedie, which is by humble estimation of our selves, by living well, not by lurking well: by conversing in the light of the common weale with equals, not by complotting in darke conventicles against superiors.[8]

Equally tendentious is what we read on the title-page of the translation of Appian as *An Auncient Historie and exquisite Chronicle of the Romanes Warres, both Civile and Foren* in 1578;

> In the which is declared:
> Their greedy desire to conquere others.
> Their mortall malice to destroy themselves.
> Their seeking of matters to make warre abroade.
> Their picking of quarels to fall out at home.
> All the degrees of Sedition, and all the effects of Ambition.
> A firme determination of Fate, thorowe all the changes of Fortune.
> And finally, an evident demonstration, That peoples rule must give
>   place, and Princes power prevayle.

This kind of material (the ordinary stuff of Roman history in the sixteenth century) does not lend itself to chatter about the majesty of the Roman people. In fact, the kind of classical dignity which we associate perhaps with Addison's *Cato* or Kemble's impersonation of Coriolanus is not to be taken for granted in Shakespeare's time. The beginning of Virgil's *Aeneid,* with its simple yet sonorous *arma virumque cano,* might by us be taken as expressive of true Roman dignity. Richard Stanyhurst, however, in his translation of Virgil in 1582 rendered it:

> Now manhood and garboyles I chaunt. . . .

[8] Sig. A 2.

"Garboyles," it will be remembered, was Antony's favourite word to describe the military and political exploits of Fulvia.

So much for Roman history as "garboyles." Secondly, besides the "garboyles" and encouraging them, there was a limitation in viewpoint due to the fact that the moral purpose of history in general, and of Roman history in particular, was directed towards *monarchs*. When Richard Reynoldes published his *Chronicle of all the noble Emperours of the Romaines, from Julius Caesar orderly. . . . Setting forth the great power, and devine providence of almighty God, in preserving the godly Princes and common wealthes* in 1571, he gave the usual panegyric: "An historie is the glasse of Princes, the image most lively bothe of vertue and vice, the learned theatre or spectacle of all the worlde, the councell house of Princes, the trier of all truthes, a witnes of all tymes and ages . . ." and so forth. The really important and interesting and relevant political lessons were those connected with *princes*. It was this that turned the attention away from republican Rome to monarchical Rome: the Rome of the Twelve Caesars and their successors. Republican Rome was not nearly so useful for models of political morality, because in sixteenth-century Europe republics happened to be rather rare. (Venice, the important one, was peculiar, not to say unique, anyway.) Republics were scarce. But there were aspiring Roman Emperors all over the place.

Sometimes the political lesson was a very simple one. In dedicating his *Auncient Historie and exquisite Chronicle of the Romanes Warres* in 1578, the translator states:

> How God plagueth them that conspire againste theyr Prince, this Historie declareth at the full. For all of them, that coniured against *Caius Caesar*, not one did escape violent death. The which this Author hathe a pleasure to declare, bycause he would affray all men from disloyaltie toward their Soveraigne.

We need not, perhaps, put too much emphasis upon this argument, because the book was being dedicated to the Captain of the Queen's Majesty's Guard. But more sophisticated writers showed the same interest. Sir Walter Raleigh in his *History of the World* on occasions pointed the suitable political moral. But the problems that interested him and set him off on one of his discussions were those relevant to the political situation in the sixteenth and early seventeenth centuries. The story of Coriolanus, for example, does not interest him at all; he compresses Livy's fine narrative into nothingness, though he spares a few words for Coriolanus's mother and wife who prevailed upon him "with a pitiful tune of deprecation."[9] But the problem of the growth of tyr-

[9] *The History of the World*, iv, vii,§i; *Works* (Oxford, 1832), v, 531–2.

anny fascinates him. He never got as far as Julius Caesar. He had to wind up his *History* at the beginning of the second century B.C. But he gets Caesar into his discussion. The problem of the difference between a benevolent monarchy and an odious tyranny, and the gradations by which the one may merge into the other—that was the real interest; and Imperial Rome was the true material for that.

So that, in spite of literary admiration for Cicero, the Romans in the imagination of the sixteenth century were Suetonian and Tacitan rather than Plutarchan. An occasional eccentric enthusiasm for one or both of the two Brutuses does not weigh against the fact that it was the busts of the Twelve Caesars that decorated almost every palace in Europe. And it required a considerable intellectual feat to substitute the Plutarchan vision of Rome (mostly republican) for the customary line of the Imperial Caesars. Montaigne and Shakespeare were capable of that feat. Not many others were. The Roman stuff that got into *A Mirror for Magistrates* naturally came from Suetonius and historians of the later Caesars. One of the educators of Europe in the sixteenth century was the Spaniard Antonio de Guevara. His *Dial of Princes* (which was a substitute for the still unprinted *Meditations* of the Emperor Marcus Aurelius) was translated by North with as much enthusiasm as Plutarch was. Guevara, whose platitudinous remarks on politics and morals—he was a worthy master for Polonius—gave him a European reputation, naturally turned to Imperial Rome to illustrate his maxims and observations on life. The Emperor Marcus Aurelius was his model of virtue (though he included love-letters from the Emperor to a variety of young women in Rome—which seems rather an incongruous thing to do for the over-virtuous author of the *Meditations*); and when Guevara wanted examples of vices as well as virtue, to give more varied moral and political lessons, he again naturally turned to the Roman monarchs. His *Decada*, in fact, gives lives from Trajan onwards. Among them appears a blood-curdling life of a certain Emperor Bassianus, a name which we shall not remember from our reading of Gibbon, but one with which we are thoroughly familiar from *Titus Andronicus*. This account of Bassianus is a shocking thing, translated with considerable energy into English in 1577 by Edward Hellowes in *A Chronicle, conteyning the lives of tenne Emperours of Rome* and dedicated to the Queen. The life of Bassianus (whom we know by his nickname of Caracalla—but Renaissance writers had too much respect for Roman Emperors to use only their vulgar nicknames) is one of almost unparalleled cruelty: how he slew his brother in the arms of his mother; how he slew half the Vestal Virgins because (so he said) they were not virgins, and then slew the other half because (so he said) they were. I will not say that it is a positive relief to pass from the life of Bassianus by Guevara to Shakespeare's

Titus Andronicus (and there to find, by the way, that Bassianus is the better of the two brothers). Still, we feel that we are in the same world. *Titus Andronicus* is Senecan, yes; and it belongs to what Mr Shandy would call "no year of our Lord"; and its *sources* probably belong to medieval legend. Yet, as made into the play we know, it is also a not untypical piece of Roman history, or would seem to be so to anyone who came fresh from reading Guevara. Not the most high and palmy state of Rome, certainly. But an authentic Rome, and a Rome from which the usual political lessons could be drawn. *Titus* was entered in the Stationers' Register in 1594 as "a Noble Roman Historye," and it was published the same year as a "Most Lamentable Romaine Tragedie," and by sixteenth-century standards the claim was justified. One could say almost without paradox that, in many respects, *Titus Andronicus* is a more typical Roman play, a more characteristic piece of Roman history, than the three great plays of Shakespeare which are generally grouped under that name. The Elizabethans had far less of a low opinion of the Low Empire than we have learned to have. In fact, many of the qualities of Romanity are in *Titus*. The garboils; the stoical or Senecal endurance; the many historical properties: senators and tribunes and patricians. It was obviously *intended* to be a faithful picture of Roman civilization. Indeed, the political institutions in *Titus* are a subject that has been rather neglected.[10] They are certainly peculiar, and cannot be placed at any known period in Roman history, as can those in *Coriolanus* or *Julius Caesar;* and they afford a strange contrast with the care and authenticity of those later plays. In *Titus Andronicus* Rome seems to be, at times, a free commonwealth, with the usual mixture of patrician and plebeian institutions. Titus is himself elected emperor of Rome on account of his merits, because the senate and people do not recognize an hereditary principle of succession. But Titus disclaims the honour in favour of the late Emperor's elder (and worser) son. Titus is a devoted adherent (not to say a maniacal one) of the hereditary monarchical principle in a commonwealth that only partly takes it into account, and he eventually acknowledges his mistake. He encourages, by his subservience, the despotic rule on which Saturninus embarks, passing to a world of Byzantine intrigue, in which the barbarians (Southern and Northern, Moors and Goths), both by personalities and armies, exert their baneful or beneficent influence. And finally, by popular acclaim, Lucius is elected emperor "to order well the state" (says the second Quarto). Now, all these elements of the political situation can be found in Roman history, but not combined in this way. The play does not assume a political situation known to Roman history; it is, rather, a summary of

[10] William Watkiss Lloyd in 1856 made some pertinent remarks (*Critical Essays on the Plays of Shakespeare* [1894], p. 352).

Roman politics. It is not so much that any particular set of political institutions is assumed in *Titus,* but rather that it includes *all* the political institutions that Rome ever had. The author seems anxious, not to get it all right, but to get it all in. It has been suggested that *Titus Andronicus* was the work of a fairly well-informed scholar. It seems to be a quintessence of impressions derived from an eager reading of Roman history rather than a real effort at verisimilitude. Still, I think that *Titus* would easily be recognized as typical Roman history by a sixteenth-century audience; the claim that it was a "noble Roman history" was a just one.

Bearing this in mind, one can see why Plutarch was no rival to Suetonius (and his imitators and followers) as a source of impressions of the Romans. Suetonius's rag-bag of gossip, scandal, piquant and spicy *personalia,* provided the material for a large proportion of the plays written on Roman themes, including a number of University plays. Indeed the estimate of the popularity of Plutarch in the sixteenth century seems to have been rather exaggerated—at least, the popularity of Plutarch's *Lives.* It was Plutarch's *Moralia* which were most admired, and most influential, those essays on such subjects as "Tranquillity of Mind," and "Whether Virtue can be Taught," and so forth, which constantly provided exercises for translations, including one by the Queen herself. These things came home to men's business and bosoms far more than the parallel lives of the Greeks and Romans, and were admired for much the same reason as Dr Johnson's *Ramblers* and Martin Tupper's *Proverbial Philosophy:* they perfectly hit the moral preoccupations of the time; and were the model for Montaigne, and thence for Bacon. It was really the eighteenth century that was the great age of Plutarch's *Lives,* when there were two complete new translations, many partial ones, and frequent convenient reprints. In Shakespeare's time the *Lives* were confined to large and cumbrous folios. We, when we want to study the relation between Shakespeare's Roman plays and Plutarch's lives, can turn to those handy selections prepared for the purpose by Skeat or Tucker Brooke or Carr. Or, if we are prompted by curiosity or conscience to set about reading the whole thing, we can turn to the manageable volumes of the Tudor Translations or to the handy little pocket volumes of the Temple Classics. But Shakespeare, when he read Plutarch, could not turn to a volume of selections illustrating Shakespeare's Roman plays. He had to take a very heavy folio in his hands. We have to read 1010 folio pages in the 1579 edition before we come to the death of Cleopatra. (It need not be suggested that Shakespeare read 1010 folio pages before *he* came to the death of Cleopatra.) It is certainly not a literary experience comparable with picking up a novelette like *Pandosto* or *Rosalynde,* or reading a little book about the Continual Factions,

Tumults and Massacres of the Romans. It was rather a serious thing for a busy man of the theatre to do. It was probably the most serious experience that Shakespeare had of the bookish kind.

In Shakespeare's three principal Roman plays we see a steadily advancing independence of thought in the reconsideration of the Roman world. In *Julius Caesar,* it seems to me, he is almost precisely in step with sound Renaissance opinion on the subject. There has been a good deal of discussion of this play because of a supposed ambiguity in the author's attitude to the two principal characters. It has been suggested, on the one hand, that Brutus is intended to be a short-sighted political blunderer who foolishly or even wickedly struck down the foremost man in all the world; Dante and survivals of medieval opinion in the sixteenth century can be quoted here. We have, on the contrary, been told, on very high authority in Shakespeare studies, that Shakespeare followed the Renaissance admiration for Brutus and detestation for Caesar. It has also been suggested that Shakespeare left the exact degrees of guilt and merit in Caesar and Brutus deliberately ambiguous in the play, to give a sense of depth, to keep the audience guessing and so make the whole dramatic situation more telling. But all this, it seems to me, obscures the fact that the reassessment and reconsideration of such famous historical figures was a common literary activity in the Renaissance, not merely in poetry and drama (where licence is acceptable), but in plain prose, the writing of history. It seems hardly legitimate to talk about "tradition," to refer to "traditional" opinions about Caesar and Brutus, when in fact the characters of each of them had been the subject of constant discussion. In the nineteenth century you could weigh up the varying views of Caesar held by Mommsen or Froude or Anthony Trollope or Napoleon III of France, and read their entertaining books on the subject. It was not so very different in the sixteenth century. I am not suggesting that Shakespeare read the great works on the life and character of Julius Caesar by Hubert Goltz (1563) or by Stefano Schiappalaria (1578) where everything about him was collected and collated and assessed and criticized. But other people did. And Shakespeare, writing a play of the subject, could hardly live in such intellectual isolation as to be unaware of the discussion. It would, I think, be quite wrong to suggest by quotation from any one writer such as Montaigne that Caesar was generally agreed to be a detestable character. On the contrary, the problem was acknowledged to be a complicated and fascinating one; and the discussion began early, and in ancient times. Men have often disputed (wrote Seneca in his *De Beneficiis,* a work translated both by Arthur Golding and by Thomas Lodge), whether Brutus did right or wrong. "For mine owne part, although I esteemed *Brutus* in all other thinges a wise and vertuous man, yet meseemeth that in this he committed a great errour"; and Seneca goes on to explain the error: Brutus

> imagined that such a Citie as this might repossesse her ancient honour, and former lustre, when vertue and the primitive Lawes were either abolished, or wholly extinguished; Or that Iustice, Right, and Law, should be inviolably observed in such a place, where he had seene so many thousand men at shocke and battell, not to the intent to discerne whether they were to obay and serve, but to resolve under whom they ought to serve and obay. Oh how great oblivion possessed this man! how much forgot he both the nature of affaires, and the state of his Citie! to suppose that by the death of one man there should not some other start up after him, that would usurpe over the common-weale.[11]

Likewise William Fulbecke (writing in 1586, though his book was not published until 1601), while seeing the calamities Caesar was bringing upon the Roman state, could not praise Brutus for permitting himself to participate in political assassinations:

> M. Brutus, the chiefe actor in Caesars tragedie, was in counsel deepe, in wit profound, in plot politicke, and one that hated the principality whereof he devested Caesar. But did Brutus looke for peace by bloudshed? did he thinke to avoyd tyrannie by tumult? was there no way to wound Caesar, but by stabbing his own conscience? & no way to make Caesar odious, but by incurring the same obloquie?[12]

Fulbecke summarized his position in the controversy: "Questionlesse the Romanes should not have nourished this lyon in their Citie, or being nourished, they should not have disgraced him."

In writing *Julius Caesar* and *Antony and Cleopatra* Shakespeare was keeping within a safe body of story. Those persons had been dignified by tragedies in many countries of Europe and many times before Shakespeare arose and drove all competitors from the field. But with *Coriolanus* it was different. There was apparently no previous play on the subject.[13] It was more of a deliberate literary and artistic choice than either of the other two Roman plays. He must have discovered Coriolanus in Plutarch. As for Caesar and Cleopatra, he presumably went to Plutarch knowing that they were good subjects for plays. But no one had directed him to Coriolanus. The story was hardly well known and not particularly attractive. The story of the ingratitude he suffered, the revenge he purposed and renounced, was told by Livy, and, along with one or two other stories of Roman womenfolk (Lucretia, Virginia), it was turned into a *novella* in Painter's *Pallace of Pleasure;* there is a mention in *Titus Andronicus.* More than *Julius Caesar* or than *Antony and Cleopatra, Coriolanus* (perhaps by the rivalry or stimulation of Ben

---

[11] Lodge's translation in *The Workes of Lucius Annaeus Seneca, Both Morall and Naturall* (1614), pp. 30–1; *Of Benefits,* II, xx.
[12] *Op. cit.* sig. Z I^v.
[13] Except a German one in Latin: *Coriolanus* by Hermann Kirchner (Marburg, 1599).

Jonson) shows a great deal of care to get things right, to preserve Roman manners and customs and allusions. We have, of course, the usual Roman officials, and political and religious customs familiarly referred to; and we have the Roman mythology and pantheon. But we are also given a good deal of Roman history worked into the background. Even the eighteenth-century editors who took a toothcomb through the play for mistaken references to English customs could find very little; and it requires considerable pedantry to check these. Moreover, in *Coriolanus* there is some effort to make literary allusions appropriate. The ladies know their Homer and the Tale of Troy. The personal names used are all authentically derived from somewhere in Plutarch; Shakespeare has turned the pages to find something suitable. He is taking great care. He is on his mettle. Dozens of poetasters could write plays on Julius Caesar or on Cleopatra. Dozens did. But to write *Coriolanus* was one of the great feats of the historical imagination in Renaissance Europe.

Setting aside poetical and theatrical considerations, and merely referring to the artist's ability to "create a world" (as the saying is), we may ask if there was anything in prose or verse, in Elizabethan or Jacobean literature, which bears the same marks of careful and thoughtful consideration of the ancient world, a deliberate effort of a critical intelligence to give a consistent picture of it, as there is in Shakespeare's plays. Of course, Ben Jonson's *Catiline* and *Sejanus* at once suggest themselves. The comparison between Shakespeare's and Ben Jonson's Roman plays is a chronic one, an inevitable one, and it is nearly always, I suppose, made to Jonson's disadvantage. At least it had its origin in their own time; for Leonard Digges tells us, in his verses before the 1640 *Poems,* that audiences were ravished by such scenes as the quarrel between Brutus and Cassius, when they would not brook a line of tedious (though well-laboured) *Catiline.* Of course, Ben Jonson's two plays are superior to any other Roman plays of the period outside Shakespeare (those of Lodge, Chapman, Massinger, Marston, or Webster, or the several interesting anonymous ones). But when Ben Jonson's are compared with Shakespeare's, as they cruelly must, their defect is a lack not so much of art as of sophistication. There is a certain naïvety about Ben Jonson's understanding of Roman history. Of course, in a way, there is more obvious learning about *Catiline* and *Sejanus* than about Shakespeare's Roman plays. There must have been a great deal of notebook work, a great deal of mosaic work. It is possible to sit in the British Museum with the texts of the classical writers which Jonson used around you and watch him making his play as you follow up his references (not all, I think, at first hand). But the defect of Jonson's *Sejanus* is lack of homogeneity of style and material. Jonson mixes the gossip of Suetonius with the gloomily penetrating and disillusioned comments on men and their motives by Tacitus. It is the old story; "who reads incessantly and to his reading brings not a spirit and judgment equal or superior" is liable to lose the advantages of his reading. After all, it doesn't require very much effort to *seem* learned. What is so difficult to acquire is the judgment in dealing with the material in which one is learned. This is not something that can in any way be tested by collecting misspellings of classical proper names in an author whose works have been unfairly printed from his foul papers and prompt-book copies. Shakespeare brought a judgment equal or superior to whatever ancient authors he read however he read them. Ben Jonson did not; his dogged and determined scholarship was not ripe enough; he had the books but not always the spirit with which to read them. There are occasions when we can legitimately place parts of their plays side by side. Consider the portents which accompanied the death of Julius Caesar, something which obviously interested Shakespeare very much. His description of them in *Hamlet* is unforgettable. His introduction of them in *Julius Caesar* is beautifully done. Some of the excitable Romans are prepared to believe any yarn about lions and supernatural fires and so forth. The amiable and unperturbed Cicero asks Casca:

> Why are you breathless? and why stare you so?

And he answers Casca's fustian about "a tempest dropping fire" with mild scepticism:

> Why, saw you any thing more wonderful?

His response to the contagious panic which Casca has acquired from

> a hundred ghastly women,
> Transformed with their fear; who swore they saw
> Men all in fire walk up and down the streets,

is to be quite unimpressed by anything that a lot of hysterical old women *swore they saw;* and he then leaves, with the remark that the weather is too bad for a walk that evening:

> Good night then, Casca: this disturbed sky
> Is not to walk in.

Compare this with the account of the portents that accompany the conspirators' oath and the blood-drinking in *Catiline*. (Jonson got little of it from the excellent Sallust but from an inferior source.) It is given no connexion with the varying emotions of the observers, there is no sceptical note: it merely seems to be there because "mine author hath it so." Indeed there is something medieval about it, and about Jonson's treatment of his characters in *Catiline*. He takes sides emphatically. He does what some critics would like Shakespeare to do in *Julius Caesar;* that is to tell us plainly which is the good man and which is the bad

man. There is a sort of pre-Renaissance naïvety about Jonson's setting
up Catiline as an example of unmitigated villany and Cicero as an example of unmitigated virtue. It is comparable with what you find in
Chaucer or in Lydgate about the slaying of the glorious and victorious
Julius Caesar by that wicked Judas-like figure called Brutus Cassius with
bodkins hid in his sleeve. There is a sense of unreality about it, a recurring feeling that Ben Jonson doesn't really know what he is talking
about—the feeling of hollowness you get when Jonson starts praising
Shakespeare by shouting

> Call forth thund'ring *Æschilus,*
> *Euripides,* and *Sophocles* to us,
> *Pacuvius, Accius,* him of *Cordova* dead,
> To life againe, to heare thy Buskin tread,
> And shake a Stage. . . .

Is this the writing of a well-informed person? We can stand for Seneca,
of course. But it is hard to include the Greek tragedians, too little known
and too little available to make the comparison intelligent; and as for
Accius and Pacuvius, there could be few criticisms more pointless than
to ask anybody to call forth their meagre fragments, those ghostly
writers, mere names in biographical dictionaries. Perhaps it is only Ben
Jonson's fun. I would like to think so. But I doubt it. I fear he wants
to be impressive. Like a medieval poet, he has licence to mention the
names of great authors without their books.

There may very well be, in Shakespeare's writings, a good many ves-
tiges of the medieval world-picture. His mind may have been encum-
bered, or steadied, by several objects, orts, and relics of an earlier kind
of intellectual culture. But it is scarcely perceptible in his Roman plays,
which can be brought to the judgment bar of the Renaissance revivifi-
cation of the ancient world, and will stand the comparison with the
major achievements of Renaissance Humanism (as Ben Jonson's will
not). We find there a writer who seems in the intellectual current of
his times. Shakespeare had what might be described as the scholarship
of the educated creative writer—the ability to go and find out the best
that is known and thought in his day; to get it quickly (as a busy writer
must, for Shakespeare wrote more than a million words in twenty years);
to get it without much trouble and without constant access to good col-
lections of books (as a busy man of the theatre must, one often on tour
and keeping up two homes); and to deal with his sources of information with intelligence and discrimination. The favourite notions of learning get around in ways past tracing. Anyone who is writing a play or a
book on any subject has by that very fact a peculiar alertness and sensitivity to information and attitudes about his subject. Shakespeare did
not write in isolation. He had friends. It would be an improbable

hypothesis that he worked cut off from the intellectual life of his times. Indeed, all investigations of the content of his plays prove the obvious: that he was peculiarly sensitive to the intellectual tendencies of his age, in all spheres of thought. His scholarship was of a better quality than Jonson's, because (one might guess) he was a better listener, not so self-assertive in the company of his betters, and was therefore more able, with that incomparable celerity of mind of his, to profit from any well-informed acquaintance.

Finally, in understanding the picture of the ancient world in these plays, the part played by Shakespeare himself in creating our notions of the ancient Romans should not be forgotten. It has become difficult to see the plays straight, to see the thing in itself as it really is, because we are all in the power of Shakespeare's imagination, a power which has been exercised for several generations and from which it is scarcely possible to extricate ourselves. It is well known, I believe, that Shakespeare practically created the fairies; he was responsible for having impressed them on the imagination, the dainty, delightful, beneficent beings which have become part of the popular mythology. To suggest that Shakespeare also practically created the ancient Romans might be regarded as irresponsible. Still, the effect that Shakespeare has had on the way the Romans exist in our imaginations is something that might well be explored. We have had in England no great historian of Rome to impose his vision of the Roman world upon readers. Gibbon begins too late; and the English historians of Rome who wrote in the sixteenth, seventeenth and eighteenth centuries are mediocre and practically un-read. We have had, on the one hand, no Mommsen; on the other, we have had no Racine, no Poussin, no David, no Napoleon. But since the early nineteenth century generations of schoolboys have been trained on *Julius Caesar* and *Coriolanus*. When English gradually penetrated into the schools as a reputable subject, it was in the sheep's clothing of Shakespeare's Roman plays that it entered the well-guarded fold; and so gave the *coup de grâce* to classical education in England. It can hardly be doubted that Shakespeare's *Julius Caesar* has had more effect than Caesar's own *Commentaries* in creating our impressions of his person-ality. Indeed, Shakespeare has had no serious rival on the subject of Ancient Rome. Neither *All for Love* nor *Cato* has stood the test of time and changing tastes. Neither the importation of *Ben Hur* from America nor the importation of *Quo Vadis* from Poland has affected Shakespeare's domination over the imagination. Besides, they belong to the wrong period. Novel writers have generally turned to the age of the Twelve Caesars, rather than to the Republic, for precisely the same reasons as did Shakespeare's contemporary playwrights; it is so much more lurid; there are so many more "garboyles." The spirit of Suetonius lives on. Shakespeare, perhaps, chose with a better instinct or with surer taste.

MAURICE CHARNEY

Style in the Roman Plays

ALTHOUGH the Roman plays have some strong similarities as a group—their use of "Roman" costume, their favorable Roman idea of suicide, their common source in Plutarch—they are stylistically quite different. The strongest contrast is between the styles of *Julius Caesar* and *Antony and Cleopatra*, which I should like to consider before going on to discuss *Coriolanus*. Actually, the Roman world in *Antony and Cleopatra* is very much like that in *Julius Caesar*, but it is "overreached" by the world of Empire and the splendors and perils of Egypt. Antony abandons the Roman style and values of Octavius Caesar—they are public, political, and objective as in *Julius Caesar*—and enters into the Egyptian style and values of Cleopatra. These two plays show the working of Shakespeare's imagination in two different moods: in *Julius Caesar* he seems to be deliberately limiting his imaginative resources, while in *Antony and Cleopatra* he appears to be trying to extend them "past the size of dreaming."

Perhaps the most characteristic example of Shakespeare's dramatic style in *Julius Caesar* is the quarrel scene (IV,iii). The verbal imagery here is fragmentary and undeveloped, while there is a brilliant presentational imagery of familiar objects and the rituals of daily life. The scene penetrates into the personal, domestic, and unheroic world of Brutus, and its disciplined use of limited means represents the "Roman" style of the play at its best.

The quarrel between Brutus and Cassius brings us closer than we have ever come to Brutus in his ordinary life. Only once before, in the scene in Brutus' "orchard" (II, i), have we seen the tragic protagonist so personally, but this was no more than a troubled glimpse. In essence, the quarrel between Brutus and Cassius is a completely external affair:

Reprinted by permission of the publishers from Maurice Charney, *Shakespeare's Roman Plays: The Function of Imagery in the Drama*, Cambridge, Mass.: Harvard University Press, Copyright, 1961, by The President and Fellows of Harvard College. Footnotes 3, 4, 8, 14, 21, 23, 28, 32, 33 omitted from original edition.

an elaborate mixture of petulant accusation and lengthy self-justification. It abates with a confession of weakness and then a handshake (4.3.117), a visual sign of reconciliation (compare *Coriolanus* 5.3.182 s.d.).

We pass into a new mood when Brutus orders Lucius to bring a bowl of wine. It is a meditative mood with a strong note of sorrow, as Brutus reveals the secret he has kept hidden:

> *Cass.* I did not think you could have been so angry.
> *Bru.* O Cassius, I am sick of many griefs.
> *Cass.* Of your philosophy you make no use
> If you give place to accidental evils.
> *Bru.* No man bears sorrow better. Portia is dead.
> *Cass.* Ha! Portia?
> *Bru.* She is dead.   (4.3.143–49)

The revelation comes forcefully and unexpectedly: the soft music of "No man bears sorrow better" is suspended in a pause on the "r" of "better"—then the absolutely clear-cut fact: "Portia is dead." The last two lines are an echo of this rhythm, as Cassius questions and Brutus reiterates. At this point Brutus' boy, Lucius, enters "with wine and tapers" (4.3.157 s.d.), and the revelation is solemnized by the drinking of wine. This is another stage ritual for reconciliation, and it recalls II,ii, where Caesar invites the conspirators to "go in and taste some wine with me . . ." (2.2.126).

As Cassius, Titinius, and Messala are about to leave, Brutus calls for his dressing gown, which he presumably puts on after the others have gone (he is wearing it at 4.3.253). The investiture with the gown begins the scene proper of Caesar's Ghost, and it is filled with a remarkable compassion. In the acting of this scene, Brutus might remove some part of his military dress before he puts on the gown to indicate a change in role: he is no longer the Roman general and conspirator, but only a private citizen, troubled in mind and weary in body and about to go to sleep. The putting on of the gown would signify this transformation (compare the disarming of Antony in *Antony and Cleopatra*). Brutus now appears in his personal and domestic role, like Caesar in his "nightgown" (or dressing gown) at the opening of II,ii.[1]

After the intense and exhausting emotion of the quarrel with Cassius, Brutus' mind turns naturally from abstract logic to the common concerns of life. He will not have Varro and Claudius "stand" watch in his tent, but provides them with cushions so that they may sleep. When Lucius dozes off while playing, Brutus carefully takes away his instrument lest

[1] When Caesar goes to the Capitol, however, he changes from gown to robe (2.2.107) to indicate his public role in visual terms. See L. C. Knights, "Shakespeare and Political Wisdom: A Note on the Personalism of *Julius Caesar* and *Coriolanus*," *Sewanee Review*, LXI (1953), 44 and n. 1.

he break it. The boy falls asleep easily and involuntarily, while the care-worn Brutus must go through a long and elaborate ritual to woo sleep (compare *Henry V* 4.1.274–301). He finds a book he has been looking for in the pocket of his gown, and when he finally settles himself he opens it to the page with the "leaf turn'd down/ Where I left reading" (4.3.273–74). All this wealth of detail—the gown, the cushions for the guards, the boy's falling asleep and his instrument taken away, the book with the dog-eared page found in the pocket of the gown—enters the consciousness of Brutus in a sudden Proustian abundance and prepares his mind for the entrance of the Ghost. In symbolic terms the Ghost of Caesar seems to "explode" into this intensely human scene. By a series of images of daily human concern, the inner consciousness of Brutus has been revealed to us, and we are not surprised to find that the spirit of the murdered Caesar has been brooding there since the quarrel with Cassius (see 4.3.19ff, 58ff, 105ff). The figure of the Ghost on stage is the external embodiment of Brutus' conscience and guilt, and the creation of a psychological atmosphere has served to identify the ghost within and the ghost without. By doing so, Shakespeare has endowed the fairly crude stage convention of the ghost with dramatic and psychological overtones, a development he will pursue further in *Hamlet*.

This scene illustrates at their best certain general features of the style of *Julius Caesar*. Most notable is the sharply limited vocabulary of the play. Only the quite short *Comedy of Errors* and *The Two Gentlemen of Verona* use a smaller stock of words.[2] Despite the fact that *Julius Caesar* was probably written just after *Henry V* and shortly before *Hamlet*, its language is strikingly different, especially from that of *Hamlet*, which "contains much the largest and most expressive vocabulary" in the Shakespeare canon. Hart thinks that this peculiarity in the diction of *Julius Caesar* represents "the result of an experiment, fortunately not repeated, of curbing the author's natural exuberance of expression and restraining his fondness for metaphor and word-coining."

The imagery of *Julius Caesar* is also quite limited. In Wells's count this play is twenty-sixth in volume of imagery, while *Antony and Cleopatra* is third.[3] And Spurgeon finds that *Julius Caesar* has less than a third the ratio of images to text that is present in *Antony and Cleopatra*.[4] However one may differ with the methods of classification of Wells or

---

[2] *Julius Caesar* (2,450 lines) has a vocabulary of 2,218 words, while *The Comedy of Errors* (1,753 lines) has 2,037, and *The Two Gentlemen of Verona* (2,193 lines) has 2,153. See Alfred Hart, "Vocabularies of Shakespeare's Plays," *Review of English Studies*, XIX (1943), 132 (Table I) and 135.

[3] Henry W. Wells, *Poetic Imagery: Illustrated from Elizabethan Literature*, N. Y., 1924, p. 219.

[4] Caroline F. E. Spurgeon, *Shakespeare's Imagery and What it Tells Us*, N. Y., 1935, Appendix II, pp. 361–62. *Julius Caesar* has 83 images for 2,450 lines of text, while *Antony and Cleopatra* has 266 images for 3,016 lines of text.

Spurgeon, the comparative figures are significant. In Acts IV and V of
Julius Caesar the carefully developed themes of the first part of the play
(blood, fire, storm) are almost abandoned.[5] There are also, especially
in these two acts, long passages that are virtually without a conscious
verbal imagery; the quarrel scene, for example, makes little use of
verbal images for its effect. Typical of this almost imageless diction is
the proscription scene which opens Act IV. Here the new Triumvirs
decide the fate of the Roman Republic:

> *Ant.* These many, then, shall die; their names are prick'd.
> *Oct.* Your brother too must die. Consent you, Lepidus?
> *Lep.* I do consent—
> *Oct.*   Prick him down, Antony.
> *Lep.* Upon condition Publius shall not live,
> Who is your sister's son, Mark Antony.
> *Ant.* He shall not live. Look, with a spot I damn him.   (4.1.1–6)

In these six lines human lives are bargained away and the business of
the Empire is begun, but the only images are the damning "spots" that
are "prick'd" down. As in *Coriolanus,* the pressure of public affairs does
not permit one to luxuriate in images.

The deliberate limiting of imaginative resources in *Julius Caesar* seems
to indicate a stylistic experiment on Shakespeare's part. He appears to
be attempting a special "Roman" style for the play, one that can express the clarity of thought and forthrightness of action in the Roman
subject matter. The "limited perfection" of this "Roman" style is perhaps best described by A. C. Bradley:

> Neither thought on the one side, nor expression on the other, seems to have
> any tendency to outrun or contend with its fellow. We receive an impression
> of easy mastery and complete harmony, but not so strong an impression of
> inner power bursting into outer life. Shakespeare's style is perhaps nowhere
> else so free from defects, and yet almost every one of his subsequent plays
> contains writing which is greater. To speak familiarly, we feel in *Julius
> Caesar* that, although not even Shakespeare could better the style he has
> chosen, he has not let himself go.

Bradley relates the style to its theme, so that the play is seen as "a
deliberate endeavour after a dignified and unadorned simplicity—a
Roman simplicity perhaps."[6] J. A. K. Thomson describes this style in
somewhat more positive terms:

[5] It is on this basis that one may take issue with the statement of R. A. Foakes: "The
imagery of words and action points to the imaginative and dramatic unity of the play as
consisting in the completion of the circle of events beginning and ending the rebellion"
("An Approach to *Julius Caesar,*" *Shakespeare Quarterly,* V [1954], 270). The play is
clearly an "imaginative and dramatic unity," but this is difficult to demonstrate through
its imagery.
[6] A. C. Bradley, *Shakespearean Tragedy,* 2 ed., London, 1905, pp. 85–86.

It is clear that he [Shakespeare] had formed for himself the notion of a style corresponding to the Renaissance conception of the Roman character, which in turn was influenced by the Greek conception of the Spartan character, with its martial virility and laconic speech. This is the style he uses in *Julius Caesar*. It is remarkably effective, and one does somehow feel, when Brutus or Cassius or Casca is speaking, that this is rather how a Roman would speak.[7]

This sort of writing consciously avoids the brilliance of *Antony and Cleopatra*, yet in that play, too, the Roman world is set forth in an austere imagery of hard, cold, material objects and the practical business of state; it is only the imagery of Egypt that is luxuriant. The "Roman" style is the natural speaking voice of Octavius Caesar as it is of Coriolanus, for whom it is a mark of integrity to be "ill-school'd/ In bolted language" (3.1.321–22).

The sense of order, limitation, and control in the "Roman" style of *Julius Caesar* is expressed in the rhetorical form of close analogy, especially the simile. This form uses explicit and carefully worked-out comparisons, and there is an attempt to indicate just what specific aspects of the vehicle (image proper) are to be applied to the tenor (idea). A very clear example is Titinius' eulogy for the dead Cassius:

> O setting sun,
> As in thy red rays thou dost sink to night,
> So in his red blood Cassius' day is set!
> The sun of Rome is set.   (5.3.60–63)

The formula for this image is quite simple and commonplace: the life of man is represented by the course of the sun in a single day, and death is therefore a sunset. Further, the red rays of the setting sun are like the red blood of Cassius' death wound. Not only is an analogy drawn between the individual and the cosmos, but the state is brought in as a third plane of being. The parts of the analogy are clearly identified by the "as . . . so" form of their relation, which makes the application of the analogy very specific and limited. Within this narrow imaginative framework, the image functions as a completed system, whose meanings are self-explained and self-pointed.[8] The balance and symmetry of the figure are particularly useful in a play such as *Julius Caesar*, where the dramatic action turns so significantly on the correspondences between microcosm and macrocosm: "The heavens themselves blaze forth the death of princes" (2.2.31).

By the time of *Antony and Cleopatra*, Shakespeare has more or less

---

[7] J. A. K. Thomson, *Shakespeare and the Classics*, London, 1953, p. 193.
[8] Another example of this kind of analogy is Brutus' argument for immediate battle at Philippi: "There is a tide in the affairs of men . . ." (4.3.218ff). The far-fetched "conceits" in the play, such as 3.2.181–86 and 5.1.32–40, also illustrate the analogy form.

abandoned the analogy form of *Julius Caesar*. We may see this contrast in style in the very unorthodox and dramatic way he now uses similes. In Cleopatra's final speech, for example, the similes make a slow, rich music of monosyllables: "As sweet as balm, as soft as air, as gentle—" (5.2.314). There is an hypnotic sense of falling asleep, in which it is dramatically just to leave the final figure incomplete—Cleopatra follows the turn of her thought to "O Antony!" (5.2.315). These similes dramatize the effect of the asp-bite as described by Plutarch; it

> causeth onely a heauiness of the head, without swounding or complaining, and bringeth a great desire also to sleepe, with a litle swet in the face, and so by litle and litle taketh away the senses & vitall powers, no liuing creature perceiuing that the patients feele any paine. For they are so sorie when any bodie awaketh them, and taketh them vp; as those that being taken out of a sound sleep, are very heauie and desirous to sleepe.[9]

Antony uses a similar type of figure in his speech to Eros in IV,xiv. The changing shapes of the clouds present a pageant of Antony's dissolution:

> That which is now a horse, even with a thought
> The rack dislimns, and makes it indistinct
> As water is in water.   (4.14.9–11)

So Antony himself is "indistinct/ As water is in water" and "cannot hold this visible shape" (4.14.14). The strong Roman sense of reality is slipping away from him, and the paradoxical simile is used to emphasize the process. These similes push beyond the ordinary limits of the analogy form to an area of hyperbole and symbol.

The personifications in the two plays also indicate a strong contrast in style. In *Julius Caesar* they function as a specific allegory for their subjects, and they are highly formal and rhetorical in tone, as in Messala's address to Error after the death of Cassius:

> O hateful Error, Melancholy's child,
> Why dost thou show to the apt thoughts of men
> The things that are not? O Error, soon conceiv'd,
> Thou never com'st unto a happy birth,
> But kill'st the mother that engend'red thee!   (5.3.67–71)

The use of abstract nouns as human entities is typical of Shakespeare's earlier manner, which is also suggested by the stiffness and deliberateness of the apostrophe. Conspiracy (2.1.77–85), danger (2.2.44–48), and constancy (2.4.6–7) are likewise personified.

The few personifications in *Antony and Cleopatra* have a much more vivid dramatic function, which is best exemplified by Cleopatra's dialogue with the Messenger from Antony:

[9] *Four Chapters of North's Plutarch*, ed. F. A. Leo, London, 1878, p. 1002.

> *Mess.*   Madam, he's well.
> *Cleo.*   Well said.
> *Mess.* And friends with Caesar.
> *Cleo.*   Th'art an honest man.
> *Mess.* Caesar and he are greater friends than ever.
> *Cleo.* Make thee a fortune from me!
> *Mess.*   But yet, madam—
> *Cleo.* I do not like 'but yet.' It does allay
> The good precedence. Fie upon 'but yet'!
> 'But yet' is as a jailer to bring forth
> Some monstrous malefactor.   (2.5.46–53)

Cleopatra pounces on "but yet" and endows it with human attributes. These two simple conjunctions become a jailer leading forth his prisoner to be hanged. By providing an occasion for Cleopatra to personify her fears, these colorless words assume dramatic significance. Similarly, when Antony is about to depart for Rome, Cleopatra vainly searches for something to say, then bursts out: "O, my oblivion is a very Antony,/ And I am all forgotten!" (1.3.90–91). Oblivion is personified as "a very Antony," the supreme example of forgetfulness because he is leaving Cleopatra and going to Rome. Cleopatra is "forgotten" in not being able to remember what she has to say and by the departing Antony. The play on these two senses makes Antony both subject and object, and the figure fits very nicely into the dramatic action. These personifications, unlike those in *Julius Caesar*, arise very naturally out of their dramatic contexts; they are in no sense set in formal speeches.

The dramatic use of similes and personifications in *Antony and Cleopatra* is part of a larger stylistic purpose very different from the ordered perfection of *Julius Caesar*. The characteristic figure in *Antony and Cleopatra* is the hyperbole, or what Puttenham in his *Arte of English Poesie* (1589) calls "for his immoderate excesse . . . the ouer reacher" or "the loud lyer," and he defines it as "by incredible comparison giuing credit."[10] In Greek "hyperbole" is *a throwing beyond: an overshooting, superiority, excess in anything . . .*" (Lidell-Scott Dictionary). It would include the ideas of extravagance and boldness as well as exaggeration and overstatement. In essence, hyperbole is the reaching-out of the imagination for superlatives. This is I think what Coleridge means when he calls the style of *Antony and Cleopatra* "*feliciter audax*"—literally, "felicitously bold or audacious," but perhaps best rendered by Coleridge's phrase, "happy valiancy of style."[11]

This type of style is demanded by the spaciousness and scope of the play's themes. Perhaps the best example is Cleopatra's dream of Antony:

[10] George Puttenham, *The Arte of English Poesie*, ed. Gladys Doidge Willcock and Alice Walker, Cambridge, 1936, p. 191.
[11] *Coleridge's Shakespearean Criticism*, ed. Thomas Middleton Raysor, London, 1930, I, 86.

> His face was as the heav'ns, and therein stuck
> A sun and moon, which kept their course and lighted
> The little O, the earth.   (5.2.79–81)

The image of Antony becomes the whole cosmos, and this earth is only a "little O" in comparison—we cannot imagine in higher terms. Cleopatra continues: "His legs bestrid the ocean: his rear'd arm/ Crested the world" (5.2.82–83). This is the Marlovian strain of invidious comparison in which man is literally made the measure of all things. Cleopatra goes so far as to question the reality of her dream, as if it were beyond our mortal sense of possibility:

> Think you there was or might be such a man
> As this I dreamt of?
> *Dol.*   Gentle madam, no.
> *Cleo.* You lie, up to the hearing of the gods!
> But, if there be or ever were one such,
> It's past the size of dreaming. Nature wants stuff
> To vie strange forms with fancy; yet, t'imagine
> An Antony were nature's piece 'gainst fancy,
> Condemning shadows quite.   (5.2.93–100)

The image of Antony is "past the size of dreaming." It is unrealizable because reality ("Nature") cannot present all the forms imagination ("fancy," a kind of dreaming) can conceive. But even to think that the forms of imagination may actually exist is an argument for "Nature." We may take this statement—"Nature wants stuff/ To vie strange forms with fancy"—as a key to the character of the style. The imagination acts as hyperbole: it throws beyond, overshoots, is superior to, and in excess of nature, yet it cannot go past the size of dreaming, and therefore must remain implicit in the dramatic action and words. Where *Julius Caesar* limits and defines its figures and insists on the proper logical application of vehicle to tenor, *Antony and Cleopatra* uses a figurative language, the "strange forms" of "fancy," that tries to force itself beyond the bounds of mere "Nature."

The "hyperbolical" quality of *Antony and Cleopatra* is also seen in a special kind of superlative. When Antony tells Cleopatra, "Now for the love of Love and her soft hours . . ." (1.1.44), the doubling of the noun with "of" serves as an intensifier: it is an attempt to get at the quintessence. Antony is Cleopatra's "man of men" (1.5.72), as if only he among men could represent Man. He is also her "Lord of lords!" (4.8.16), and his sons are proclaimed "kings of kings" (3.6.13). This grammatical form echoes in the mind when we hear Antony say that Cleopatra

> Like a right gypsy hath at fast and loose
> Beguil'd me to the very heart of loss!   (4.12.28–29)

No loss can be imagined greater; it is an absolute, the essence and the life of loss.

The range of diction in *Antony and Cleopatra* is very wide, and it shows an extravagant juxtaposing of latinate and colloquial words, as in Cleopatra's speech to the asp:

> Come, thou mortal wretch,
> With thy sharp teeth this knot intrinsicate
> Of life at once untie. Poor venomous fool,
> Be angry, and dispatch.   (5.2.306–09)

"Intrinsicate" was considered a pedantic, "inkhorn" term in its time, a fit object for satire in Marston's *The Scourge of Villanie* (1599). When his poem "shall come into the late perfumed fist of iudiciall *Torquatus* . . . he will vouchsafe it, some of his new-minted Epithets, (as *Reall, Intrinsecate, Delphicke,*). . . ."[12] "Intrinsicate" was often used for "intricate" and meant much the same thing: "involved," "complicated," "entangled." But it also suggests a connection with "intrinsic," which refers to the essential nature of a thing. Life is the intrinsic knot—intricate, entangled, essential—which the asp, as death the lover, will at once untie. Alongside this uncommon word, "intrinsicate," are such familiar terms of endearment as "mortal wretch" and "Poor venomous fool." The use of the colloquial in Cleopatra's speech to the asp appeals to the common human emotions of tragedy, while the latinate has a heightening effect. Charmian's words on the death of her mistress also illustrate this two-fold quality:

> Now boast thee, death, in thy possession lies
> A lass unparallel'd. Downy windows, close;
> And golden Phoebus never be beheld
> Of eyes again so royal!   (5.2.318–21)

The homely and familiar "lass" is placed between the long latinate words "possession" and "unparallel'd." It recalls the Cleopatra of

> No more but e'en a woman, and commanded
> By such poor passion as the maid that milks
> And does the meanest chares.   (4.15.73–75)

The effect of "lass"—a common, lowly word—is immediately countered by the periphrasis of "Downy windows" for eyes and the mythological

---

12 John Marston, Preface to *The Scourge of Villanie* (1599), ed. G. B. Harrison, London, 1925, p. 9. See I. A. Richards' comment on "intrinsicate" in *The Philosophy of Rhetoric*, N. Y., 1936, pp. 64–65.

reference to "golden Phoebus."[13] The verbal context is further enriched by a covert allusion. Cleopatra, the "lass unparallel'd," now triumphs over Caesar, the "ass/ Unpolicied" (5.2.310–11)—the half-rhyme deliberately pairs these latinate-colloquial phrases.[14]

Going beyond the effects of rhetoric, we may explore the "hyperbolical" style of *Antony and Cleopatra* in a more extended example. Cleopatra's "infinite variety"[15] is a leading hyperbole in the play, and it draws its strength as much from the poetic language lavished on Cleopatra as from the presented image of her character—the role demands an "infinite variety" of gesture and stage action. The explication of this elaborate hyperbole may serve as a parallel to the analysis of the scene of Caesar's Ghost; in both places there is a very characteristic expression of the play's style.

The ambivalent tone of "infinite variety" is first established by Enobarbus right after his splendid speech about Cleopatra in her barge on the Cydnus. He assures Maecenas that Antony cannot break off from his "enchanting queen":

> Never! He will not.
> Age cannot wither her nor custom stale
> Her infinite variety. Other women cloy
> The appetites they feed, but she makes hungry
> Where most she satisfies; for vilest things
> Become themselves in her, that the holy priests
> Bless her when she is riggish.   (2.2.239–45)

Cleopatra is outside the withering toils of age and custom and cloying appetite, for "vilest things/ Become themselves in her," achieve their apotheosis and inner perfection. She is even blessed when she plays the strumpet ("is riggish")—this is the strange issue of the "holy palmers' kiss" of *Romeo and Juliet* (1.5.102). We have been prepared for Enobarbus' statement by many previous expressions of Cleopatra's variousness and her capacity to exploit the range of emotions. She is Antony's

[13] See John Middleton Murry, *Shakespeare*, N. Y., 1936, p. 298. Another example, very obvious and powerful, of this double effect is in Macbeth's harrowing consciousness of guilt:
> "Will all great Neptune's ocean wash this blood
> Clean from my hand? No. This my hand will rather
> The multitudinous seas incarnadine,
> Making the green one red."   (2.2.60–63)
The simple "green" and "red" restate "multitudinous seas" and "incarnadine" and act as a relief to these learned words. See John Crowe Ransom, "On Shakespeare's Language," *Sewanee Review*, LV (1947), 181–98.
[14] See George Rylands, "Shakespeare's Poetic Energy," *Proceedings of the British Academy 1951*, XXXVII, 101.
[15] Peter G. Phialas notes in his New Yale Shakespeare edition (New Haven, 1955, pp. 142–43) that the phrase "infinite varietie" occurs in Florio's Montaigne (Modern Library edition, 1933, p. 108).

> wrangling queen!
> Whom every thing becomes—to chide, to laugh,
> To weep. . . .   (1.1.48–50)

She knows how to manipulate her sentiments and to stimulate passion by "infinite variety." As she tells the incredulous Charmian in her message to Antony:

> If you find him sad,
> Say I am dancing; if in mirth, report
> That I am sudden sick.   (1.3.3–5)

This is beyond Charmian's comprehension, but Cleopatra is herself a "heavenly mingle" (1.5.59), and she knows the art to "make defect perfection" (2.2.236).

These paradoxical aspects of Cleopatra may be demonstrated in II,v, where her "infinite variety" is seen as roving desire searching for objects. We begin with the consciously poetic and languorous tone of *Twelfth Night:* "Give me some music! music, moody food/ Of us that trade in love" (2.5.1–2). The music is called for, and Mardian the Eunuch enters, but Cleopatra is no longer interested in hearing him sing: "Let it alone! Let's to billiards" (2.5.3). Now begins a series of sexual puns in the style of Shakespeare's early comedies; Cleopatra explores the witty possibilities of "play":

> *Cleo.* As well a woman with an eunuch play'd
> As with a woman. Come, you'll play with me, sir?
> *Mar.* As well as I can, madam.
> *Cleo.* And when good will is show'd, though 't come too short,
> The actor may plead pardon.   (2.5.5–9)

But she quickly tires of this verbal sport and has a new whim:

> Give me mine angle! we'll to th' river. There,
> My music playing far off, I will betray
> Tawny-finn'd fishes. My bended hook shall pierce
> Their slimy jaws; and as I draw them up,
> I'll think them every one an Antony,
> And say, 'Ah, ha! y'are caught!'   (2.5.10–15)

The suggestion of music at the opening of the scene is taken up again, but the mood is entirely different. The absent Antony is "caught" or "hooked" in the physically violent image of the slimy-jawed fish, which is much transmuted from the incident in Plutarch of the salt fish attached as a jest to Antony's line.

Once struck, the note of passion is intensified with the appearance of the Messenger:

> O, from Italy!
> Ram thou thy fruitful tidings in mine ears,
> That long time have been barren.   (2.5.23–25)

It is a sudden sexual fury to have Antony himself in the tidings about him. When the Messenger tells his news of Antony's marriage, he is struck down by Cleopatra (2.5.61 s.d., 62 s.d.), haled up and down (2.5.64 s.d.), and threatened with a knife (2.5.73 s.d.). The luxuriant poetic tone of the passage has now issued into the physical violence of the stage action. This is all part of the style of Cleopatra's "infinite variety," which runs the gamut from "music, moody food" to "Rogue, thou hast liv'd too long" with the stage direction *"Draw a knife."*

In contrast to this scene we have the "infinite variety" of Cleopatra's suicide, which is not quite done in the "high Roman fashion" (4.15.87), but with a priestly deliberateness and an aesthetic enjoyment of robe and crown and the effect of the asp-bite. Shakespeare here takes advantage of all the richness of the Elizabethan staging to enforce the poetic splendor of Cleopatra's final scene. She is to be shown "like a queen" (5.2.227) in elaborate stage ritual and costume, and we know from Henslowe's account books and other sources how important gorgeous robes were to an Elizabethan production.

In her death Caesar affirms her magnificence:

> she looks like sleep,
> As she would catch another Antony
> In her strong toil of grace.   (5.2.349–51)

Part of the effectiveness of this passage rests in the manner of portrayal. Cleopatra must really look "like sleep," with an indefinable expression of grace—perhaps a smile. In Elizabethan English "grace" is a complex word whose meanings range from physical attraction and charm of personal manner to pre-eminence of nobility, moral rightness, and divine blessing. Cleopatra's "strong toil of grace" is a union of the queen who "beggar'd all description" (2.2.203), and the "serpent of old Nile" (1.5.25)—she could "catch another Antony" now as she caught the first one. We recall Cleopatra fishing in II,v; there the hooked fish was Antony, over whom she uttered the triumphant cry, " 'Ah, ha! y'are caught!' " (2.5.15). We should not overlook the violence in Cleopatra's "strong toil of grace" and its ability to "catch." The word "toil," for example, refers to a net or trap to snare game. Although Cleopatra is heightened by her death, her character and motives remain in a certain ambiguity even at the end. She is always both "queen" (female monarch) and "quean" (wench, whore), and in this covert pun[16] lies the secret of her attraction.

The rhapsodic and transcendental aspects of "infinite variety" are only too plain. Yet there is a strong sense in which the hyperboles of the play are constantly undercut. This is perhaps what Coleridge means when he says that Cleopatra's passion "springs out of the habitual craving of a licentious nature, and that it is supported and reinforced by voluntary stimulus and sought-for associations, instead of blossoming out of spontaneous emotion." Such terms as "habitual," "voluntary," and "sought-for" convey a sense of the effort and ennui involved. But Coleridge safeguards the balance of his judgment by noting that "the sense of criminality in her passion is lessened by our insight into its depth and energy. . . ."[17] This is precisely the paradox of Cleopatra's "infinite variety," that it not only suggests an unlimited creative vitality, but also artifice and boredom. New pleasures are essential to a life of pleasure, as Antony says in the first scene of the play (where the whole Egypt-Rome conflict is stated in extreme form): "There's not a minute of our lives should stretch/ Without some pleasure now" (1.1.46–47). The concern for the new pleasure of every "minute" suggests Pater, who proposes in the Conclusion to *The Renaissance* "to give nothing but the highest quality to your moments as they pass, and simply for those moments' sake." Thus, behind the appearances of splendor and fulfillment in Egypt lies a burdensome compulsion: the life of the senses must have "infinite variety" or cease to exist.

---

16 Helge Kökeritz discusses the possibility of this pun, but regards it as "dubious." It is possible in colloquial speech, but not in the polite speech that Shakespeare uses (*Shakespeare's Pronunciation*, New Haven, 1953, p. 88). E. J. Dobson agrees that "the use of the raised sound was a vulgarism," but notes that it "might occasionally make its way into the speech of higher classes . . ." (*English Pronunciation 1500–1700*, Oxford, 1957, II, 640). Dobson also indicates that "queen" and "quean" appear as homophones on a number of contemporary lists.

Whether or not this pun was actually intended on the Elizabethan stage, it seems to be implied when Antony says, "I must from this enchanting queen break off" (1.2.132), and it is also an innuendo in the exchange between Pompey and Enobarbus in II,vi:

> "*Pom.* And I have heard Apollodorus carried—
> *Eno.* No more of that! He did so.
> *Pom.*   What, I pray you?
> *Eno.* A certain queen to Caesar in a mattress." (2.6.69–71)

We can perhaps see an instance here of covert puns setting off meanings already present in our minds. Thomas Heywood very obviously plays on "queen" and "quean" in the card-game of *A Woman Kilde with Kindnesse* (probably performed in 1603—see Chambers, *Elizabethan Stage*, III, 342):

> "*Wend.* I am a Knaue.
> *Nicke.* Ile sweare it.
> *Anne.* I a Queene.
> *Fr.* A quean thou shouldst say: wel the cards are mine,
> They are the grosest paire that ere I felt."

(See *The Dramatic Works of Thomas Heywood*, London, J. Pearson, 1874, II, 123.)

17 *Coleridge's Shakespearean Criticism*, I, 86. Compare the "moral realism" of L. C. Knights, "On the Tragedy of Antony and Cleopatra," *Scrutiny*, XVI (1949), 318–23, and D. A. Traversi, *An Approach to Shakespeare*, 2 ed., Garden City, N. Y., 1956, pp. 235–61.

Among Shakespeare's plays, *Antony and Cleopatra* is one of the richest in imagery and stylistic effects and *Julius Caesar* one of the most sparse. The two plays offer an illustrative contrast between a carefully limited and controlled "Roman" style and a hyperbolical and evocative "Egyptian" style. The imagery in *Antony and Cleopatra* tends to be implicit and its meanings suggested rather than stated. In this sense we may speak of its style as elliptical and complex, with an ability to suspend many ideas without seeking to resolve them into one. Its style demonstrates, to a remarkable degree, Shakespeare's "negative capability." This is not a quality that is much evident in *Julius Caesar*, yet the sharpness and clarity of detail in that play is a unique achievement. It proceeds deliberately rather than expansively, and it produces its effects, as in the appearance of Caesar's Ghost to Brutus, with an astonishing simplicity. There is a sense of distinct outline and completed form in this play that is absent from *Antony and Cleopatra*, but its perfection is attained at the expense of imaginative intensity and fullness of implication. The "Roman" style of *Julius Caesar* seems to involve Shakespeare in some basic contradictions, and he never again so consciously restricts his imaginative powers.

The style of *Coriolanus* stands in sharp contrast to both the other Roman plays, but perhaps most to *Antony and Cleopatra*, which was probably written only a year or so earlier. We no longer find the richness and complexity of imagery of *Antony and Cleopatra*, but a curiously cold, aloof, and objective world. In this respect the sense of control in *Coriolanus* reminds us somewhat of *Julius Caesar*, although the two plays cannot be compared in the relative mastery of their dramatic verse.[18] Both plays also use a similar two-part form, but *Coriolanus* rises by a series of mounting climaxes to the high point of Coriolanus' yielding in V,iii, whereas *Julius Caesar* never builds to a second climax as strong as the murder of Caesar in the third act—this creates a certain imbalance in the development of the action. Despite the poetic and structural skill of *Coriolanus*, the play appears to be odd and anomalous and to point ahead to the last plays rather than back to the period of the great tragedies. It has not only not attracted critics, but it has seemed to represent an exhaustion of Shakespeare's powers. One way to answer these judgments is to examine the play in terms of its dramatic purposes; the strict application of expression to function makes its style quite different from that of *Julius Caesar* or *Antony and Cleopatra*.

As a basic premise we need to agree that the style of *Coriolanus* is closely linked to the character of the protagonist, about whom A. C. Bradley has said, "If Lear's thunderstorm had beat upon his head, he

[18] See Traversi, *An Approach to Shakespeare*, pp. 216–34.

would merely have set his teeth."[19] Coriolanus is an unreflective man
of action. His tragedy is massive and overwhelming, almost like fate,
and it does not touch us very personally. We see him setting his teeth
against the storm of Fortune when he appears in humble guise at the
house of his former enemy, Aufidius. He expresses this great change
from Rome's defender to Rome's chief enemy in terms of chance trivial-
ities. Just as fast-sworn friends, "on a dissension of a doit" (4.4.17) become enemies,

> So fellest foes,
> Whose passions and whose plots have broke their sleep
> To take the one the other, by some chance,
> Some trick not worth an egg, shall grow dear friends
> And interjoin their issues. So with me.
> My birthplace hate I, and my love's upon
> The enemy town.   (4.4.18–24)

Enright finds this soliloquy strange because, "coming at the turn of the
play, at the very hinge of the tragic action, it should refer us to 'some
trick not worth an egg.' "[20] At a similar juncture Macbeth and Othello
react entirely differently.

We have an even stronger example at the end of the play of the in-
adequacy of Coriolanus as a tragic protagonist. Although he yields to
the family group, there is never any real recognition of the tragic folly
of his betrayal; his climactic words are simply a realization of his own
doom:

> O my mother, mother! O!
> You have won a happy victory to Rome;
> But for your son—believe it, O believe it!—
> Most dangerously you have with him prevail'd,
> If not most mortal to him. But let it come.   (5.3.185–89)

There is an awareness of the tragic consequences of mercy here rather
than any true self-awareness. The words have none of the quality of
Lear's emergence from madness: "Pray, do not mock me./ I am a very
foolish fond old man . . ." (4.7.59–60). Although the character of
Coriolanus is consistent throughout, his next appearance, proud and
choleric in Corioles (V,vi), comes as a surprise. Accustomed as we are
to the effects of tragedy, we are not ready to accept the fact that his
yielding seems to have had no influence on his moral being. But neither
Coriolanus nor any of the persons in this play is either inward or meditative or lyric, and there is not much self-awareness or tragic recognition. Actually, only Menenius uses figurative language freely and natu-

---

[19] A. C. Bradley, "Coriolanus," *Proceedings of the British Academy 1911–1912*, V, 459.
[20] D. J. Enright, "*Coriolanus:* Tragedy or Debate?" *Essays in Criticism*, IV (1954), 16–17.

rally, as in the fable of belly and members, but his role is limited to that of conciliator. In this atmosphere a rich verbal imagery would defeat the dramatic purpose, whereas in such a play as *Richard II* it is just this rich vein of poetic fancy that calls attention to the ineffectual and histrionic nature of the king.

When Coriolanus does use figures of speech, he inclines to similes rather than metaphors, since they provide a simpler and more explicit form of expression. Both the vehicle and tenor of the image are very carefully balanced and limited, usually by the connectives "like" or "as" (I count ninety-three similes in the play, fifty-seven with "as" and thirty-six with "like"). The similes do not suggest new areas of meaning, but give points already stated an added force and vividness. Their function is illustrative rather than expressive. In this respect *Coriolanus* seems to resemble *Julius Caesar* and Shakespeare's earlier plays, for the trend of Shakespeare's development is away from the simile form and toward a dramatically integrated type of metaphor.[21]

Volumnia makes good use of illustrative simile when she instructs her son in his role before the people: "Now humble as the ripest mulberry/ That will not hold the handling . . ." (3.2.79–80). Coriolanus must be "humble" before the people, and the simile emphasizes the exact sort of humility that is expected. Although the mulberry image makes a vivid and original illustration, it is an embellishment of the basic meaning and not at all indispensable. But the similes in *Antony and Cleopatra*—for example, Antony's "indistinct/ As water is in water" (4.14.10–11)—are themselves the meaning of the passages in which they occur and are not in any way dispensable. This sensitive image of the "ripest mulberry" has an important dramatic function. Its highly imaginative character suggests a false tone in what Volumnia is saying. In its context the image is overwrought, for Volumnia knows her son cannot feign any sort of humility, no less the supreme humility of the "ripest mulberry." It is too self-conscious and lush an image and hints that there is a servile, dishonorable aspect in what Volumnia is proposing. This type of figure raises interesting questions about the function of poetic language in the drama. If the mulberry image appeared isolated from its context in an anthology of lyric poetry, it would certainly seem striking and original, yet in the play its effect is insidious. The poetic quality of the image has been diverted to dramatic ends.

Another example of this principle is in Coriolanus' injunction against flattery in I,ix:

---

[21] See W. H. Clemen, *The Development of Shakespeare's Imagery*, London, 1951, p. 5. This is one of Clemen's theses about Shakespeare's development.

> When drums and trumpets shall
> I' th' field prove flatterers, let courts and cities be
> Made all of false-fac'd soothing! When steel grows
> Soft as the parasite's silk, let him be made
> An overture for th' wars!   (1.9.42–46)

In the overturning of order that flattery brings, the steel of the soldier (probably his mail coat) will become as soft as the silk of the parasite. It is a vivid contrast of textures, but its imaginative tone is used to suggest the luxury of peace—as if one would expect the silk-clad parasite at court but not the steel-coated man of war to use similes. This pejorative connotation of silk is echoed in the final scene of the play when Coriolanus is accused of "Breaking his oath and resolution like/ A twist of rotten silk . . ." (5.6.94–95).

The images of peace and civil life put an unexpected music into Coriolanus' verse, although he uses them contemptuously. To prevent flattery, he terms his wounds "Scratches with briers,/ Scars to move laughter only" (3.3.51–52), which recalls his earlier speech in the Capitol as he escapes from Cominius' oration:

> I had rather have one scratch my head i' th' sun
> When the alarum were struck than idly sit
> To hear my nothings monster'd.   (2.2.79–81)

This passage is a graphic illustration of what it means to "voluptuously surfeit out of action" (1.3.28). War is "sprightly, waking, audible, and full of vent," while peace is "a very apoplexy, lethargy; mull'd, deaf, sleepy, insensible . . ." (4.5.237–39). In terms of these values (war is the positive force, peace the negative),[22] we find that the love imagery of the play is curiously transferred to military contexts. In I,vi Marcius greets Cominius in the language of the wedding-night:

> O, let me clip ye
> In arms as sound as when I woo'd, in heart
> As merry as when our nuptial day was done
> And tapers burn'd to bedward!   (1.6.29–32)

And in IV,v Aufidius welcomes his former enemy in these same epithalamial terms:

> But that I see thee here,
> Thou noble thing, more dances my rapt heart
> Than when I first my wedded mistress saw
> Bestride my threshold.   (4.5.120–23)

But there is none of this sort of imagery between Coriolanus and his wife Virgilia. In his first dialogue with her, for example, he addresses

---

[22] See Paul A. Jorgensen, *Shakespeare's Military World*, Berkeley, 1956, chap. v.

her as his "gracious silence" (2.1.192) and asks somewhat bluntly: "Wouldst thou have laugh'd had I come coffin'd home/ That weep'st to see me triumph?" (2.1.193–94). The military context evokes a spontaneously vivid imagery that ceases when we move "From th' casque to th' cushion" (4.7.43).

Coriolanus' own attitude to words helps to shape the character of the verbal imagery in the play. Suspecting he will have the worst of it, he refuses to parry arguments with the Tribune Brutus, for "oft,/ When blows have made me stay, I fled from words" (2.2.75–76). Unlike Hamlet or Richard II or even Othello, Coriolanus has a natural antipathy to eloquence that goes beyond the Elizabethan convention that a soldier should be a plain, if not rude, speaker.[23] As Menenius tells the patricians, Coriolanus' aversion to words is part of his hatred of flattery: "His heart's his mouth;/ What his breast forges, that his tongue must vent . . ." (3.1.257–58). He is "ill-school'd/ In bolted language . . ." and "meal and bran together/ He throws without distinction" (3.1.321–23). There is no subtlety in this man, no use of language as an exploration of consciousness. He says what he thinks and feels and that is the end of it, for words are simply a means to express his bluff honesty. Remember Antony's ironic claim at the height of his oration: "I am no orator, as Brutus is . . ." (3.2.222). Coriolanus is emphatically "no orator," and in a play so thoroughly political as this, the inability to make speeches is a claim to integrity.

Coriolanus is also peculiarly oppressed by the reality of words, a weakness the fluent Tribunes and Aufidius know how to turn to their own ends. These antagonists of Coriolanus have, by the way, a striking similarity of function in the two parts of the play. Both display that extempore grasp of circumstance that is the mark of the Machiavel, and the "plebeian malignity and tribunitian insolence"[24] of Brutus and Sicinius are matched by Aufidius' guiding principle: "I'll potch at him some way./ Or wrath or craft may get him" (1.10.15–16). In III,i, for example, Sicinius baits Coriolanus in typical fashion:

> It is a mind
> That shall remain a poison where it is,
> Not poison any further.   (3.1.86–88)

Coriolanus seizes on this "shall" as if it were a menacing entity:

> Shall remain?
> Hear you this Triton of the minnows? Mark you
> His absolute 'shall'?
> Com.   'Twas from the canon.
> Cor.   'Shall'?   (3.1.88–90)

[23] *Ibid.*, chap. vi.
[24] *Johnson on Shakespeare,* ed. Walter Raleigh, London, 1908, p. 179.

And Coriolanus continues to rage against the "peremptory 'shall'" (3.1.94), the "popular 'shall,'" (3.1.106), which is made to symbolize the whole patrician-plebeian conflict. In terms of the actual situation, Coriolanus' rage is excessive and strident; he is "fleeing from words" (2.2.76) rather than realities.

Aufidius uses the same trick as the Tribunes in V,vi, where he tempts Coriolanus to his doom with three contemptuous words: "traitor," "Marcius," and "boy." Coriolanus recoils from the verbal concussion and repeats the words unbelievingly as if they had power over him:

> Boy? False hound!
> If you have writ your annals true, 'tis there,
> That, like an eagle in a dovecote, I
> Flutter'd your Volscians in Corioles.
> Alone I did it. Boy?   (5.6.112–16)

For the moment, the word and the thing are confounded, producing a crisis that can only be resolved by violence. The situation here is the reverse of that in *Antony and Cleopatra,* where Caesar mocks at Antony's insults: "He calls me boy, and chides as he had power/ To beat me out of Egypt" (4.1.1–2). The imperturbability of Caesar cannot be ruffled by mere words.

Coriolanus' normal speaking voice is often harsh and vituperative. In his tirades against the people he uses a few repeated image themes (especially food, disease, and animals), but our interest is not so much in the images themselves as in their expletive force. After the Romans are beaten to their trenches by the Volscians, for example, "Enter *Marcius,* cursing" (1.4.29 s.d.), and his volley of abuse begins:

> All the contagion of the South light on you,
> You shames of Rome! you herd of—Biles and plagues
> Plaster you o'er, that you may be abhorr'd
> Farther than seen and one infect another
> Against the wind a mile! You souls of geese
> That bear the shapes of men, how have you run
> From slaves that apes would beat! Pluto and hell!
> (1.4.30–36)

What is important here is not the catalogue of disease and animal imagery, but the "thunder-like percussion" (1.4.59) of Marcius' wrath. The breaking off in "you herd of—" is not felt as a gap, but as part of a natural rhythm in which the histrionic stress is on sound rather than sense. These images are therefore "illustrative" because they are used as examples of Marcius' anger, and no single image nor the sequence of the group is absolutely necessary. We have the same sort of effect in Marcius' second speech in the play, an extended harangue to the plebeians:

> He that trusts to you,
> Where he should find you lions, finds you hares;
> Where foxes, geese. You are no surer, no,
> Than is the coal of fire upon the ice
> Or hailstone in the sun. . . .   (1.1.174–78)

These are metaphors but they could as easily have been similes, for the analogy that is drawn is very explicit and limited. The animals have traditional, proverbial associations that are fairly well fixed: the lion is valiant, the hare fearful, while the fox represents shrewdness and craft, and the goose foolish simplicity. We do not feel any breadth of meaning in these images. But we must remember that it is Marcius who is speaking, and he is neither a poet nor a politician, but only a straightforward man of war. He tags plebeian faults with what is for him a suitable imagery, and if it seems familiar and trite, that in itself is a comment on his image-making powers.

It is significant, too, that the thirty-six lines of soliloquy in *Coriolanus* —the same number as in *As You Like It*—represent the minimal use of this device in Shakespeare. By itself, this proves nothing, but it keeps us aware of the lack of inwardness in the play and the fact that Coriolanus is the least articulate of Shakespeare's tragic heroes. At an opposite pole is the brooding, meditative Hamlet, who resorts to the soliloquy as a "natural" form of expression. The few soliloquies in *Coriolanus* have a very particular dramatic effect. In a play so full of politics it is not often that we see a lone figure on stage speaking as if to himself. We have been accustomed to seeing troops moving about and crowds of plebeians and patricians wrangling with each other. In this context the soliloquy, the stage image of isolation, emphasizes Coriolanus' own inner state. The two soliloquies in IV,iv, for example, call attention to the spiritual alienation of Coriolanus as an exile and traitor in the country of the Volscians. In II,iii his proud soliloquy in the gown of humility sets him completely apart from his plebeian petitioners. He speaks to himself on stage not to unburden his conscience nor to express his inner purposes, but because he feels himself to be a lone and humiliated figure.

The style of *Coriolanus* is not so much "Roman," implying as this does a Stoic self-control, as objective and public. This is seen very vividly in the great amount of public ceremony in the play, with its accompanying music or noise. The ominous shouts of "mutinous *Citizens*" open the action, and these are reinforced by "*Shouts within*" (1.1.47 s.d.) from the mob on the other side of the city. We then have an elaborate range of sound directions for the battle scenes: "*They sound a parley*" (1.4.12 s.d.), "*Drum afar off*" (1.4.15 s.d.), "*Alarum far off*" (1.4.19 s.d.), "*Alarum, as in battle*" (1.8. s.d.), "*Flourish. Alarum. A retreat is sounded.*" (1.9 s.d.), and "*A flourish. Cornets.* Enter *Tullus Aufidius* bloody, with two or three *Soldiers.*" (1.10 s.d.). These directions graphically convey the changing fortunes of war. We also have a number of acclamations of Marcius' valor: "*They all shout and wave their swords, take him up in their arms and cast up their caps*" (1.6.75 s.d.) and "*A long flourish. They all cry,* 'Marcius! Marcius!' *cast up their caps and lances*" (1.9.40 s.d.). In Coriolanus' triumphal procession there is "*A shout and flourish*" (2.1.172 s.d.), "*A sennet. Trumpets sound.*" (2.1.178. s.d.) and "*Flourish. Cornets. Exeunt in state, as before.*" (2.1.220 s.d.). In the conflict between Coriolanus and the plebeians in Act III we have confused shouting as "*They all bustle about Coriolanus*" (3.1.185 s.d.), and when he is banished, "*They all shout and throw up their caps*" (3.3.135 s.d.). Coriolanus' decision to spare Rome is celebrated by musical jubilation: "*Trumpets, hautboys, drums beat, all together*" (5.4.51 s.d.), "*Sound still with the shouts*" (5.4.60 s.d.), and "*A flourish with drums and trumpets*" (5.5.7. s.d.) The final scene of the play also puts strong insistence on public ceremony as "*Drums and trumpets sound, with great shouts of the people* (5.6.48 s.d.), and Coriolanus enters "marching with *Drum* and *Colours* . . ." (5.6.69 s.d.). As in *Hamlet,* the play ends with solemn music: "*A dead march sounded*" (5.6.155 s.d.)

The public style of *Coriolanus,* so forcibly conveyed by the sound directions, is in some sense an expression of the imaginative limitations of the play; the characters use language and imagery that are natural and appropriate to them. Coriolanus himself renounces rhetoric and seems to equate a plain style with integrity, for the heroic virtues of war and the soldier do not demand an elaborate poetic imagery. Perhaps part of the difficulty in appreciating this play stems from an overemphasis on verbal imagery. If we consider the play from a dramatic point of view, it has surprising force and vitality, as the production directed by John Houseman at the Phoenix Theater in 1954 seemed to indicate. The poetic speech is remarkably tight and sinewy, from Volumnia's familiar "Pow, waw!" (2.1.157) to Marcius' formal renunciation of "acclamations hyperbolical" (1.9.50). There is also a brilliant use of short choric scenes which comment on the main action without making obtrusive analogies; for dramatic economy, I,iii and IV,iii are among the best scenes of this sort in all of Shakespeare. It is along these dramatic lines, I think, that we may understand the otherwise bewildering remark of Eliot that *Coriolanus* is, "with *Antony and Cleopatra,* Shakespeare's most assured artistic success."[25]

25 T. S. Eliot, "Hamlet," in *Selected Essays 1917–1932,* N. Y., 1932, p. 124. See also Eliot's unfinished *Coriolan,* which is based on Shakespeare's play (*The Complete Poems and Plays 1909–1950,* N. Y., 1952, pp. 85–89).

EDWARD DOWDEN

The Character of Caesar

THE CONSPIRACY has been conceived and hatched by Cassius. The one thing wanting to the conspirators, as he perceives, is moral elevation, and that prestige which would be lent to the enterprise by a disinterested and lofty soul like that of Brutus. The time is the feast of Lupercal, and Antony is to run in the games. Cæsar passes by, and as he passes a soothsayer calls in shrill tones from the press of people, "Beware the Ides of March." Cæsar summons him forward, gazes in his face, and dismisses him with authoritative gesture, "He is a dreamer; let us leave him: pass." It is evidently intended that Cæsar shall have a foible for supposing that he can read off character from the faces of men:

> Yond Cassius has a lean and hungry look.

Cæsar need not condescend to the ordinary ways of obtaining acquaintance with facts. He asks no question of the soothsayer. He takes the royal road to knowledge—intuition. This self-indulgence of his own foibles is, as it were, symbolized by his physical infirmity, which he admits in lordly fashion—"Come on my right hand, for this ear is deaf." Cæsar is entitled to own such a foible as deafness; it may pass well with Cæsar. If men would have him hear them, let them come to his right ear. Meanwhile, things may be whispered which it were well for him if he strained an ear—right or left—to catch. In Shakspere's rendering of the character of Cæsar, which has considerably bewildered his critics, one thought of the poet would seem to be this—that unless a man continually keeps himself in relation with facts, and with his present person and character, he may become to himself legendary and mythical. The real man Cæsar disappears for himself under the greatness of the Cæsar myth. He forgets himself as he actually is, and knows only the vast legendary power named Cæsar. He is a *numen* to himself, speaking of Cæsar in the third person, as if of some power above and

From *Shakspere: A Critical Study of His Mind and Art*, third edition, New York, 1881, pp. 252–56. First published 1875. Title supplied by the present editor.

behind his consciousness. And at this very moment—so ironical is the time-spirit—Cassius is cruelly insisting to Brutus upon all those infirmities which prove this god no more than a pitiful mortal.

Julius Cæsar appears in only three scenes of the play. In the first scene of the third act he dies. Where he does appear, the poet seems anxious to insist upon the weakness rather than the strength of Cæsar. He swoons when the crown is offered to him, and upon his recovery enacts a piece of stagy heroism; he suffers from the falling-sickness; he is deaf; his body does not retain its early vigor. He is subject to the vain hopes and vain alarms of superstition. His manner of speech is pompous and arrogant; he accepts flattery as a right; he vacillates, while professing unalterable constancy; he has lost in part his gift of perceiving facts, and of dealing efficiently with men and with events. Why is this? And why is the play, notwithstanding, "Julius Caesar"? Why did Shakespere decide to represent in such a light the chief man of the Roman world? . . .

Julius Cæsar is indeed protagonist of the tragedy; but it is not the Cæsar whose bodily presence is weak, whose mind is declining in strength and sure-footed energy, the Cæsar who stands exposed to all the accidents of fortune. This bodily presence of Cæsar is but of secondary importance, and may be supplied when it actually passes away, by Octavius as its substitute. It is the spirit of Cæsar which is the dominant power of the tragedy; against this—the spirit of Cæsar—Brutus fought; but Brutus, who forever errs in practical politics, succeeded only in striking down Cæsar's body; he who had been weak now rises as pure spirit, strong and terrible, and avenges himself upon the conspirators. The contrast between the weakness of Cæsar's bodily presence in the first half of the play, and the might of his spiritual presence in the latter half of the play, is emphasized, and perhaps over-emphasized, by Shakspere. It was the error of Brutus that he failed to perceive wherein lay the true Cæsarean power, and acted with short-sighted eagerness and violence. Mark Antony, over the dead body of his lord, announces what is to follow:

> Over thy wounds now do I prophesy—
>
> .   .   .   .   .   .
>
> A curse shall light upon the limbs of men;
> Domestic fury and fierce civil strife
> Shall cumber all the parts of Italy;
>
> .   .   .   .   .   .
>
> And Cæsar's spirit, ranging for revenge,
> With Ate by his side come hot from hell,
> Shall in these confines with a monarch's voice
> Cry "Havoc," and let slip the dogs of war.

The ghost of Cæsar (designated by Plutarch only the "evil spirit" of Brutus), which appears on the night before the battle of Philippi, serves as a kind of visible symbol of the vast posthumous power of the dictator. Cassius dies with the words—

> Cæsar, thou art revenged,
> Even with the sword that killed thee.

Brutus, when he looks upon the dead face of his brother, exclaims,

> O Julius Cæsar, thou art mighty yet!
> Thy spirit walks abroad, and turns our swords
> In our own proper entrails.

Finally, the little effort of the aristocrat republicans sinks to the ground, foiled and crushed by the force which they had hoped to abolish with one violent blow. Brutus dies:

> Cæsar, now be still:
> I kill'd not thee with half so good a will.

Brutus dies; and Octavius lives to reap the fruit whose seed had been sown by his great predecessor. With strict propriety, therefore, the play bears the name of *Julius Cæsar*.

RICHARD G. MOULTON

How the Play of Julius Caesar Works to a Climax at the Centre

A STUDY IN PASSION AND MOVEMENT

THE preceding chapters have been confined to two of the main elements in dramatic effect, Character and Plot: the third remains to be illustrated. Amongst other devices of public amusement the experiment has been tried of arranging a game of chess to be played by living pieces on a monster board; if we suppose that in the midst of such a game the real combative instincts of the living pieces should be suddenly aroused, that the knight should in grim earnest plunge his spear into his nearest opponent, and that missiles should actually be discharged from the castles, then the shock produced in the feelings of the bystanders by such a change would serve to bring out with emphasis the distinction between Plot and the third element of dramatic effect, Passion. Plot is an interest of a purely intellectual kind, it traces laws, principles, order, and design in the incidents of life. Passion, on the other hand, depends on the human character of the personages involved; it consists in the effects produced on the spectator's emotional nature as his sympathy follows the characters through the incidents of the plot; it is War as distinguished from *Kriegspiel*. Effects of such Passion are numerous and various: the present study is concerned with its *Movement*. This Movement comprehends a class of dramatic effects differing in one obvious particular from the effects considered so far. Character-Interpretation and Plot are both analytical in their nature; the play has to be taken to pieces and details selected from various parts have to be put together to give the idea of a complete character, or to make up some single thread of design. Movement, on the contrary, follows the actual order of the events as they take place in the play itself. The emotional effects produced by such events as they succeed one another will not be uniform and monotonous; the skill of the dramatist will lie in concentrating

From *Shakespeare as a Dramatic Artist*, third edition, Oxford, 1906, chapter IX and chart on p. 406 of appendix. First published 1885.

effect at some points and relieving it at others; and to watch such play of passion through the progress of the action will be a leading dramatic interest. Now we have already had occasion to notice the prominence which Shakespeare in his dramatic construction gives to the central point of a play; symmetry more than sensation is the effect which has an attraction for his genius, and the finale to which the action is to lead is not more important to him than the balancing of the whole drama about a turning-point in the middle. Accordingly it is not surprising to find that in the Passion-Movement of his dramas a similar plan of construction is often followed; that all other variations are subordinated to one great Climax of Passion at the centre. To repeat an illustration already applied to Plot: the movement of the passion seems to follow the form of a regular arch, commencing in calmness, rising through emotional strain to a summit of agitation at the centre, then through the rest of the play declining into a calmness of a different kind. It is the purpose of this and the next studies to illustrate this kind of movement in two very different plays. *Julius Cæsar* has the simplest of plots; our attention is engaged with a strain of emotion which is made to rise gradually to a climax at the centre, and then equally gradually to decline. *Lear,* on the contrary, is amongst the most intricate of Shakespeare's plays; nevertheless the dramatist contrives to keep the same simple form of emotional effect, and its complex passions unite in producing a concentration of emotional agitation in a few central scenes.

The passion in the play of *Julius Cæsar* gathers around the conspirators, and follows them through the mutations of their fortunes. If however we are to catch the different parts of the action in their proper proportions we must remember the character of these conspirators, and especially of their leaders Brutus and Cassius. These are actuated in what they do not by personal motives but by devotion to the public good and the idea of republican liberty; accordingly in following their career we must not look too exclusively at their personal success and failure. The exact key to the movement of the drama will be given by fixing attention upon the *justification of the conspirators' cause* in the minds of the audience; and it is this which is found to rise gradually to its height in the centre of the play, and from that point to decline to the end. I have pointed out in the preceding study how the issue at stake in *Julius Cæsar* amounts to a conflict between the outer and inner life, between devotion to a public enterprise and such sympathy with the claims of individual humanity as is specially fostered by the cultivation of the inner nature. The issue is reflected in words of Brutus already quoted:

> The abuse of greatness is, when it disjoins
> Remorse from power.

Brutus applies this as a test to Cæsar's action, and is forced to acquit him: but is not Brutus here laying down the very principle of which his own error in the play is the violation? The assassin's dagger puts Brutus and the conspirators in the position of power; while "remorse"—the word in Shakespearean English means human sympathy—is the due of their victim Cæsar, whose rights to justice as a man, and to more than justice as the friend of Brutus, the conspirators have the responsibility of balancing against the claims of a political cause. These claims of justice and humanity are deliberately ignored by the stoicism of Brutus, while the rest of the conspirators are blinded to them by the mists of political enthusiasm; this outraged human sympathy asserts itself after Cæsar's death in a monstrous form in the passions of the mob, which are guided by the skill of Antony to the destruction of the assassins. Of course both the original violation of the balance between the two lives and the subsequent reaction are equally corrupt. The stoicism of Brutus, with its suppression of the inner sympathies, arrives practically at the principle—destined in the future history of the world to be the basis of a yet greater crime—that it is expedient that one man should die rather than that a whole people should perish. On the other hand, Antony trades upon the fickle violence of the populace, and uses it as much for personal ends as for vengeance. This demoralisation of both the sides of character is the result of their divorce. Such is the essence of this play if its action be looked at as a whole; but it belongs to the movement of dramatic passion that we see the action only in its separate parts at different times. Through the first half of the play, while the justification of the conspirators' cause is rising, the other side of the question is carefully hidden from us; from the point of the assassination the suppressed element starts into prominence, and sweeps our sympathies along with it to its triumph at the conclusion of the play.

In following the movement of the drama the action seems to divide itself into stages. In the first of these stages, which comprehends the first two scenes, the conspiracy is only forming; the sympathy with which the spectator follows the details is entirely free from emotional agitation; passion so far is indistinguishable from mere interest. The opening scene strikes appropriately the key-note of the whole action. In it we see the tribunes of the people—officers whose whole *raison d'être* is to be the mouthpiece of the commonalty—restraining their own clients from the noisy honours they are disposed to pay to Cæsar. To the justification in our eyes of a conspiracy against Cæsar, there could not be a better starting-point than this hint that the popular worship of Cæsar, which has made him what he is, is itself reaching its reaction-point. Such a suggestion moreover makes the whole play one complete *wave* of popular fickleness from crest to crest.

The second is the scene upon which the dramatist mainly relies for the *crescendo* in the justification of the conspirators. It is a long scene, elaborately contrived so as to keep the conspirators and their cause before us at their very best, and the victim at his very worst. Cassius is the life and spirit of this scene, as he is of the whole republican movement. Cassius is excellent soil for republican principles. The "rash humour" his mother gave him would predispose him to impatience of those social inequalities and conventional distinctions against which republicanism sets itself. Again he is a hard-thinking man, to whom the perfect realisation of an ideal theory would be as palpable an aim as the more practical purposes of other men. He is a Roman moreover, at once proud of his nation as the greatest in the world, and aware that this national greatness had been through all history bound up with the maintenance of a republican constitution. His republicanism gives to Cassius the dignity that is always given to a character by a grand passion, whether for a cause, a woman, or an idea—the unification of a whole life in a single aim, by which the separate strings of a man's nature are, as it were, tuned into harmony. In the present scene Cassius is expounding the cause which is his life-object. Nor is this all. Cassius was politician enough to adapt himself to his hearers, and could hold up the lower motives to those who would be influenced by them; but in the present case it is the "honourable metal" of a Brutus that he has to work upon, and his exposition of republicanism must be adapted to the highest possible standard. Accordingly, in the language of the scene we find the idea of human equality expressed in its most ideal form. Without it Cassius thinks life not worth living.

> I had as lief not be as live to be
> In awe of such a thing as I myself.
> I was born free as Cæsar; so were you;
> We both have fed as well, and we can both
> Endure the winter's cold as well as he.

The examples follow of the flood and fever incidents, which show how the majesty of Cæsar vanished before the violence of natural forces and the prostration of disease.

> And this man
> Is now become a god, and Cassius is
> A wretched creature and must bend his body,
> If Cæsar carelessly but nod on him.

In the eye of the state, individuals are so many members of a class, in precisely the way that their names are so many examples of the proper noun.

> Brutus and Cæsar: what should be in that "Cæsar"?
> Why should that name be sounded more than yours?
> Write them together, yours is as fair a name;
> Sound them, it doth become the mouth as well;
> Weigh them, it is as heavy; conjure with them,
> Brutus will start a spirit as soon as Cæsar.
> Now, in the names of all the gods at once,
> Upon what meat doth this our Cæsar feed,
> That he is grown so great?

And this exposition of the conspirators' cause in its highest form is at the same time thrown into yet higher relief by a background to the scene, in which the victim is presented at his worst. All through the conversation between Brutus and Cassius, the shouting of the mob reminds of the scene which is at the moment going on in the Capitol, while the conversation is interrupted for a time by the returning procession of Cæsar. In this action behind the scenes which thus mingles with the main incident Cæsar is committing the one fault of his life; this is the fault of "treason," which can be justified only by being successful and so becoming "revolution," whereas Cæsar is failing, and deserving to fail from the vacillating hesitation with which he sins. Moreover, unfavourable as such incidents would be in themselves to our sympathy with Cæsar, yet it is not the actual facts that we are permitted to see, but they are further distorted by the medium through which they reach us—the cynicism of Casca which belittles and disparages all he relates.

Bru. Tell us the manner of it, gentle Casca.

Casca. I can as well be hanged as tell the manner of it: it was mere foolery; I did not mark it. I saw Mark Antony offer him a crown;—yet 'twas not a crown neither, 'twas one of these coronets:—and, as I told you, he put it by once: but, for all that, to my thinking, he would fain have had it. Then he offered it to him again; then he put it by again: but, to my thinking, he was very loath to lay his fingers off it. And then he offer'd it the third time; he put it the third time by: and still as he refused it, the rabblement hooted and clapped their chapped hands and threw up their sweaty night-caps and uttered such a deal of stinking breath because Cæsar had refused the crown that it had almost choked Cæsar; for he swounded and fell down at it: and, for mine own part, I durst not laugh, for fear of opening my lips and receiving the bad air. . . . When he came to himself again, he said, If he had done or said anything amiss, he desired their worships to think it was his infirmity. Three or four wenches, where I stood, cried, "Alas, good soul!" and forgave him with all their hearts; but there 's no heed to be taken of them; if Cæsar had stabbed their mothers they would have done no less.

At the end of the scene Brutus is won, and we pass immediately into the second stage of the action: the conspiracy is now formed and developing, and the emotional strain begins. The adhesion of Brutus has given us confidence that the conspiracy will be effective, and we have only to *wait* for the issue. This mere notion of *waiting* is itself enough to introduce an element of agitation into the passion sufficient to mark off this stage of the action from the preceding. How powerful suspense is for this purpose we have expressed in the words of the play itself:

> Between the acting of a dreadful thing
> And the first motion, all the interim is
> Like a phantasma, or a hideous dream:
> The Genius and the mortal instruments
> Are then in council; and the state of man,
> Like to a little kingdom, suffers then
> The nature of an insurrection.

But besides the suspense there is a special device for securing the agitation proper to this stage of the passion: throughout there is maintained a Dramatic Background of night, storm, and supernatural portents.

The conception of nature as exhibiting sympathy with sudden turns in human affairs is one of the most fundamental instincts of poetry. To cite notable instances: it is this which accompanies with storm and whirlwind the climax to the *Book of Job,* and which leads Milton to make the whole universe sensible of Adam's transgression:

> Earth trembl'd from her entrails, as again
> In pangs, and Nature gave a second groan;
> Sky lowr'd, and muttering thunder, some sad drops
> Wept at completing of the mortal sin
> Original.

So too the other end of the world's history has its appropriate accompaniments: "the sun shall be darkened and the moon shall not give her light, and the stars shall be falling from heaven." There is a *vagueness* of terror inseparable from these outbursts of nature, so mysterious in their causes and aims. They are actually the most mighty of forces—for human artillery is feeble beside the earthquake—yet they are invisible: the wind works its havoc without the keenest eye being able to perceive it, and the lightning is never seen till it has struck. Again, there is something weird in the feeling that the most frightful powers in the material universe are all *soft things.* The empty air becomes the irresistible wind; the fluid and yielding water wears down the hard and massive rock and determines the shape of the earth; impalpable fire that is blown about in every direction can be roused till it devours the solidest constructions of human skill; while the most powerful agencies of all, electricity and atomic force, are imperceptible to any of the senses and are known

only by their results. This uncanny terror attaching to the union between force and softness is the inspiration of one of Homer's most unique
episodes, in which the bewildered Achilles, struggling with the river-
god, finds the strength and skill of the finished warrior vain against the
ever-rising water, and bitterly feels the violation of the natural order—

> That strong might fall by strong, where now weak water's luxury
> Must make my death blush.

To the terrible in nature are added portents of the supernatural, sudden
violations of the uniformity of nature, the principle upon which all sci-
ence is founded. The solitary bird of night has been seen in the crowded
Capitol; fire has played around a human hand without destroying it;
lions, forgetting their fierceness, have mingled with men; clouds drop
fire instead of rain; graves are giving up their dead; the chance shapes
of clouds take distinctness to suggest tumult on the earth. Such phenomena of nature and the supernatural, agitating from their appeal at
once to fear and mystery, and associated by the fancy with the terrible
in human events, have made a deep impression upon primitive thought;
and the impression has descended by generations of inherited tradition
until, whatever may be the attitude of the intellect to the phenomena
themselves, their associations in the emotional nature are of agitation.
They thus become appropriate as a Dramatic Background to an agitated
passion in the scenes themselves, calling out the emotional effect by a
vague sympathy, much as a musical note may set in vibration a distant
string that is in unison with it.

This device then is used by Shakespeare in the second stage of the
present play. We see the warning terrors through the eyes of men of
the time, and their force is measured by the fact that they shake the
cynical Casca into eloquence.

> Are not you moved, when all the sway of earth
> Shakes like a thing unfirm? O Cicero,
> I have seen tempests, when the scolding winds
> Have rived the knotty oaks, and I have seen
> The ambitious ocean swell and rage and foam,
> To be exalted with the threatening clouds:
> But never till to-night, never till now,
> Did I go through a tempest dropping fire.
> Either there is a civil strife in heaven,
> Or else the world, too saucy with the gods,
> Incenses them to send destruction.

And the idea thus started at the commencement is kept before our minds
throughout this stage of the drama by perpetual allusions, however slight,
to the sky and external nature. Brutus reads the secret missives by the

light of exhalations whizzing through the air; when some of the conspirators step aside, to occupy a few moments while the rest are con-
ferring apart, it is to the sky their thoughts naturally seem to turn, and
they with difficulty can make out the East from the West; the discussion
of the conspirators includes the effect on Cæsar of the night's prodigies.
Later Portia remonstrates against her husband's exposure to the raw and
dank morning, to the rheumy and unpurged air; even when daylight
has fully returned, the conversation is of Calpurnia's dream and the
terrible prodigies.

Against this background are displayed, first single figures of Cassius
and other conspirators; then Brutus alone in calm deliberation: then the
whole band of conspirators, their wild excitement side by side with
Brutus's immovable moderation. Then the Conspiracy Scene fades in
the early morning light into a display of Brutus in his softer relations;
and with complete return of day changes to the house of Cæsar on the
fatal morning. Cæsar also is displayed in contact with the supernatural,
as represented by Calpurnia's terrors and repeated messages of omens
that forbid his venturing upon public action for that day. Cæsar faces
all this with his usual loftiness of mind; yet the scene is so contrived
that, as far as immediate effect is concerned, this very loftiness is made
to tell against him. The unflinching courage that overrides and inter-
prets otherwise the prodigies and warnings seems presumption to us
who know the reality of the danger. It is the same with his yielding to
the humour of his wife. Why should he not? his is not the conscious
weakness that must be firm to show that it is not afraid. Yet when, upon
Decius's explaining away the dream and satisfying Calpurnia's fears,
Cæsar's own attraction to danger leads him to persevere in his first
intention, this change of purpose seems to us, who have heard Decius's
boast that he can o'ersway Cæsar with flattery, a confirmation of
Cæsar's weakness. So in accordance with the purpose that reigns through
the first half of the play the victim is made to appear at his worst: the
passing effect of the scene is to suggest weakness in Cæsar, while it is
in fact furnishing elements which, upon reflection, go to build up a
character of strength. On the other hand, throughout this stage the
justification of the conspirators' cause gains by their confidence and their
high tone; in particular by the way in which they interpret to their own
advantage the supernatural element. Cassius feels the wildness of the
night as in perfect harmony with his own spirit.

> For my part, I have walk'd about the streets,
> Submitting me unto the perilous night,
> And, thus unbraced, Casca, as you see,
> Have bared my bosom to the thunder-stone;

> And when the cross blue lightning seem'd to open
> The breast of heaven, I did present myself
> Even in the aim and very flash of it.

And it needs only a word from him to communicate his confidence to his comrades.

> *Cassius.* Now could I, Casca, name to thee a man
>   Most like this dreadful night,
>   That thunders, lightens, opens graves, and roars
>   As doth the lion in the Capitol,
>   A man no mightier than thyself or me
>   In personal action, yet prodigious grown
>   And fearful, as these strange eruptions are—
> *Casca.* 'Tis Cæsar that you mean; is it not, Cassius?

The third stage of the action brings us to the climax of the passion; the strain upon our emotions now rises to a height of agitation. The exact commencement of the crisis seems to be marked by the soothsayer's words at the opening of Act III. Cæsar observes on entering the Capitol the soothsayer who had warned him to beware of this very day.

> *Cæsar.* The ides of March are come.
> *Sooth.* Ay, Cæsar; but not gone.

Such words seem to measure out a narrow area of time in which the crisis is to work itself out. There is however no distinct break between different stages of a dramatic movement like that in the present play; and two short incidents have preceded this scene which have served as emotional devices to bring about a distinct advance in the intensification of the strain. In the first, Artemidorus appeared reading a letter of warning which he purposed to present to Cæsar on his way to the fatal spot. In the Capitol Scene he presents it, while the ready Decius hastens to interpose another petition to take off Cæsar's attention. Artemidorus conjures Cæsar to read his first for "it touches him nearer"; but the imperial chivalry of Cæsar forbids:

> What touches us ourself shall be last served.

The momentary hope of rescue is dashed. In the second incident Portia has been displayed completely unnerved by the weight of a secret to the anxiety of which she is not equal; she sends messengers to the Capitol and recalls them as she recollects that she dare give them no message; her agitation has communicated itself to us, besides suggesting the fear that it may betray to others what she is anxious to conceal. Our sympathy has thus been tossed from side to side, although in its general direction it still moves on the side of the conspirators. In the crisis itself the agitation becomes painful as the entrance of Popilius Lena and his secret communication to Cæsar cause a panic that threatens to wreck the whole plot on the verge of its success. Brutus's nerve sustains even this trial, and the way for the accomplishment of the deed is again clear. Emotional devices like these have carried the passion up to a climax of agitation; and the conspirators now advance to present their pretended suit and achieve the bloody deed. To the last the double effect of Cæsar's demeanour continues. Considered in itself, his unrelenting firmness of principle exhibits the highest model of a ruler; yet to us, who know the purpose lurking behind the hypocritical intercession of the conspirators, Cæsar's self-confidence resembles the infatuation that goes before Nemesis. He scorns the fickle politicians before him as mere wandering sparks of heavenly fire, while he is left alone as a pole-star of true-fixed and resting quality:—and in answer to his presumptuous boast that he can never be moved come the blows of the assassins which strike him down; while there is a flash of irony as he is seen to have fallen beside the statue of Pompey, and the marble seems to gleam in cold triumph over the rival at last lying bleeding at its feet. The assassination is accomplished, the cause of the conspirators is won: pity notwithstanding we are swept along with the current of their enthusiasm; and the justification that has been steadily rising from the commencement reaches its climax as, their adversaries dispersing in terror, the conspirators dip their hands in their victim's blood, and make their triumphant appeal to the whole world and all time.

> *Cassius.* Stoop, then, and wash. How many ages hence
>   Shall this our lofty scene be acted over
>   In states unborn and accents yet unknown!
> *Brutus.* How many times shall Cæsar bleed in sport,
>   That now on Pompey's basis lies along,
>   No worthier than the dust!
> *Cassius.*   So oft as that shall be,
>   So often shall the knot of us be call'd
>   The men that gave their country LIBERTY!

Enter a servant: this simple stage-direction is the "catastrophe," the turning-round of the whole action; the arch has reached its apex and the Reaction has begun. So instantaneous is the change, that though it is only the servant of Antony who speaks, yet the first words of his message ring with the peculiar tone of subtly-poised sentences which are inseparably associated with Antony's eloquence; it is like the first announcement of that which is to be a final theme in music, and from this point this tone dominates the scene to the very end.

> Thus he bade me say:
> Brutus is noble, wise, valiant, and honest,
> Cæsar was mighty, bold, royal, and loving,
> Say I love Brutus, and I honour him;
> Say I fear'd Cæsar, honour'd him, and lov'd him.
> If Brutus will vouchsafe that Antony
> May safely come to him, and be resolv'd
> How Cæsar hath deserved to lie in death,
> Mark Antony shall not love Cæsar dead
> So well as Brutus living.

In the whole Shakespearean Drama there is nowhere such a swift swing-ing round of a dramatic action as is here marked by this sudden up-springing of the suppressed individuality in Antony's character, hitherto so colourless that he has been spared by the conspirators as a mere limb of Cæsar. The tone of exultant triumph in the conspirators has in an instant given place to Cassius's "misgiving" as Brutus grants Antony an audience; and when Antony enters, Brutus's first words to him fall into the form of apology. The quick subtlety of Antony's intellect has grasped the whole situation, and with irresistible force he slowly feels his way towards using the conspirators' aid for crushing themselves and aveng-ing their victim. The bewilderment of the conspirators in the presence of this unlooked-for force is seen in Cassius' unavailing attempt to bring Antony to the point, as to what compact he will make with them. Antony, on the contrary, reads his men with such nicety that he can indulge himself in sailing close to the wind, and grasps fervently the hands of the assassins while he pours out a flood of bitter grief over the corpse. It is not hypocrisy, nor a trick to gain time, this conciliation of his enemies. Steeped in the political spirit of the age, Antony knows, as no other man, the mob which governs Rome, and is conscious of the mighty engine he possesses in his oratory to sway that mob in what direction he pleases; when his bold plan has succeeded, and his adver-saries have consented to meet him in contest of oratory, then ironical conciliation becomes the natural relief to his pent-up passion.

> Friends am I with you all and love you all,
> *Upon this hope, that you shall give me reasons*
> Why and wherein Cæsar was dangerous.

It is as he feels the sense of innate oratorical power and of the oppor-tunity his enemies have given to that power, that he exaggerates his temporary amity with the men he is about to crush: it is the execu-tioner arranging his victim comfortably on the rack before he proceeds to apply the levers. Already the passion of the drama has fallen under the guidance of Antony. The view of Cæsar as an innocent victim is now allowed full play upon our sympathies when Antony, left alone with the corpse, can drop the artificial mask and give vent to his love and vengeance. The success of the conspiracy had begun to decline as we marked Brutus's ill-timed generosity to Antony in granting him the funeral oration; it crumbles away through the cold unnatural euphuism of Brutus's speech in its defence; it is hurried to its ruin when Antony at last exercises his spell upon the Roman people and upon the reader. The speech of Antony, with its mastery of every phase of feeling, is a perfect sonata upon the instrument of the human emotions. Its opening theme is sympathy with bereavement, against which are working as if in conflict anticipations of future themes, doubt and compunction. A distinct change of movement comes with the first introduction of what is to be the final subject, the mention of the will. But when this new movement has worked up from curiosity to impatience, there is a diversion: the mention of the victory over the Nervii turns the emotions in the direction of historic pride, which harmonises well with the opposite emotions roused as the orator fingers hole after hole in Cæsar's mantle made by the daggers of his false friends, and so leads up to a sudden shock when he uncovers the body itself and displays the popular idol and its bloody defacement. Then the finale begins: the forgotten theme of the will is again started, and from a burst of gratitude the passion quickens and intensifies to rage, to fury, to mutiny. The mob is won to the Reaction; and the curtain that falls upon the third Act rises for a moment to display the populace tearing a man to pieces simply because he bears the same name as one of the conspirators.

The final stage of the action works out the development of an inevitable fate. The emotional strain now ceases, and, as in the first stage, the passion is of the calmer order, the calmness in this case of pity balanced by a sense of justice. From the opening of the fourth Act the decline in the justification of the conspirators is intimated by the logic of events. The first scene exhibits to us the triumvirate that now governs Rome, and shows that in this triumvirate Antony is supreme: with the man who is the embodiment of the Reaction thus appearing at the head of the world, the fall of the conspirators is seen to be inevitable. The decline of our sympathy with them continues in the following scenes. The Quarrel Scene shows how low the tone of Cassius has fallen since he has dealt with assassination as a political weapon; and even Brutus's moderation has hardened into unpleasing harshness. There is at this point plenty of relief to such unpleasing effects: there is the exhibition of the tender side of Brutus's character as shown in his relations with his page, and the display of friendship maintained between Brutus and Cassius amid falling fortunes. But such incidents as these have a different effect upon us from that which they would have had at an earlier period; the justification of the conspirators has so far declined that now attractive touches in them serve only to increase the pathos of a fate which, however, our sympathy no longer seeks to resist. We get a supernatural foreshadowing of the end in the appearance to Brutus of Cæsar's Ghost, and the omen Cassius sees of the eagles that had consorted his army to Philippi giving place to ravens, crows, and kites on the morning of battle: this lends the authority of the invisible world to our sense that the conspirators' cause is doomed. And judicial blindness overtakes them as Brutus's authority in council overweighs in point after point the shrewder advice of Cassius. Through the scenes of the fifth Act we see the republican leaders fighting on without hope. The last remnant of justification for their cause ceases as the conspirators themselves seem to acknowledge their error and fate. Cassius as he feels his death-blow recognizes the very weapon with which he had committed the crime:

> Cæsar, thou art revenged,
> Even with the sword that kill'd thee.

And at last even the firm spirit of Brutus yields:

> O Julius Cæsar, thou art mighty yet!
> Thy spirit walks abroad, and turns our swords
> In our own proper entrails.

JULIUS CÆSAR

A Passion-Drama

Scheme of Actions
Main Nemesis Action: Rise and Fall of the Republican Conspirators.
   (Sub-Action to the Rise [Character-decline]: The Victim Cæsar.
) Sub-Action to the Fall [Character-rise]: The Avenger Antony.
Enveloping Action: The Roman Mob.

Economy
Balance about the Centre: the Rise by the Fall, the Sub-Action to the Rise
by the Sub-Action to the Fall.

Movement
Passion-Movement, with Similar Motion between the Main and Sub-Actions.
[The form of the Main is distributed between the two Sub-Actions.]
Motive Force: The Main Action, slightly assisted by the Enveloping Action.

Turning-points
The Centre of Plot and Catastrophe coincide: iii. i. between 121 and 122.

HAROLD S. WILSON

THE ORDER OF NATURE
Julius Caesar

IN JULIUS CAESAR, Shakespeare makes a fresh start in the tragic form. The play differs radically from the tragedy that precedes it chronologically, *Romeo and Juliet,* in subject-matter, in the tragic conception, and, for the most part, in technical execution. *Romeo and Juliet* belongs to the matter of romance, matter that Shakespeare could freely alter to suit his conception, as he did by inventing characters and complications not found in his source, by directing the action in a schematic pattern that emphasizes the parts played by chance and a higher destiny and that shows a providential purpose controlling the whole action. *Hamlet* and *Othello* are likewise the matter of romance and here again Shakespeare shapes the matter to suit the design of his Christian conception, of providence and divine justice; *Macbeth* is so freely compounded of different materials found in Holinshed and elsewhere that we may consider it in the same way.

Julius Caesar draws upon the historical authority of Plutarch, as do the later Roman tragedies, an authority which the Elizabethans held in great veneration. Shakespeare doubtless felt freer to alter the materials of Holinshed for his dramatic purposes;[1] at least, his Roman plays follow Plutarch for the most part with close fidelity.[2] Furthermore, the very name of tragedy, for Shakespeare's age, summoned up the authority both of ancient matter and of ancient dramatic form—the formal precedent, that is, of Seneca mainly, which makes itself felt throughout the tragedies of Shakespeare, as in those of Chapman and others of Shakespeare's contemporaries. The treating of familiar themes drawn from

From *On the Design of Shakespearian Tragedy,* 1957, pp. 85–97. Reprinted by permission of the University of Toronto Press. Footnotes 1 and 11 omitted. Title supplied by the present editor.
[1] An interesting reflection of the veneration felt for ancient historical authorities in Shakespeare's age occurs in a marginal Latin note (here translated) of Gabriel Harvey in his folio copy of Livy (Basel, 1555): "We have no historians nowadays of the stature of Livy and Tacitus. Grafton, Stow, and Holinshed are mere asses compared with them. These writers lack a sound historical method and any comprehensive view of history. Better things may be expected of Camden and Hakluyt."
[2] See M. W. MacCallum, *Shakespeare's Roman Plays and their Background* (London, 1910).

ancient history and "climbing to the height of Seneca his style" became almost as much an obligation for the popular dramatist of the end of Elizabeth's reign as it was within the coterie of the Countess of Pembroke. It was to be expected that Shakespeare, as a practising dramatist, would turn his hand to something in the classical manner, or what would be accepted as the classical manner. Actually, the treatment of the theme would be in the tradition of the living theatre of Shakespeare's day, and just as truly aimed at popular appeal as was *Romeo and Juliet* or *Hamlet:* in the hands of Shakespeare the treatment would be incomparably more skilful than the academic exercises of the English Senecans; but it would also, and necessarily, bid for the attention of the learned—Ben Jonson's scornful comment about "Caesar did never wrong but with just cause" is well known—and Shakespeare doubtless felt some constraint in undertaking it. Certainly, it is one of his most careful pieces of workmanship, as we now have it.

The play centres upon what Shakespeare's age probably considered the most famous event of ancient history, as it was set forth in the pages of their favourite moralist among the ancient historians, whom Shakespeare read in Sir Thomas North's fine version. It was a theme full of political and moral import for Shakespeare's time, the story of the assassination of a dictator, the grandeur of whose personality has impressed succeeding ages like that of no other man. Caesar's murder changed the mightiest of states from a republic of free men who ruled the world to an empire which rapidly degenerated into tyranny. So Shakespeare endeavoured to comprehend it.

His task, in constructing a tragedy upon this theme, was one of historical interpretation. Undoubtedly Shakespeare made a careful effort of historical imagination for *Julius Caesar* and his other Roman plays, thinking himself back into the time of Cicero and Brutus, Cleopatra and Octavius Caesar, Aufidius and Coriolanus, trying to feel their motives and to think their thoughts, as he found them suggested in Plutarch. Shakespeare's Romans are by no means Elizabethans; they are *men,* of course, as Dr. Johnson remarked; for Shakespeare, human nature is universally the same; but Shakespeare's Romans do not have the outlook and attitudes of Christians, nor do they recognize the same political motives and values as Elizabethans, or share recognizably kindred tastes. Shakespeare, in fact, is very careful in *Julius Caesar* and the other Roman plays to avoid anachronisms—witness the difference in such plays as *Troilus and Cressida* (where the atmosphere is mediaeval) or in *The Winter's Tale* (where anachronism seems to be a calculated part of the effect). He is not so learned as Ben Jonson; there is no special attempt to create historical atmosphere; but Shakespeare is clearly trying to interpret the actual motives and point of view of historical persons in

Julius Caesar, Antony and Cleopatra, and *Coriolanus,* to make us understand, with his artist's imagination, how the events which Plutarch records, in his interesting but limited historian's way, really came about. He takes minor liberties with Plutarch's data—especially with the chronology, in the service of his dramatic narrative—as he did with the events of the English history plays; but he is remarkably faithful, on the whole, to the main lines of Plutarch's narrative, even to the extent of transferring whole passages of North's prose into verse, almost word for word, as has often been remarked.

To the writing of *Julius Caesar,* Shakespeare brought the rich experience of the English history plays he had already produced. *Julius Caesar* belongs to the period of the two parts of *Henry IV* and *Henry V* and contains minor reminiscences of *1 Henry IV.*[3] There is the same effort of historical imagination; but *Julius Caesar* lacks the immediacy and warmth of patriotic feeling that we sense throughout the plays dealing with English history. There is a cool detachment about *Julius Caesar,* a dispassionate study of incident and motive and character. Human nature is displayed with profound insight, as always with Shakespeare; but the actors move in a context of political concepts in some degree alien to Shakespeare the Elizabethan and patriot of the English histories; and there is a pervasive irony, characteristic of Shakespeare's dealings with antiquity generally, which controls the mood of the whole.

In this mood of ironic contemplation, of disinterested reflection upon the great persons and happenings of an age that had vanished, Shakespeare follows the pattern of events with a clear and untroubled gaze. It is a pattern of moral causes and their effects in this world. There are no theological, no metaphysical preconceptions. The world of *Julius Caesar*—as of *Antony and Cleopatra* and *Coriolanus*—is the natural order of man, which is a moral order, but the religious sanction of that order is not invoked. It is simply man's world as he knows it by the light of natural reason—as Plutarch knew it, and Julius Caesar, Brutus, Cassius, and the rest. In this world there are no significant chains of accident, as we have observed them in *Romeo and Juliet* and *Hamlet.* The moments of choice are clear and emphatic: Brutus's soliloquy (II, i), Caesar's disregard of Calphurnia's foreboding dream, Brutus's overbearing Cassius's judgment about Antony and about the battle of Philippi; even the lack of judgment in the Roman mob has its sequent penalty. The action does, of course, imply a superhuman order of justice and retribution; only we must not think of sin and punishment, if they carry

---

3 Brutus's appeal to "honour" (I, ii, 85–89) curiously recalls Hotspur's more extravagant boast (*1 Henry IV,* I, iii, 201 ff.); and the portents of *Julius Caesar* are somewhat reminiscent of Glendower's account of the upheaval of nature at his birth, the one account perhaps a smiling parody of the other. Cf. also Hotspur's interview with Lady Percy (*1 Henry IV,* II, iii, 39 ff.) and Brutus's with Portia (*Julius Caesar,* II, i, 233 ff.).

any Christian implications for us, but rather of *ate* (the mad folly that comes upon proud men), *hybris* (arrogance), and *nemesis* (the inescapable consequences of *ate* and *hybris*). Shakespeare invokes no other explanation of events, and even these Greek conceptions we must invoke for ourselves; but they best fit the course of events in Shakespeare's Roman plays. What he shows us is a moral pattern of human history, a sequence of human causes and their effects. The supernatural portents in *Julius Caesar*, even the ghost of Caesar before Philippi, are not agents in the drama. They are present for atmospheric effect, and because they figure in Plutarch's account; we may take them as symbolic of the moral event, or not, as we please; but they do not determine anything. The moral outcome is clearly enough determined by the characters of the drama as they feel and think and act before our eyes.

The unifying principle of conception and execution in *Julius Caesar* has troubled a good many critics, the fate of Caesar and that of Brutus (or Brutus and Cassius) being thought to constitute two centres of interest not altogether reconciled; and Fleay's suggestion that we should regard the play as an amalgamation of two earlier ones—a "Death of Caesar" and a "Revenge of Caesar"—has been followed by even wilder hypotheses.[4] There are those who regard the play as essentially Brutus's tragedy,[5] and those for whom the theme is "Caesar and Caesarism."[6] Nor is Professor Kittredge's view that the supernaturalism of the play is the clue to its unity very satisfactory: "Caesar vanquishes Brutus and Cassius at Philippi as truly as he vanquishes Pompey at Pharsalus. Antony and Octavius are not Caesar's avengers; they are merely Caesar's agents; he avenges himself. . . . Caesar, alive or dead, pervades and operates the drama—and not less after his death than in his life."[7] This view exaggerates the importance of the theme of revenge, which is hardly more than incidental to the action; and whether we regard the act of revenge as Caesar's or his successors', such an interpretation differs but little from Fleay's suggestion. Dover Wilson seems much nearer the mark in stressing the political implications, for the play is in some sense Rome's tragedy, as much as Brutus's or Caesar's. But we must necessarily take account of Brutus's centrality in the action, for he is the most impressive figure in it, and the spotlight is on him at the end.

Actually, the play is more complex than any of these suggestions would indicate. We feel its unity readily enough as we read it or see it

[4] F. G. Fleay, *A Chronicle History of the Life and Work of William Shakespeare* (London, 1886), pp. 215, 252; J. M. Robertson, *The Shakespeare Canon*, I (London, 1922), 66 ff.; see the judicious summing-up of E. K. Chambers, *William Shakespeare*, I, 398–99.
[5] A recent example is Willard Farnham, *Shakespeare's Tragic Frontier*, pp. 3–4.
[6] Dover Wilson, introduction to the New Cambridge edition of *Julius Caesar* (Cambridge, 1949), p. xxi.
[7] *The Tragedy of Julius Caesar*, ed. G. L. Kittredge (Boston, etc., 1939), p. xiii.

acted, but when we try to find a verbal approximation for this effect, we may easily overlook some of the significant interrelations of its parts. We may try to express the unity of its theme in a question: Was the murder of Caesar justified? The implied answer develops two levels of significance—like *The Faerie Queene*, except that *Julius Caesar* does not employ the method of allegory. The political issue provides the major and enveloping theme that comprehends all the actors in their relation to the state; among them Caesar is the dominant figure, for he is the occasion of the action, influences its course whether living or dead (as Professor Kittredge has said), and illustrates the tendency, in a republic, for the ablest man to seek absolute power, and the consequent struggle, the anarchy and reversion to a worse form of tyranny which may ensue upon his overthrow. The political tragedy of the Roman state and of Caesar are, for the purposes of the play, identical; the play is thus well named, because the fortunes of Rome reach their highest point, and their turning point, in the fall of Caesar. This political tragedy involves as a consequence the moral tragedy of Brutus; and Brutus's moral tragedy, in turn, is mirrored in Caesar's; for Brutus's act is no better justified in its outcome than Caesar's aims, perhaps less justified. Brutus's wrong choice arises from the "flaw" (in the sense of an ineluctable blindness) of his character. "The noblest Roman of them all," he is nevertheless blind to his own limitations and the guiding motives of other men; with steadfast confidence in his own ideals and his own rightness, he misses the mark completely and without realizing that he has done so. The overweening pride of Caesar during his last days shows us the ground of Brutus's fears for the future and influences his decision: had Caesar not been ambitious, Brutus had never fallen. The fault of one provokes the fault of the other. And yet, the political argument holds as a generalization, without depending upon the personal characters of the protagonists; for if Caesar had not aspired to absolute power, so the political argument would go, sooner or later some other would: he would have found his opposer, and in the resulting conflict Rome would still have fallen. The principals are exemplary of a profound comment upon states and upon individuals; and the two themes, the political and the moral, parallel and complement each other in an ironic yet deeply understanding study of the blindness and futility of men's strivings as they try to act according to their own righteousness and to impose their personal wills in a universe which sets little store by merely human pretensions.

Julius Caesar opens with the tribunes' foreboding of Caesar's mounting ambition and the contrasting irresponsibility of the plebeian crowd; it closes with the victory of the triumvirate over Brutus and Cassius. This is cause and effect, the epitome of the political scale of the action.

In between these poles, we have the fall of Caesar and the moral tragedy of Brutus which it entails. The fall of Brutus parallels that of Caesar; Caesar falls through obstinate pride and Brutus through his own blindness—the Greek *hybris* comprehends both varieties of human culpability. But both of these men, in their falls, show us what is happening to the Roman state. Having made himself dictator, Caesar, "the greatest man in all this world," naturally aspires to the final step, the absolute and permanent power of a king; and ironically, it is just such a benevolent autocrat as he would make that the careless Roman populace need to rule them, and, in their fickleness, would readily welcome. Brutus, in attempting to uphold the traditional republican ideals of Rome by leading the conspiracy against Caesar, actually delivers Rome into the power of the opportunist Antony and the coldly astute Octavius, neither of whom has either the disinterested devotion to his country of Brutus or the magnanimity of Caesar. Such is the pattern of human history that *Julius Caesar* presents to us.

The portrait of Caesar in his last days which the play affords, of a man physically infirm—even Cassius's exaggeration of these infirmities (I, ii, 100 ff.), though we discern his envy of Caesar's greatness in the account, has its derogatory weight—easily swayed by Calphurnia's fears or Decius's flattery, and vain to the point of infatuation, has been variously accounted for. The traits of the braggart, for instance, have been traced to the Senecan *Julius Caesar* of Muretus and the tradition descending therefrom;[8] and, as Granville Barker has remarked, Caesar must be played down if he is to die in the third act, or the play would end in anticlimax.[9] Yet more significant is the fact that Shakespeare does choose to kill Caesar in the middle of the play rather than at the end. Evidently, Shakespeare does not take sides, nor is the play simply a study of characters in conflict. Caesar's character in the play is more than a device of dramatic balance or a heritage of Senecan bias; it is part of Shakespeare's reading of the tragic pattern of history, a pattern in which no man, however great, is entirely self-sufficient.

Something of Caesar's true stature emerges from the spell his spirit casts over the drama: he seems to us greater dead than living. With Caesar living, there is no particular subtlety. His is the fault of pride, of *hybris* in its familiar classical lineaments. "What, is the fellow mad?" asks Caesar, with blandly unconscious irony, as Artemidorus presses the paper upon him informing him of the conspiracy. And the extraordinary vaunt of

[8] H. M. Ayres, "Shakespeare's *Julius Caesar* in the Light of Some Other Versions," *Publications of the Modern Language Association of America*, XXV (1910), 183–227.
[9] Granville-Barker, *Prefaces to Shakespeare*, II (Princeton, 1951), 373.

> But I am constant as the Northern Star,
> Of whose true-fix'd and resting quality
> There is no fellow in the firmament . . .

seems in itself enough to provoke the thrusts of the conspirators. This is all heightened for dramatic effect, no doubt, for it is hard to believe that the Caesar of the *Commentaries* ever talked in quite this vein; though in the calculated understatements of Caesar's surviving accounts of his conquests we may perhaps catch an echo of the Thrasonical *veni, vidi, vici,* which, together with his genius for politics, his intellect, and his magnanimity, we may consider, as Shakespeare apparently did, to constitute the complex nature of the man.

Caesar, Brutus, and Cassius are the greatest figures of the play; Octavius, and even Antony, are minor by comparison. Caesar's arrogance and Caesar's fall are the occasion, or the provocation, for the fall of Cassius and Brutus. The dominant note of Cassius's character is plainly envy:

> Such men as he be never at heart's ease,
> Whiles they behold a greater than themselves.

He is the sort of man who takes everything personally, always prone to suppose that someone has slighted or injured him, even his best friends.

> I have not from your eyes that gentleness
> And show of love as I was wont to have,

are his opening words to Brutus (I, ii, 33–34); and he begins the quarrel scene,

> Most noble brother, you have done me wrong!

Especially revealing is his soliloquy after he has first broached the conspiracy to Brutus:

> If I were Brutus now and he were Cassius,
> He should not humour me. . . .

The personal favour of Caesar would, for him, have overborne his resentment of Caesar's tyrannous ways, or so he thinks, for the sake of asserting to himself his superior shrewdness. Yet his resentment of Caesar is something more than personal spite. Cassius, we eventually come to feel, is indeed, as Brutus calls him, "The last of all the Romans" (meaning the great ones), excepting Brutus himself. Cassius is able, far abler than Brutus as a tactician; he is brave; in his way, he is devoted to the ideal of Roman freedom; he is warm-hearted, and knows something of his own faults; and most of us probably feel that, as a friend, we should much prefer the choleric and not altogether high-souled Cassius to the noble Brutus—at least, as Shakespeare imagines them. But Cassius's faults are enough, and more than enough, to bring about his downfall. We recognize the justice and inevitability of his end:

> Caesar, thou art reveng'd
> Even with the sword that kill'd thee;

and the irony of it, for he has despaired of the fluctuating battle too soon.

The justice and the irony of Brutus's end are very much subtler. His integrity is unimpeachable. In his personal character, he approaches Plato's ideal of the philosopher-statesman, disinterested and unsusceptible to passion, devoted to the welfare of his country, the *res publica* which his ancestors had founded and which he is ready to defend at whatever personal cost. No one can doubt that he joins the conspiracy through devotion to his republican principles which, he honestly thinks, are jeopardized by Caesar's continued existence, and despite his friendship and admiration for the man. What Brutus feels about Caesar as a man we may gather from his incidental tributes to him: "O that we then could come by Caesar's spirit, And not dismember Caesar" (II, i, 169–70); "I, that did love Caesar when I struck him" (III, i, 182); "The foremost man of all this world" (IV, iii, 22). Brutus's friendship for Cassius is of the same stuff. "You love me not!" cries Cassius, at the height of their quarrel, when he has been humiliated to the breaking point by Brutus's inflexible insistence upon Cassius's deviations from Brutus's strict code of honourable dealing; and Brutus's reply comes with chilling emphasis: "I do not like your faults." Brutus cares less for persons than for ideas; he has an unshakable conviction of his own virtue; and he demands that the same virtue should be in other men:

> There is no terror, Cassius, in your threats;
> For I am arm'd so strong in honesty
> That they pass by me as the idle wind
> Which I respect not.

His view of the conspiracy is of like simplicity:

> Did not great Julius bleed for justice sake?
> What villain touch'd his body that did stab
> And not for justice?

which we may place beside Antony's final verdict:

> All the conspirators save only he
> Did what they did in envy of great Caesar.

Brutus's motives are unselfish; his integrity is complete; and yet he is infatuated, with an infatuation like Caesar's in degree, if not in kind —indeed, more terrible, because Caesar's vanity (as Shakespeare imag-

ines it) has something of a child's boastfulness,[10] while Brutus's opinion
of his own honesty is well founded.[11] His fault lies in his superb confidence. The ancients taught that no mortal could afford such self-
sufficiency: "Think as a mortal," the maxim has it;[12] and Brutus's pride
is of the type that Montaigne so strongly censured in the peroration to
the most famous of his essays.[13]

Brutus's pride betrays him. Once in the conspiracy, his reputation,
and his sublime assurance of his own rightness (an assurance which
Cassius, for all his passionate intensity, never dreamed of possessing,
or of questioning in Brutus, either), impose him as the leader. With
unerring insight, Shakespeare fixes upon this trait to explain Brutus's
fatal mistake as he found it described in Plutarch:

> All the conspirators but Brutus, determining upon this matter, thought it
> good also to kill Antonius, because he was a wicked man, and that in nature
> favoured tyranny; besides also, for that he was in great estimation with
> soldiers, having been conversant of long time amongst them: and specially
> having a mind bent to great enterprises, he was also of great authority at
> that time, being Consul with Caesar. But Brutus would not agree to it.
> First, for that he said it was not honest: secondly, because he told them
> there was hope of change in him. For he did not mistrust, but that Antonius,
> being a noble-minded and courageous man (when he should know that
> Caesar was dead) would willingly help his country to recover her liberty,
> having them as an example unto him, to follow their courage and virtue.
> So Brutus by this means saved Antonius's life. . . .[14]

To this flagrant misjudgment of Plutarch's Brutus, Shakespeare adds the
weight of Brutus's assurance as he overbears the shrewder judgment of
Cassius not merely in the matter of sparing Antony (II, i, 162 ff.) but

---

[10] For example, the rant of

> Danger knows full well
> That Caesar is more dangerous than he.
> We are two lions litter'd in one day,
> And I the elder and more terrible.

And yet, in real life such absurdity is not incompatible with greatness. We cannot doubt
Shakespeare's just estimate of Caesar's greatness; but he had a lively sense of the ridiculous-
ness of his more extravagant pretensions, and, doubtless, of the more extravagant worship of
his memory, as his casual allusions elsewhere than in *Julius Caesar* suggest—"The hook-
nos'd fellow of Rome," *2 Henry IV*, IV, iii, 45; "Caesar's thrasonical brag of 'I came, saw,
and overcame,' " *As You Like It*, V, ii, 34. We may likewise recall that Polonius did once
enact Julius Caesar (*Hamlet* III, ii, 105 ff.).
[11] Cassius understands Brutus best, as his masterful handling of him in I, ii shows. We
might say that Cassius here flatters Brutus; and yet it is not so much that Brutus is subject
to flattery as that he sincerely believes himself to be the model of virtue that Cassius
describes—and with some justification; and Cassius really believes all that he says in compliment to Brutus, too.
[12] See Pindar, *Isthm.* V, 16; Paul Elmer More, "Nemesis, or the Divine Envy," *Shelburne
Essays, Second Series* (New York and London, 1905), pp. 219 ff.; E. R. Dodds, *The Greeks
and the Irrational* (Berkeley and Los Angeles, 1951), pp. 29 ff.
[13] Montaigne, "Apologie de Raimond Sebond," *Essais*, II, xii, *ad fin.*
[14] "The Life of Marcus Brutus," in *Shakespeare's Plutarch*, ed. C. F. Tucker Brooke
(London, 1909), I, 133–34; cf. II, 20.

in the plan of tactics for their last battle as well (IV, iii, 196 ff.).[15] And
the crowning irony is Brutus's unawareness of his fault, or of the venality
that vitiates his cause. This blindness is that "missing of the mark"
(ἁμάρτημα) which is at least part of what Aristotle had in mind in that
troublesome passage of the *Poetics* on dramatic character,[16] and which,
in the severest tragic conception of the Greeks, above all of Sophocles,
the gods punish as inevitably as the faults of passion. As Granville-
Barker excellently puts it, "it is not . . . passions that blind [Brutus], but
principles";[17] and his fault is more awe-inspiring than the passion of
Cassius because it is the excess of his virtue: in his serene sense of that
virtue, he never knows that he does wrong.

In Brutus, we cannot trace a process of ennoblement through suffering, as we can in Hamlet, and perhaps even in Mark Antony of *Antony
and Cleopatra*. The end of *Julius Caesar* shows, among other things,
how unchanged Brutus is by all that has happened. We can hardly feel
sorry for him. His motives, his principles, his acts are all of a piece
throughout, and he dies in defence of the same principle of Roman
liberty that had led him in the first place to join the conspirators. He
commits suicide against his Stoic code (V, i, 100 ff.), but this is to
avoid what for a Roman was unbearable disgrace, to be led as a victim
in a Roman triumph. It is perhaps a final irony that the rational Brutus
should be influenced by the ghost of Caesar to take his life at Philippi.
But Brutus's suicide was also his last act in defence of liberty, and in
this sense the final assertion of his principles.

Brutus's tragedy is personal in its cause, human blindness, but it is
not deep personal tragedy, the tragedy of divided motives; the deeper
tragedy lies in the public consequences of his acts. In a great crisis of
the world's history, Brutus, despite his complete personal integrity,
lacked the wisdom necessary to the high role he felt called upon to fill,
adjudicator in the issue of what form of government made for justice.
He committed murder, and without achieving the results he hoped for.
The consequences, like nemesis, were civil war for Rome, death for
Brutus and the other conspirators, and an eventual reign of tyranny
compared with which the rule of Julius Caesar had been benevolent and
wise.

---

[15] Such reiterated or parallel episodes (II, i, 155 ff.; IV, iii, 196 ff.), already noticed as
part of the technique of *Romeo and Juliet*, are an occasional feature of the technique of
Julius Caesar. Cf. Cassius's flattery of Brutus (I, ii, 55 ff.) with Decius's flattery of Caesar
(II, ii, 92 ff.); Cassius's interpretation of the portents of the storm to Casca (I, iii, 57 ff.)
with Decius's interpretation of Calphurnia's dream (II, ii, 83 ff.); and the passages between
(*a*) Brutus and Portia, (*b*) Brutus and his servant Lucius, which reiterate the point of
Brutus's sensibility as the necessary qualification of his otherwise inflexible temper to make
him recognizably human.
[16] Aristotle, *Poetics*, 1453a, 10, 16.
[17] Granville-Barker, *Prefaces to Shakespeare*, II, 390.

In the political consequences of the play lies its ultimate significance. If Brutus had been at all venal—if, as the analogy of Cassius suggests to us, the personal favour he enjoyed from Caesar had weighed with him more than the cause of liberty—his personal tragedy might have been avoided. His plight is that he had the virtue of disinterestedness without the wisdom—that is, the understanding of himself and other men—necessary to give his disinterestedness political effectiveness. He is as noble, essentially, as a man can be; his tragedy is that he is, after all, human, and he aspired to play the role of a god.

Brutus commands our admiration rather than our full sympathy. At bottom, he was infatuated, no better than a fool—as Caesar was in a different way, and as many another great man has been, before and since; and when they die through their own folly, we cannot deplore their loss. What is most fully tragic about the play is the effect of Brutus's conduct, for it influenced the lives of all his fellow beings, the Roman commonweal. Ironically, his act of killing Caesar brought upon Rome the very tyranny he planned to do away with. Yet we cannot say that the tyranny which followed is wholly Brutus's fault, either. He became the guiding spirit of the conspiracy, and so we may speak as if it were his agency. But he was not its cause. If Brutus and Cassius had not murdered Caesar, others probably would have; for his arrogance (in a state accustomed to the maximum of liberty for the citizens) cried out for such a check.

This is the design, then, of political events and their outcome which Shakespeare presents to us in the play. The human ideal of liberty is incompatible with the limits of human wisdom, the human capacity of self-knowledge and self-rule. This fact is tragic for the noble-minded idealist like Brutus and for the great statesman like Caesar; and it is tragic for the state, for each member of it has his share of responsibility in the catastrophe, from Caesar and Brutus, Caesar's supporters and Brutus's supporters, on down to the humblest of the Roman mob, who make holiday when Caesar triumphs over the sons of Pompey and would indifferently accept Caesar or Brutus for their king.

This play contains perhaps the most philosophical of all Shakespeare's dramatic interpretations of human history. Plainly, it is the most detached; there was nothing to engage Shakespeare's partisanship, and he views both the imperial ambitions of Caesar and the republican ardour of Brutus with a gravely ironic impartiality. The irony is deeply understanding; he studies not only the vicissitudes of the Roman state in its moment of greatest crisis but also the personal tragedies of its citizens. Brutus and Caesar, Cassius and Antony, Titinius and Lucilius and even the slave Strato who holds the sword for Brutus are all vividly realized for us as human beings. The detachment, the serene and impartial understanding of the artist and the thinker—for this is more a play of thought than of passion—is the leading quality of this work; and, as we grow older, at least, it leaves us filled with admiration for the artist's genius but comparatively unmoved—unmoved, that is, compared with the effects we experience in the great tragedies that followed *Julius Caesar*. It is an excellent play for young students, because here they may discover the beautiful comprehensiveness of Shakespeare's mind and the constructive genius of his dramatic art displayed with relative simplicity, without the subtler ambiguities of motive he delighted to study in the psychologically more complex of his tragedies and without the headier intoxication of his most splendid poetry. There was nothing in the theme of *Julius Caesar* to arouse Shakespeare's highest poetic energies, most deeply stirred by romantic rather than historical themes. On the other hand, we find a simplicity of style admirably suited to the subject, a severe logic of construction,[18] and a pervasive irony in the development of the motives and the action not unworthy to rank with the work of the supreme master of dramatic irony, Sophocles. *Julius Caesar* is far from the greatest of Shakespeare's own tragedies; nor is it so learned an invocation of classical antiquity as Ben Jonson's *Sejanus:* yet it is a very much greater play. It is, among English plays, the one best informed with the qualities we call "classical"—a perfection of structure, a severe and restrained beauty of style, deeply contemplative insight. In this sense, it is the best classical tragedy in English.

[18] The cavil against the great quarrel scene of Act IV, which Bradley thought failed to advance the action, has been shown to be an unwarranted objection by a number of commentators, notably Kittredge, *The Tragedy of Julius Caesar*, notes to IV, iii; and Dover Wilson, *Julius Caesar*, New Cambridge ed., p. xx.

ERNEST SCHANZER

The Tragedy of Shakespeare's Brutus

WHILE SHAKESPEARE'S Cassius, Caesar, and Antony owe little to their prototypes in Plutarch, his Brutus is substantially Plutarch's Brutus. Yet even here, for all that makes Brutus a *dramatic* character as distinct from a copy-book hero, his divided mind, his self-deception, his final tragic disillusion, Shakespeare received no hints from Plutarch.

It is a mistake to see Brutus as the unworldly scholar, blind to political realities, devoid of a knowledge of life, called from his books to assume a task for which he is not fitted. This view was dear to Romantic critics, who liked to present this phantom Brutus as Shakespeare's first sketch in preparation for their phantom Hamlet. Shakespeare shows Brutus to be a bad judge of character, but as by no means devoid of political shrewdness and practical wisdom. For instance, in Plutarch it is Antony who suggests that Caesar's "body should be honourably buried, and not in hugger mugger, lest the people might thereby take occasion to be worse offended if they did otherwise." (*Brutus*, pp. 136–7).[1] Shakespeare transfers the argument to Brutus, making him declare:

> What Antony shall speak, I will protest
> He speaks by leave and by permission,
> And that we are contented Caesar shall
> Have all true rites and lawful ceremonies.
> It shall advantage more than do us wrong.
> (3. 1. 239 ff.)

That Shakespeare regarded the argument as by no means "fatuous," as one critic calls it, but as shrewd practical politics, is shown by his putting a variation of it a few years later into the mouth of his arch-politician Claudius:

From *ELH*, XXII (1955), 1–15. Reprinted by permission of The Johns Hopkins Press and the author. Essay revised by the author for this edition.
[1] All page-references are to *Shakespeare's Plutarch*, ed. Tucker Brooke, 2 vol., in the *Shakespeare's Library* series.

> the people muddied,
> Thick and unwholesome in their thoughts and whispers
> For good Polonius' death—and we have done but greenly
> In hugger-mugger to inter him.   (*Hamlet*, 4. 5. 80 ff.)

(The "hugger-mugger" shows that Shakespeare had that very passage from Plutarch at the back of his mind when writing these lines, a striking example of how North's more vivid idioms were garnered up in the poet's memory, to be brought out when some similarity of situation recalled them.) Brutus' advice is in itself sound enough and would have justified itself with anyone except Antony, whom he so fatally misjudges.

Again, I cannot agree with critics who speak of Brutus's oration as an example of his political naïveté, of the scholar's inability to understand the emotions of the mob, or to present his case effectually. It seems to me, on the contrary, an extremely shrewd and highly effective piece of oratory. In his soliloquy Brutus could find nothing with which to reproach Caesar except his desire for the crown. The murder is in his eyes purely preventive, designed to protect the commonwealth from the kind of person Caesar is likely to become upon the acquisition of greater powers. To win the support of a mob clamouring for satisfaction with no better arguments to justify the murder of their hero is clearly no simple matter. How does Brutus achieve it? He begins by subtly, unobtrusively, flattering his audience. The very fact that he does not talk down to them, will not speak their language, as Antony does, is a compliment to their intelligence. And even if they cannot quite follow him in his clipped, carefully patterned sentences, they can at least make out that the noble Brutus asks them to respect his honour, to censure him in their wisdom, to be his judges. Nothing could be more flattering except his next suggestion, that among them there may be a dear friend of Caesar's. Then comes the assertion, true as we know it to be, but therefore none the less effective, that only a superior love for his country made him slay his dearest friend. Still no charge has been brought against Caesar. Then suddenly the question is sprung on them: "Had you rather Caesar were living, and die all slaves, than that Caesar were dead, to live all free men?" That the alternative may be quite unreal will not occur to the crowd under the influence of Brutus's oratory. At last an accusation is brought forward, but one of the vaguest sort: Caesar was ambitious. And at once, before they have time to ask for evidence, there follows the series of rhetorical questions which so ingeniously forestall any objections from his audience:

> Who is here so base that would be a bondman? If any, speak; for him have
> I offended. Who is here so rude that would not be a Roman? If any, speak;

for him have I offended. Who is here so vile that will not love his country?
If any, speak; for him have I offended. I pause for a reply.   (3. 2. 30 ff.)

Nothing could be more skilful. He has brought only the vaguest charge
against Caesar and yet effectively blocked all further questions from the
crowd, shown himself the saviour of his country, and gained the love
and admiration of the people. The speech is kept as short as possible,
so that detailed accusations would seem out of place, and, in closing,
the people are hurriedly referred for facts to the records in the Capitol,
with a final display of fairmindedness: "The question of his death is
enrolled in the Capitol; his glory not extenuated, wherein he was worthy;
nor his offences enforced, for which he suffered death." Brutus con-
cludes with a parting glance at the benefit which the people will derive
from Caesar's death, and with an expression of his willingness to die for
his country. The whole speech is as shrewdly contrived and, as the
response of the people shows, quite as effective as Antony's. And Brutus's
is really the far more difficult task. For he has to defend the murder of
"the foremost man of all this world" on a charge which he cannot sub-
stantiate. All that Antony needs to do is to discredit Brutus's allegation
of Caesar's ambition in order to nullify his entire argument. The fact
that all that Brutus says appears to him strictly true and is sincerely
felt in no way lessens the extraordinary skill of the speech.

At other times, too, in the play Brutus does not show himself devoid
of practical wisdom. The reasons he gives for marching to Philippi may
be mistaken, but they certainly show no lack of an eye for the expedient
and politic. Altogether, I think we must banish the myth of the un-
practical dreamer from our image of Brutus's character.

It would seem that just as in Hamlet Shakespeare represents the
Renaissance ideal of the encyclopaedic man, the "uomo universale," in
Brutus he represents the ideal of the harmonious man, whose gentleness,
courtesy, and love of music all bear witness to his "well-tempered"
nature. It is to this quality in him that Antony pays his final tribute:

> His life was gentle, and the elements
> So mixed in him that Nature might stand up
> And say to all the world "This was a man."   (5. 5. 73 ff.)

Yet both Hamlet and Brutus are depicted from their first appearance as
wrenched from their ordinary selves, steeped in melancholy, so that their
normal nature is largely veiled from us, and is chiefly glimpsed through
the tribute of others, an Antony or an Ophelia. Brutus, the harmonious
man, is ironically shown to us throughout the first half of the play rent
by discordant emotions, and later, in the quarrel-scene, "like sweet bells
jangled, out of tune and harsh." Of the civil war in Brutus, resulting
from the conflict between personal and political loyalties, we learn upon

his first appearance, when he speaks to Cassius of "poor Brutus with himself at war," and of his being vexed "of late with passions of some difference" (i. e. with conflicting emotions). It is echoed and amplified by the tempests that precede the assassination and which appear to Casca to spring from "civil strife in heaven" (1. 3. 11). And finally, in fulfilment of Antony's terrible prophecy, the civil war spreads from microcosm and macrocosm to the body politic, finding its culmination at Philippi and its reflection even in the quarrel-scene between Brutus and Cassius. Brutus's inner conflict continues until the assassination, taking on a nightmare quality, and somewhat altering its nature. For while the earlier conflict seems caused mainly by rival loyalties, by warring principles, after Brutus's decision is reached it is the deed itself, now revealed to his imagination in all its stark horror, that causes his feelings to rebel against the decision which his intellect has made. This, I take it, is the meaning of the much disputed

> Between the acting of a dreadful thing
> And the first motion all the interim is
> Like a phantasma or a hideous dream:
> The Genius and the mortal instruments
> Are then in council, and the state of man
> Like to a little kingdom suffers then
> The nature of an insurrection. (2. 1. 63 ff.)

While his mind considers the various possible ways of carrying out the murder (pictured as a council meeting between man's presiding genius, his intellect, and the mortal instruments, the means of bringing about the death), his instincts and passions are in revolt against the decision of their ruler. Brutus finds himself no longer in a state of civil war, where rival principles, each with their army of followers, are engaging in battle, but in a state of insurrection, in which his whole instinctive, emotional, and imaginative being rises in revulsion against the decision which his intellect has made. His gentle, frank, and generous nature is in revolt not only against the deed itself, but against the whole conspiracy, with all the secrecy and deceitfulness that it entails. This is how he greets the announcement of the arrival of his fellow-conspirators:

> They are the faction. O conspiracy,
> Sham'st thou to show thy dangerous brow by night,
> When evils are most free? O, then, by day
> Where wilt thou find a cavern dark enough
> To mask thy monstrous visage? Seek none, conspiracy,
> Hide it in smiles and affability:
> For if thou path, thy native semblance on,
> Not Erebus itself were dim enough
> To hide thee from prevention. (2. 1. 77 ff.)

To save himself from these nightmare realizations he plunges headlong into self-deception. In his soliloquy he had acquitted Caesar of all high-handed, tyrannical acts:

> And, to speak truth of Caesar,
> I have not known when his affections swayed
> More than his reason.   (2. 1. 19 ff.)

A little later, in the company of the conspirators, he tries to work himself up into a conviction that Caesar is already a full-blown tyrant.[2]

> No. Not an oath: if not the face of men,
> The sufferance of our souls, the time's abuse—
> If these be motives weak, break off betimes,
> And every man hence to his idle bed;
> So let high-sighted tyranny range on
> Till each man drop by lottery.   (2. 1. 114 ff.)

Caesar here is no longer the serpent's egg of his soliloquy, nor Flavius's young hawk whose growing feathers must be plucked betimes (1. 1. 75 ff.), but a full grown falcon, scouring for prey.

Like Othello, Brutus tries to free himself both from the guilt and from the sheer physical horror of the murder by adopting a ritualistic and an aesthetic attitude towards it.

> Let's kill him boldly, but not wrathfully.
> Let's carve him as a dish fit for the gods,
> Not hew him as a carcass fit for hounds.   (2. 1. 172 ff.)

> Yet I'll not shed her blood;
> Nor scar that whiter skin of hers than snow,
> And smooth as monumental alabaster.   (5. 2. 3 ff.)

Both these "honourable murderers" picture the deed as an act of sacrifice. "Let us be sacrificers but not butchers, Caius." It is not a husband murdering his wife, not a friend murdering his "best lover" and benefactor; they are "purgers, not murderers." "It is the cause, it is the cause, my soul." Caesar must be killed beautifully, ceremonially.

The ritualistic bathing of their hands in Caesar's blood, suggested by Brutus after the murder, carries this further, and, incidentally, fulfils Calpurnia's prophetic dream.

> Stoop, Romans, stoop,
> And let us bathe our hands in Caesar's blood
> Up to the elbows, and besmear our swords.   (3. 1. 106 ff.)

[2] This element of self-delusion in Brutus has already been pointed out by Sir Mark Hunter, *Trans. Royal Soc. Lit.*, X (1931), pp. 136 ff., and by Mr. J. I. M. Stewart in his *Character and Motive in Shakespeare*, pp. 51 ff.

But, ironically, the action suggests another ritual, far removed from that which Brutus has in mind, the custom of huntsmen at the kill to steep their hands in the blood of their victim. It is to this bloody rite that Antony refers:

> Here wast thou bayed, brave hart,
> Here didst thou fall, and here thy hunters stand,
> Signed in thy spoil and crimsoned in thy lethe.   (3. 1. 204 ff.)[3]

Whereas Brutus pictures to himself the murder as a ceremonial slaying of the sacrificial beast on the altar of the commonweal, Antony sees it as the bloody slaughter of the noble stag, the King of the Forest, for the sake of his spoil. For under cover of the metaphor Antony can dare to accuse the conspirators to their face of killing Caesar for the sake of plunder, the other significance of "spoil." But fearing he has gone too far he at once insinuates a piece of flattery, as is his wont throughout this scene:

> How like a deer strucken by many princes
> Dost thou here lie.   (3. 1. 209–210)

But from Antony's soliloquy we realize that even the hunting-metaphor was a form of flattery. "O, pardon me, thou bleeding piece of earth, / That I am meek and gentle with these butchers." It is an ironic comment on Brutus's illusions and his "Let us be sacrificers, but not butchers, Caius." The assassination turns into something very different from a ritual slaying. Plutarch mentions that "divers of the conspirators did hurt themselves striking one body with so many blows" (*Caesar*, p. 102). Shakespeare makes Antony allude to this in the "flyting" scene at Philippi, when he speaks of how the conspirators' "vile daggers hacked one another in the sides of Caesar." It is not a very pretty picture. Nor does the reality of Caesar's body "marred with traitors" bear much relation to Brutus's aesthetic vision. Disconcerting to his illusions is also the conspirators' flattery of Caesar, which makes the latter speak of Metellus's "spaniel-fawning," and threaten to spurn him like a cur out of his way. It is not as priests officiating at a sacrifice that the conspirators are here seen, not even as hunters, but as hounds that fawn upon their victim before tearing it to pieces. It is to this image that Antony returns in the "flyting" scene, when he accuses them of having "fawned like hounds," "whilst damned Casca, like a cur behind, / Struck Caesar on the neck." (5. 1. 41 ff.) On one other occasion in the play Antony uses a metaphor from the hunt. In his soliloquy he envisages the war of

---

[3] Whether we accept Capell's explanation of "lethe" as "a term used by hunters to signify the blood shed by a deer at its fall"—and I can find no evidence to support it—or take it to mean "stream of death" and hence "life-blood," does not much affect the force of the image.

revenge as a savage hunting scene in which this time the conspirators are the quarry, no quarter is given, and Caesar's ghost acts as the chief huntsman:

> And Caesar's spirit, ranging for revenge,
> With Até by his side come hot from hell,
> Shall in these confines with a monarch's voice
> Cry "Havoc," and let slip the dogs of war.   (3. 1. 270 ff.)

This whole complex of hunting-metaphors was probably set off in the poet's mind by Plutarch's description of Caesar as "hacked and mangled among them, as a wild beast taken of hunters." (*Caesar*, pp. 101–2.)

The need for self-deception, which drives Brutus to picture Caesar as a dangerous tyrant and to visualize his murder as a sacrificial rite, makes him afterwards try to persuade himself that they have done a benefit not only to their country but to Caesar himself. He eagerly takes up Casca's

> Why, he that cuts off twenty years of life
> Cuts off so many years of fearing death,

exclaiming,

> Grant that, and then is death a benefit:
> So are we Caesar's friends, that have abridged
> His time of fearing death.   (3. 1. 102 ff.)

In his soliloquy we find Brutus engaged in a more subtle form of self-deception in the attempt to still his inner conflict. We are not here watching an act of choice. The choice has already been made, as the opening line makes us realize: "It must be by his death." (2. 1. 10). How Brutus arrived at this absolute "must" we are never shown. It would seem that Shakespeare wishes us to feel that the decision had nothing to do with reason and logic, that he has somehow fallen victim to Cassius's powers of persuasion without being able to accept his arguments or to share his motives. What we are watching in the soliloquy is Brutus's attempt to defend his decision before the court of his conscience. The rhythm of the verse, the disjointed sentences, the diction in such lines as "and since the quarrel / Will bear no colour for the thing he is / Fashion it thus," brings out the anxious groping for some plausible justification for the deed. Caesar's desire for the crown does not in itself appear sufficient cause to Brutus. Shakespeare's Brutus is by no means a doctrinaire republican, in contrast to the Brutus of Plutarch, who reproaches Cicero for favouring Octavius Caesar, declaring, "For our predecessors would never abide to be subject to any Master, how gentle or mild soever they were." (*Brutus*, p. 141.) Cassius's denunciation of the rule of a single man, and his reference to Lucius Brutus, who "would have brooked / Th' eternal devil to keep his state in Rome / As easily as a king" (1. 2. 159 ff.), whatever their emotional impact, have not swayed Brutus's reason. His opposition to kingship rests on his fears of the corrupting effect of power, not on the nature of its office. "He would be crowned: / How that might change his nature, there's the question." (2. 1. 12–13) It is startling to find Brutus in the remainder of his soliloquy speak of Caesar as if he were still at the beginning of his career, to hear him talk of "the bright day that brings forth the adder," of "young ambition's ladder," of Caesar as a serpent's egg. Like the reference to his "lowliness" it is wildly out of keeping with the impression of Caesar that we gather in the course of the play. It would seem that, finding nothing in the mere fact of kingship, nor anything in Caesar's past behaviour to justify the assassination, Brutus deludes himself by vastly exaggerating the gap that separates the present from the future Caesar, between the power wielded by the dictator and by the imaginary king. Once this position is taken up Brutus has no difficulty in advancing a logical argument for the assassination, and in this he is helped by his metaphor. It suggests the justification for the preventive murder, since it implies that, just as the adder, once hatched, is a menace that can no longer be controlled, so Caesar, once crowned, would be out of reach of the assassins' daggers. To safeguard the commonwealth he must therefore be destroyed while he is still accessible, even though there is the possibility that the egg may hatch a dove and not a serpent. The argument is quite cogent and contains no confusion, as some critics have claimed. But it is founded on self-deception.

By thus putting the justification for the murder on a pragmatic basis Brutus is laying the foundation for his later tragedy. Had he been a doctrinaire republican and murdered Caesar to save the republic from kingship he would have been safe, if not from inner conflicts, at least from tragic disillusion. For his purpose would have been accomplished. But by justifying the deed to himself and others on the grounds of "pity to the general wrong of Rome" (3. 1. 171), the wrong that Caesar might have committed in the future, he put himself at the mercy of events. For it is only by establishing a government under which the people suffer less wrong than they would have done under Caesar's rule that the murder can, to Brutus, be justified. And what are in fact its consequences as they are depicted in the play? They are adumbrated in Antony's prophecy: "Domestic fury and fierce civil strife / Shall cumber all the parts of Italy." "All pity choked with custom of fell deed . . ." (3. 1. 263 ff.) It is a grim comment on Brutus's words in the same scene:

And pity to the general wrong of Rome—
As fire drives out fire, so pity pity—
Hath done this deed on Caesar.   (3. 1. 171 ff.)

In the succeeding scenes we find Antony translating his prophecy into fact. We see the domestic fury unchained by him tearing the harmless Cinna to pieces, and in the next scene observe the regime that has been established in Rome in the place of Caesar's: callous, cold-blooded, and ruthless. The blood-bath of the triumvirs contrasts with Caesar's scrupulous and unselfish administration of justice of which we get glimpses in his "What touches us ourself shall be last served" (3. 1. 8), and his behaviour over the repeal of the banishment of Cimber. News reaches Brutus that seventy senators, including Cicero, have been put to death. His wife has committed suicide. And, to cap it all, his own cause has been tarnished by Cassius's malpractices. These are the fruits of the assassination. Instead of benefiting his country Brutus has, from the best of motives and the highest of principles, plunged it into ruin. This is one of the great ironies in a play full of ironic touches.

The action of *Julius Caesar* thus conforms to Aristotle's conception of *peripeteia,* an ironic turn of events which makes an action have the very opposite effects of those intended. It is found with varying degrees of prominence in all of Shakespeare's mature tragedies.

An understanding of the nature of Brutus's tragedy also helps us to comprehend why Shakespeare depicted Caesar as he did. Had he made him a full-blown tyrant there would have been no tragedy lying in wait for Brutus. Had he made him a wholly admirable figure Brutus's tragedy would have been more like that of Othello, with Brutus murdering his "best lover," misled by Cassius's Iago-like machinations, and the later terrible realization of what he has done. By depicting Caesar as he does Shakespeare takes Brutus's tragedy out of the field of personal relations into that of public life. Unlike the Brutus in *Caesar's Revenge,* Shakespeare's Brutus is not shown at the end of the play as tortured by memories of the murder of his friend and benefactor. His torments, as far as we can judge, result rather from the realization of the kind of world which he has helped to bring into being. His "best lover" is not really Caesar, or Portia, still less Cassius, but the "res publica." It is her image which has become for him "begrim'd and black" since she has gone a whoring with Antony and been besmirched by Cassius's malpractices. It is this tragic disillusion which seems to me implicit in the quarrel-scene, and which vents itself in Brutus's passionate outbursts, and in the harshness and bitterness of his recriminations. For it is Cassius who, as his associate and friend, has above all sullied for Brutus the image of his ideal republic, and contributed most to his disillusion. Hence the

virulence of the accusations, the talk of chastisement, the repeated
dwelling upon his own honesty. The mood finds at once expression upon
Brutus's first re-entry after his oration in Act 3.

> Your master, Pindarus,
> In his own charge, or by ill officers,
> Hath given me some worthy cause to wish
> Things done undone.   (4. 2. 6 ff.)

And it becomes most explicit in his passionate reminder to Cassius of
the high ideals for which Caesar has been murdered and which alone
make the assassination for him defensible:

> Remember March, the Ides of March remember!
> Did not great Julius bleed for justice' sake?
> What villain touched his body, that did stab,
> And not for justice? What, shall one of us,
> That struck the foremost man of all this world
> But for supporting robbers, shall we now
> Contaminate our fingers with base bribes;
> And sell the mighty space of our large honours
> For so much trash as may be grasped thus?
> I had rather be a dog, and bay the moon,
> Than such a Roman.   (4. 3. 18 ff.)

In the quarrel-scene, as elsewhere in the play, Brutus and Cassius talk
an entirely different language. To Cassius the quarrel is a lovers' quarrel. He cannot conceive why Brutus should be so passionately angry
over such trivial offences, has no notion that for Brutus they are bound
up with the justifiability of the entire conspiracy. He can merely see that
Brutus loves him not, and that under such conditions life to him is value-
less, so that without insincerity he can exclaim:

> There is my dagger,
> And here my naked breast; within, a heart
> Dearer than Pluto's mine, richer than gold;
> If that thou be'st a Roman, take it forth;
> I, that denied thee gold, will give my heart:
> Strike, as thou didst at Caesar; for I know,
> When thou didst hate him worst, thou lovedst him better
> Than ever thou lovedst Cassius.   (4. 3. 99 ff.)

The image of the gold echoes a very similar one used earlier in the scene
by Brutus:

> By heaven, I had rather coin my heart,
> And drop my blood for drachmas, than to wring
> From the hard hands of peasants their vile trash
> By any indirection.   (4. 3. 72 ff.)

The two images epitomise the character of the speakers. Brutus would rather die than injure his country; Cassius would rather die than live without the love of his friend. The conflict, fundamental to the play, between private and public loyalties, which is waged in Brutus's mind in the earlier part of the play, has in the quarrel-scene become externalised, and is now fought out between the representatives of the two opposing ways of life.

We see, then, that the quarrel-scene, so far from being episodic and dramatically dispensable, as Bradley thought,[4] is in many ways the most important scene in the play. Not only is it here that Brutus's tragic disillusion is most fully revealed to us, but the scene also crystallises the play's main moral issue, the rival claims of personal relations and the "res publica."

The play's unity, which has so often been impugned by critics, is really achieved in a twofold manner: By Shakespeare's adoption of the framework of an Elizabethan revenge tragedy, which makes the last two acts, with the ghost's pursuit of the murderers and his final revenge on the battlefield, an integral part of the play's structure. And, more importantly, by Shakespeare's choice of Brutus for his tragic hero. This last fact has frequently been denied by critics. Professor Charlton, for instance, goes so far as to declare that "Brutus is no more significant in the play than is Hotspur in *Henry IV*"; and that "it is impossible to fit *Julius Caesar* into Shakespeare's mode of tragedy." To him *"Julius Caesar* is a history play in exactly the same sense as are *Henry IV* and *Henry V*: i.e. it is a political play."[5] And to Professor Dover Wilson "the main issue of the play is not the conspirators' fate but the future of Rome, of liberty, of the human race, to which their fate is incidental."[6] Both these views seem to me wholly at odds with the imaginative impact of the play. The main issue of *Julius Caesar*, as I see it, is not a political but a moral issue, consisting in the conflicting claims of the world of personal relations and that of politics.[7] This issue is never for long lost sight of in the play. In Brutus's assassination of Caesar and in his quarrel with Cassius personal loyalties are sacrificed to political ideals. In Antony's feigned league of friendship with the conspirators and in his treatment of Lepidus personal relations are made the dupe of political expediency. And the same is true of Decius Brutus's relations with Caesar. Political issues, such as the future of Rome and the choice be-

---

[4] A. C. Bradley, *Shakespearean Tragedy*, p. 60.
[5] H. B. Charlton, *Shakespeare, Politics and Politicians*, English Association Pamphlet No. 72, pp. 19 ff.
[6] *Julius Caesar*, New Cambridge edition, p. xx.
[7] The importance of this issue in *Julius Caesar* has been well brought out by Professor L. C. Knights in his valuable and stimulating article on "Shakespeare and Political Wisdom," *Sewanee Review*, 61 (1953).

tween a republican and monarchic form of government, enter the play only in so far as they impinge upon the moral issue. They are, in other words, not a concern of the play itself, but merely a concern of some of the play's characters.

Its central character is Brutus, in whom the moral issue is fought out, and whose tragedy seems to me very much of the Shakespearean kind. It is on Brutus, the only person in the play who experiences any inner conflict, that our main interest is focussed from the first, and it is with an eye on him that much of the play's material is presented. Had Shakespeare's main concern been with Caesar or with political issues he would never have denied himself the stage-presentation of Antony's offer of the crown at the Lupercal. But it is its effect upon Brutus that concerns Shakespeare, so that all he needs to give us are the shouts of the populace, Brutus's anxious surmises, and Casca's taunting report. Shakespeare's presentation of the character of Caesar itself seems partly determined, as I have argued, by its bearing upon Brutus's tragedy. And the play ends with the tribute to the tragic hero, as we find it in *Hamlet, Coriolanus, Antony and Cleopatra,* and *Romeo and Juliet* (Othello and Timon provide their own epitaphs).

Julius Caesar is, in fact, the first of the poet's tragedies in what we have come to think of as the peculiarly Shakespearian mode, and in its presentation of Brutus's tragic disillusion points forward to *Troilus and Cressida* and *Timon,* to *Othello* and *Macbeth.*

SAMUEL TAYLOR COLERIDGE

NOTES ON THE TRAGEDIES
Antony and Cleopatra

SHAKESPEARE can be complimented only by comparison with himself: all other eulogies are either heterogeneous (*ex. gr.*, in relation to Milton, Spenser, etc.) or flat truisms (*ex. gr.*, to prefer him to Racine, Corneille, or even his own immediate successors, Fletcher, Massinger, etc.). The highest praise or rather form of praise, of this play which I can offer in my own mind, is the doubt which its perusal always occasions in me, whether it is not in all exhibitions of a giant power in its strength and vigor of maturity, a formidable rival of the *Macbeth, Lear, Othello,* and *Hamlet. Feliciter audax* is the motto for its style comparatively with his other works, even as it is the general motto of all his works compared with those of other poets. Be it remembered too, that this happy valiancy of style is but the representative and result of all the material excellencies so exprest.

This play should be perused in mental contrast with Romeo and Juliet;—as the love of passion and appetite opposed to the love of affection and instinct. But the art displayed in the character of Cleopatra is profound in this, especially, that the sense of criminality in her passion is lessened by our insight into its depth and energy, at the very moment that we cannot but perceive that the passion itself springs out of the habitual craving of a licentious nature, and that it is supported and reinforced by voluntary stimulus and sought-for associations, instead of blossoming out of spontaneous emotion.

But of all perhaps of Shakespeare's plays the most wonderful is the *Antony and Cleopatra.* [There are] scarcely any in which he has followed history more minutely, and yet few even of his own in which he impresses the notion of giant strength so much, perhaps none in which he impresses it more strongly. This [is] owing to the manner in which it is sustained throughout—that he *lives* in and through the play—to the numerous momentary flashes of nature counteracting the historic abstraction, in which take as a specimen the [death of Cleopatra].

From *Coleridge's Shakespearean Criticism*, edited by Thomas Middleton Raysor, Cambridge, Mass., Harvard University Press, 1930, Vol. I, 85–86. Reprinted by permission of Thomas Middleton Raysor.

HARLEY GRANVILLE-BARKER

Cleopatra

SHAKESPEARE'S CLEOPATRA had to be acted by a boy, and this did
everything to determine, not his view of the character, but his presenting of it. Think how a modern dramatist, a practical man of the theater,
with an actress for his Cleopatra, would set about the business. He
might give us the tragedy of the play's end much as Shakespeare does,
no doubt—if he could; but can we conceive him leaving Cleopatra without one single scene in which to show the sensual charm which drew
Antony to her, and back to her, which is the tragedy's very fount? Yet
this is what Shakespeare does, and with excellent reason: a boy could
not show it, except objectionably or ridiculously. He does not shirk her
sensuality, he stresses it time and again; but he has to find other ways
than the one impracticable way of bringing it home to us. What is the
best evidence we have (so to speak) of Cleopatra's physical charms?
A description of them by Enobarbus—by the misogynist Enobarbus—
given us, moreover, when she has been out of our sight for a quarter of
an hour or so. Near her or away from her, Antony himself never speaks
of them. He may make such a casual joke as

> The beds i' the East are soft.

or reflect in a fateful phrase,

> I will to Egypt . . . .
> I' the East my pleasure lies.

but Shakespeare will not run even so much risk of having a lover's
ecstasies discounted. Enobarbus may grumble out gross remarks about
her; but Antony's response, as he plans his escape, is

> She is cunning past man's thought.

The lovers are never once alone together; and the only approach to a

Reprinted from *Prefaces to Shakespeare* by Harley Granville-Barker, Vol. I, 435–48, by
permission of Princeton University Press. Copyright, 1946, by Princeton University Press.

"love-scene" comes with our first sight of them, walking in formal procession and reciting antiphonally:

CLEOPATRA.   If it be love indeed, tell me how much.
ANTONY.   There's beggary in the love that can be reckoned.
CLEOPATRA.   I'll set a bourn how far to be beloved.
ANTONY.   Then must thou needs find out new heaven, new earth.

This is convention itself. Antony's

> Here is my space.
> Kingdoms are clay: our dungy earth alike
> Feeds beast as man: the nobleness of life
> Is to do thus; when such a mutual pair
> And such a twain can do't. . . .

is pure rhetoric.[1] And the poetry of

> Now, for the love of Love and her soft hours,
> Let's not confound the time with conference harsh.
> There's not a minute of our lives should stretch
> Without some pleasure now. What sport tonight?
> CLEOPATRA. Hear the ambassadors.
> ANTONY.   Fie, wrangling queen!
> Whom everything becomes, to chide, to laugh,
> To weep; whose every passion fully strives
> To make itself in thee, fair and admired! . . .

is sensuality sublimated indeed.

Not till their passion deepens as tragedy nears does Shakespeare give it physical expression. Antony leaves her for battle with "a soldier's kiss" (it is the first the action definitely shows) and, returning triumphant, hails her with

> O thou day o' the world,
> Chain mine armed neck: leap thou, attire and all,
> Through proof of harness to my heart, and there
> Ride on the pants triumphing.

A very open and aboveboard embrace. And not till death is parting them do we reach

> I am dying, Egypt, dying; only
> I here importune death awhile, until
> Of many thousand kisses the poor last
> I lay upon thy lips.

[1] The *"embracing"* which Pope and editors after him tagged on to "thus," is not Shakespeare's direction. Whether he means the two to embrace here may be a moot point, but this sort of thing was *not* what he meant by suiting the action to the word and the word to the action.

with, for its matching and outdoing, her

> welcome, welcome! die where thou hast lived:
> Quicken with kissing: had my lips that power,
> Thus would I wear them out.

By which time, if dramatist and actors between them have not freed the imaginations of their audience from the theater's bonds, all three will have been wasting it. Throughout the play Cleopatra herself gives us glimpses enough of her sensual side.

> Thou, eunuch Mardian!
> What's your highness' pleasure?
> Not now to hear thee sing. I take no pleasure
> In aught an eunuch has: 'tis well for thee
> That, being unseminared, thy freer thoughts
> May not fly forth of Egypt.

But Shakespeare never has her turn it towards a flesh-and-blood Antony, inviting response.

His only choice, then, is to endow her with other charms for conquest: wit, coquetry, perception, subtlety, imagination, inconsequence—and this he does to the full. And had he a veritable Cleopatra to play the part, what other and what better could he do? How does a Cleopatra differ from the common run of wantons but in just such gifts as these? It would take a commonplace dramatist to insist upon the obvious, upon all that age does wither, while custom even sooner stales its infinite monotony!

It is, of course, with his magic of words that Shakespeare weaves Cleopatra's charm. To begin with, we may find ourselves somewhat conscious of the process. Though that first duet between the lovers is with good reason conventional, they seem slightly self-conscious besides; less themselves, at the moment, than advocates for themselves. Not till Cleopatra appears has this cloud about her vanished; but nothing of the sort ever masks her again.

CLEOPATRA.	Saw you my lord?
ENOBARBUS.	No, lady.
CLEOPATRA.	Was he not here?
CHARMIAN.	No, madam.
CLEOPATRA.	He was disposed to mirth; but on the sudden A Roman thought hath struck him. Enobarbus!
ENOBARBUS.	Madam.
CLEOPATRA.	Seek him and bring him hither. Where's Alexas?
ALEXAS.	Here, at your service. My lord approaches.
CLEOPATRA.	We will not look upon him; go with us.

And when she returns:

> See where he is, who's with him, what he does:
> I did not send you: if you find him sad,
> Say I am dancing: if in mirth, report
> That I am sudden sick: quick, and return.

Here is actuality; and forged in words of one syllable, mainly. This is the woman herself, quick, jealous, imperious, mischievous, malicious, flagrant, subtle; but a delicate creature, too, and the light, glib verse seems to set her on tiptoe.

For the scene with Antony, Shakespeare rallies his resources. We have the pouting

> I am sick and sullen.

the plaintive

> Help me away, dear Charmian; I shall fall:
> It cannot be thus long, the sides of nature
> Will not sustain it.

the darting ironic malice of

> I know, by that same eye, there's some good news.
> What says the married woman? You may go. . . .

and pretty pettishness suddenly throbbing into

> Why should I think you can be mine and true,
> Though you in swearing shake the throned gods,
> Who have been false to Fulvia? . . .

Then the vivid simplicities melt into a sheer magic of the music of words.

> But bid farewell and go: when you sued staying,
> Then was the time for words: no going then;
> Eternity was in our lips and eyes,
> Bliss in our brows' bent; none our parts so poor
> But was a race of heaven. . . .

And so, up the scale and down, she enchants the scene to its end.

For a moment in the middle of it we see another Cleopatra, and hear a note struck from nearer the heart of her. She is shocked by his callously calculated gloss upon Fulvia's death. Vagaries of passion she can understand, and tricks and lies to favor them. But this hard-set indifference! She takes it to herself, of course, and is not too shocked to make capital of it for her quarrel. But here, amid the lively wrangling, which is stimulus to their passion, shows a dead spot of incomprehension, the true division between them. They stare for an instant; then cover it, as lovers will. Fulvia's wrongs make the best of capital; there are poisoned pinpricks in them, and the second round of the fight leaves him helpless —but to turn and throttle her. The rules of the ring are not for Cleopatra. She takes woman's leave to play the child, and the great lady's to outdo any wench in skittishness; she matches vulgar gibing with dignity and pathos, now loses herself in inarticulate imaginings, now is simple and humble and nobly forgiving. He must leave her; she lets him go. But to the unguessed riddle that she still is he will return.

Let the actress of today note carefully how the brilliant effect of this first parade of Cleopatra is gained. There is no more action in it than the dignity of a procession provides, and the swifter coming and going and returning which ends in this duel of words danced at arm's length with her lover. There is no plot to be worked out; Antony is departing, and he departs, that is all. What we have is the transposing of a temperament into words; and it is in the changing rhythm and dissolving color of them, quite as much as in the sense, that the woman is to be found. Neither place nor time is left for the embroidery of "business," nor for the overpainting of the picture by such emotional suggestion as the author of today legitimately asks of an actress. Anything of that sort will cloud the scene quite fatally. If the shortcomings of a boy Cleopatra were plain, we can imagine his peculiar virtuosity. To the adopted graces of the great lady he would bring a delicate aloofness, which would hover, sometimes very happily, upon the edge of the absurd. With the art of acting still dominantly the art of speech—to be able to listen undistracted an audience's chief need—he would not make his mere presence disturbingly felt; above all, he could afford to lose himself unreservedly—since his native personality must be lost—in the music of the verse, and to let that speak. So in this scene must the Cleopatra of today, if *we* are not to lose far more than we gain by her. There will be the larger demands on her later, those that Shakespeare's indwelling demon made on him; he had to risk their fulfillment then, as now.

But her presenting continues for awhile to be very much of a parade. She is never, we notice, now or later, left to a soliloquy.[2] Parade fits her character (or if Shakespeare fits her character to parade the effect is the same). She is childishly extravagant, ingenuously shameless; nothing exists for her but her desires. She makes slaves of her servants, but she jokes and sports with them, too, and opens her heart to them in anger or in joy; so they adore her. It is not perhaps an exemplary Court,

---

[2] Nor is anyone else in the play for more than a few lines; another token of it as drama of action rather than of spiritual conflict. We see in this too how far Shakespeare's stagecraft had outgrown the older, conventional, plot-forwarding use of soliloquies. In his earlier plays of action they abound.

in which the Queen encourages chaff about her paramours, and turns on her lady-in-waiting with

> By Isis, I will give thee bloody teeth,
> If thou with Cæsar paragon again
> My man of men.

but it is at least a lively one, and its expansiveness would be a boon to any dramatist.

She is indeed no sluggardly sensualist; double doses of mandragora would not keep her quiet. What she cannot herself she must do by proxy; she cannot follow Antony, but her messengers gallop after him every post. Her senses stir her to potent imagery:

> O happy horse, to bear the weight of Antony!
> Do bravely, horse! for wot'st thou whom thou movest. . . .

—if perverted a little:

> now I feed myself
> With most delicious poison.

And in that

> Think on me,
> That am with Phœbus' amorous pinches black,
> And wrinkled deep in time.

there is elemental power. And if her praise of Antony for his "well-divided disposition" seems incongruous; why, a nature so sure of itself can admire the qualities it lacks.

Shakespeare shirks nothing about her. What will be left for us of her womanly charm when we have seen her haling the bringer of the news of Antony's treachery up and down by the hair of his head, and running after him, knife in hand, screaming like a fishfag? But this also is Cleopatra. He allows her here no moment of dignity, nor of fortitude in grief; only the pathos of

CLEOPATRA. In praising Antony, I have dispraised Cæsar?
CHARMIAN. Many times, madam.
CLEOPATRA.   I am paid for't now.

—which is the pathos of the whipped child, rancorous against its gods, resigned to evil. There is the moment's thought, as she calls the scared messenger back again:

> These hands do lack nobility, that they strike
> A meaner than myself; since I myself
> Have given myself the cause.

And this is a notable touch. It forecasts the Cleopatra of the play's end, who will seek her death after the "high Roman fashion"; it reveals, not inconsistency, but that antithesis in disposition which must be the making of every human equation. It is the second touch of its sort that Shakespeare gives to his picturing of her; and both, in the acting, must be stamped on our memories.[3]

The end of the scene sees her, with her maids fluttering round her, lapsed into pitifulness, into childish ineptitude. But again, something of spiritual continence sounds in its last note of all, in the

> Pity me, Charmian;
> But do not speak to me.

The complementary scene, in which the unlucky messenger is re-examined, would be more telling if it followed a little closer; but, as we have seen, Shakespeare has hereabouts an overplus of Roman material to deal with. It is pure comedy, and of the best. She is calm again, very collected, making light of her fury; but an echo of it can be heard in that sudden nasty little snarl which ends in a sigh. Charmian and Iras and Alexas have evidently had a trying time with her. They conspire to flatter her back to confidence—and she lets them. The messenger has been well coached too. But the best of the comedy is in Cleopatra's cryptic simplicity. She likes flattery for its own sake. There is a sensuality of the mind that flattery feeds. What does it matter if they lie to her; of what use is the truth? Anger is crippling; but in the glow of their adulation she uncurls and feels her lithe strength return, and this is her only need.

> All may be well enough.

Yet the words savor faintly of weariness too.

Now comes the war and her undoing. Her disillusion first; for Antony, won back, is no longer the all-conquering captain, from whom she may command Herod of Jewry's head—or Cæsar's!—nor does her own reckless generalship prove much help. We do not, as we have noted, see the reuniting of the lovers; we find her at a nagging match with Enobarbus, and turned, with her Antony, to something very like a shrew. And if to the very end she stays for him an unguessed riddle, "cunning past man's thought," there is much in which Shakespeare is content to leave her so for us—thereby to manifest her the more consummately. By what twists of impulse or of calculation is she moved through the three fateful days of swaying fortune? How ready was she to "pack cards" with Cæsar? What the final betrayal amounted to, that sent Antony raging after her, Shakespeare, it may be said, could not tell us, because

[3] The first, her stinging reproach to him for his callousness at Fulvia's death.

he did not know; and her inarticulate terror at this point may therefore show us his stagecraft at its canniest. But in retrospect all this matters dramatically very little; what does matter is that as we watch her she should defy calculation.

It is futile, we know, to apply the usual moral tests to her, of loyalty, candor, courage. Yet because she shamelessly overacts her repentance for her share in that first defeat it by no means follows that she feels none. She lends an ear to Thidias, and the message to Cæsar sounds flat treason; this is the blackest count against her. But soft speech costs nothing, and perhaps it was Cæsar who was to be tricked. Can we detect, though, a new contempt for Antony as she watches him, his fury glutted by the torment of the wretched envoy? She might respect him more had he flogged her instead! Is there in the sadly smiling

> Not know me yet?

with which she counters his spent reproach, and in her wealth of pro-test, something of the glib falsity of sated ardors? Next morning she buckles on his armor and bids him good-bye like a happy child; but, his back turned:

> He goes forth gallantly. That he and Cæsar might
> Determine this great war in single fight!
> Then, Antony—! But now—?

It is a chilling postscript.

She is like Antony in this at least—and it erects them both to figures of heroic size—that she has never learned to compromise with life, nor had to reconcile her own nature's extremes. To call her false to this or to that is to set up a standard that could have no value for her. She is true enough to the self of the moment; and, in the end, tragically true to a self left sublimated by great loss. The passionate woman has a child's desires and a child's fears, an animal's wary distrust; balance of judgment none, one would say. But often, as at this moment, she shows the shrewd scepticism of a child.

From now till we see her in the Monument and Antony is brought to die in her arms, Shakespeare sinks the figure into the main fabric of the play. He makes a moment's clear picture of the welcome to Antony returned from victory. The

> *Enter Cleopatra, attended.*

might be radiance enough; but, for surplus, we have her ecstatic

> Lord of lords!
> O infinite virtue, comest thou smiling from
> The world's great snare uncaught!

When defeat follows quickly, her collapse to terror is left, as we saw, the anatomy of a collapse and no more. Then, from being but a part of the general swift distraction, she emerges in fresh strength to positive significance again; and—this is important—as a tragic figure for the first time.

From wantonness, trickery and folly, Shakespeare means to lift her to a noble end. But, even in doing it, he shirks no jot of the truth about her. She loses none of her pristine quality. If she victimizes the complacent Dolabella with a glance or two, who shall blame her? But how far she would go in wheedling Cæsar—were there a joint to be found in that armor of cold false courtesy—who shall say? She cheats and lies to him as a matter of course, and Seleucus would fare worse with her than did that once unlucky messenger. Misfortune hardly lends her dignity, the correct Cæsar may well think as he leaves her there. He will think otherwise when he sees her again. But it is not till the supreme moment approaches that she can pretend to any calm of courage. She must sting herself to ever fresh desperation by conjured visions of the shame from which only death will set her free; we hear that "Be noble to myself," "my noble act," repeated like a charm. Yet she is herself to the end. It is the old willful childishness, tuned to a tragic key, that sounds for us in

> O Charmian, I will never go from hence.
>
> CHARMIAN.   Be comforted, dear madam.
> CLEOPATRA.   No, I will not:
> All strange and terrible events are welcome,
> But comforts we despise. . . .

and in the extravagant magnificence of her grief she is the Eastern queen, who could stir even an Enobarbus to rhapsody, and beggar all description. She has no tears for Antony.[4] The shock of his death strikes her senseless, but her spirit is unquelled. Defiant over his body:

> It were for me
> To throw my sceptre at the injurious gods;
> To tell them that this world did equal theirs
> Till they had stolen our jewel. . . .

The rest may find relief in grieving; not she!

Shakespeare allows her one touch of his favorite philosophy. She reappears, confirmed in her loss.

> My desolation does begin to make
> A better life. 'Tis paltry to be Cæsar;
> Not being Fortune, he's but Fortune's knave,
> A minister of her will. . . .

4 Throughout the play Cleopatra never weeps. Antony does.

This is the note, once struck by Brutus, sustained by Hamlet, of failure's contempt for success. We hear it in life, more commonly, from quite successful men, who also seem to find some needed comfort in the thought. It is a recurring note in all Shakespearean tragedy, this exalting of the solitary dignity of the soul; and he will not end even this most unspiritual of plays without sounding it. He passes soon to a somewhat truer Cleopatra—here is the same thought pursued, though—when she counters Dolabella's bland assurance with

> You laugh when boys or women tell their dreams.
> Is't not your trick? . . .
> I dreamt there was an Emperor Antony.
> O, such another sleep, that I might see
> But such another man!

and utterly bewilders him with the hyperbole that follows, strange contrast to Cæsar's recent decorous regret. But it is on such ridiculous heights that genius—even for wantonness—will lodge its happiness. And the next instant he appears, the manikin Cæsar, who has triumphed over her "man of men"! She stares, as if incredulous, till Dolabella has to say

> It is the emperor, madam.

Then she mocks their conqueror with her humilities. But the scene is, besides, a ghastly mockery of the Cleopatra that was. Compare it with the one in which she laughed and pouted and turned Antony round her finger. She is a trapped animal now, cringing and whining and cajoling lest the one chink of escape be stopped. There is no cajoling Cæsar. He betters her at that with his

> Feed and sleep:
> Our care and pity is so much upon you,
> That we remain your friend.

Even so might a cannibal ensure the tenderness of his coming meal. She knows; and when he is gone:

> He words me, girls, he words me, that I should not
> Be noble to myself!

One last lashing of her courage; then a flash of glorious, of transcendent vanity—

> Show me, my women, like a queen: go fetch
> My best attires: I am again for Cydnus,
> To meet Mark Antony.

—a last touch of the old frolicsomeness as she jokes with the clown, peeping the while between the fig-leaves in which the aspics lie; and she is ready.

> Give me my robe, put on my crown; I have
> Immortal longings in me: now no more
> The juice of Egypt's grape shall moist this lip.
> Yare, yare, good Iras: quick! Methinks I hear
> Antony call; I see him rouse himself
> To praise my noble act; I hear him mock
> The luck of Cæsar, which the gods give men
> To excuse their after wrath. Husband, I come:
> Now to that name my courage prove my title! . . .

The dull Octavia, with her "still conclusions," defeated and divorced!

> I am fire and air; my other elements
> I give to baser life. So; have you done?
> Come then, and take the last warmth of my lips.
> Farewell, kind Charmian, Iras, long farewell. . . .

Iras so worships her that she dies of the very grief of the leave-taking.

> Have I the aspic in my lips? Dost fall?
> If thou and nature can so gently part,
> The stroke of death is as a lover's pinch,
> Which hurts and is desired. Dost thou lie still?
> If thus thou vanishest, thou tell'st the world
> It is not worth leave-taking.

Sensuous still, still jealous; her mischievous, magnificent mockery surpassing death itself.

> This proves me base.
> If she first meet the curled Antony,
> He'll make demand of her, and spend that kiss
> Which is my heaven to have. Come, thou mortal wretch,
> With thy sharp teeth this knot intrinsicate
> Of life at once untie; poor venomous fool,
> Be angry and despatch. O, couldst thou speak,
> That I might hear thee call great Cæsar ass
> Unpolicied!

Charmian sees her uplifted, shining:

> O eastern star!

Then follows the consummate

> Peace, peace!
> Dost thou not see my baby at my breast,
> That sucks the nurse asleep?

and in another moment she is dead.

Very well, then, it is not high spiritual tragedy; but is there not something still more fundamental in the pity and terror of it? Round up a beast of prey, and see him die with a natural majesty which shames our civilized contriving. So Cleopatra dies; defiant, noble in her kind, shaming convenient righteousness, a miracle of nature that—here is the tragedy—will not be reconciled to any gospel but its own. She is herself to the very end. Her last breath fails upon the impatient

> What should I stay—?

Her last sensation is the luxury of

> As sweet as balm, as soft as air, as gentle!

And what more luminous summary could there be of such sensual womanhood than the dignity and perverse humor blended in this picture of her yielded to her death—suckling an asp? It defies praise. So, for that matter, does Charmian's

> Now boast thee, death, in thy possession lies
> A lass unparalleled.

—the one word "lass" restoring to her, even as death restores, some share of innocence and youth.

This scene shows us Shakespeare's artistry in perfection, and all gloss upon it will doubtless seem tiresome. But though the reader be teased a little, it cannot hurt him to realize that this close analysis of every turn in the showing of a character and composing of a scene—and much besides—must go to giving a play the simple due of its acting. As reader he cannot lose by knowing what demands the play's art makes on the actor's. The greater the play, the more manifold the demands! When he sees them fulfilled in the theater his enjoyment will be doubled. If they are not, he will a little know why, and so much the worse for the actor; but, at long last, so much the better.

D. A. TRAVERSI

Antony and Cleopatra

THE CRITIC of *Antony and Cleopatra* has, in offering an account of this great tragedy—for the fact of its greatness is plainly evident in purely poetic terms—to resolve a problem of approach, of the interpretation of the author's true intention. This problem has in the past produced a variety of strangely contrary solutions. Sooner or later, indeed, the critic finds himself faced by two interpretations of Shakespeare's intention in this play, each of them strongly defended and each of them arguing from elements demonstrably present in the text, whose only disadvantage is that they appear to be mutually exclusive. Is *Antony and Cleopatra*, to put the matter in other terms, a tragedy of lyrical inspiration, justifying love by presenting it as triumphant over death, or is it rather a remorseless exposure of human frailties, a presentation of spiritual possibilities dissipated through a senseless surrender to passion? Both interpretations, as we have said, can be defended; but to give each its due, to see them less as contradictory than as complementary aspects of a unified artistic creation, is as difficult as it proves, in the long run, to be necessary for a proper understanding of the play.[1]

The fact that these two readings can, in spite of their appearance of contradiction, *both* be derived from a dispassionate examination of the tragedy can be explained in the light of the past development of Shakespeare's art, as we have sought to follow it in the preceding pages, for both correspond to aspects of that development which we have already had occasion to consider. From one point of view, indeed, this tragedy is the supreme expression in Shakespeare of love as *value,* as triumphant over time through and in despite of death; from another, it exposes, again through a consideration of human relationships in love, the weakness which makes possible the downfall of the tragic hero, a weakness,

From *An Approach to Shakespeare*, second edition, Garden City, N. Y., 1956, Doubleday Anchor Books, pp. 235–61. Reprinted by permission of Sands & Co., Ltd.
[1] An interesting recent study of *Antony and Cleopatra*, included in J. F. Danby's collection of essays *Poets on Fortune's Hill* (Faber & Faber, 1952), is worth consulting, but should be balanced by a reading of Wilson Knight's argument in *The Imperial Theme*.

moreover, which is given a *social* reference by being consistently related to the presentation of a society in the advanced stages of decay. Now all these factors, positive and negative alike, have been given expression in Shakespeare's earlier plays, and the novelty of *Antony and Cleopatra* lies not in the fact of their presence, but in the manner and complexity of their interrelation. The desire to see love as a manifestation of spiritual values derives, as we have seen, from as far back at least as the sonnets, and in so far as *Antony and Cleopatra* succeeds in presenting it as such, the tragedy can be described as a positive counterpoise, given full depth and maturity, to *Troilus and Cressida*. The exposure of tragic weakness in the hero, first dramatically presented in *Othello*, gathers strength through the great plays which follow and is finally related to an explicit political study, similar in type though vastly developed in conception to that originally expressed in the later works of English history, in the Roman theme of *Coriolanus*. It is the supreme achievement, rather than the problem, of *Antony and Cleopatra* to show that these two lines of development, far from excluding one another, are in fact mutually illuminating.

The presence of these various elements, positive and negative so to call them, is admirably indicated in the short opening scene of the play, which serves, in a manner highly characteristic of the mature Shakespeare, as a kind of overture to the main action, a first brief exposition of the themes which will be developed in the course of the tragedy by relationship and contrast. The opening speech of Philo leaves us in no doubt as to the adverse estimate which we are bound, on a dispassionate, realistic view, to form of Antony's relationship to Cleopatra. His love is described as a manifestation of "dotage," which has, moreover, reached the point at which it can no longer be tolerated, at which it "overflows the measure"; his former martial virtues, through which he maintained his position of responsibility as "triple pillar of the world"— the phrase is one which will be repeatedly echoed in the course of the political action—have been shamefully abandoned, have become, in the scathing comment of the common soldier,

> the bellows and the fan
> To cool a gipsy's lust.   (I, i)

Nothing in the action to come, no poetic exaltation of the passion that animates the main protagonists, can make this first estimate irrelevant; it is part of the truth, and no later development can properly contradict it.

The entry of Antony and Cleopatra, immediately after the end of this indignant comment, at once confirms it and introduces further themes for consideration. The first exchanges of the lovers are couched in an antiphonal form that will become familiar in the passionate personal passages of this play: emotion responds to emotion in a mutual height-ening, a progressive accumulation of intensities. To Cleopatra's request that Antony should tell her "how much" is his love for her, he replies, "There's beggary in the love that can be reckon'd"; and to her further statement that she will "set a bourn how far to be beloved," he responds with a lyrical declaration that suggests infinity, transcendence in emo-tion: "Then must thou needs find out new heaven, new earth." Once more this sense of superhuman value apprehended through love is one that the play will be concerned to repeat and develop. Its final relation-ship will be to the experience of death imposed, as a consequence of their "political" failure, upon both characters at the end of the tragedy; but meanwhile its emotional force must not blind us to its irrelevance in terms of common realism. The fact that the lovers who can thus address one another are in fact persons subdued to the course of events in the world is stressed by the entry of a messenger from Rome and by the manner, remarkably discordant with the spirit of what we have just heard, of his reception. Antony's gesture in thrusting aside the new-comer in order to turn again to the mistress who has enslaved him is rather petulant, self-indulgent, than noble or generous, and Cleopatra, with the intention of playing upon his dependency, is not slow to chide him with the imagined anger of his wife or with that inferiority to the "scarce-bearded Caesar" which already rankles in his uneasy conscience. The scene, in fact, by relating the political action to emotion poetically expressed, calls in the characteristic Shakespearean way for a balance in judgment which will have to be maintained throughout the play. On the one hand, Antony's turning away from the news of the outside world serves as a background giving weight and relevance to the first opulent gesture of triumphant love which it produces in him; on the other, that gesture is subjected to criticism, seen in its double nature as splendid and yet finally mean and morally degrading. To bear in mind *both* the judgments thus simultaneously present, refusing to abandon one in order to exalt the other, is to remain faithful to the spirit of the play.

This spirit, indeed, can be confirmed by an examination of Antony's first full expression of the emotion which moves him:

> Let Rome in Tiber melt, and the wide arch
> Of the ranged empire fall! Here is my space.
> Kingdoms are clay: our dungy earth alike
> Feeds beast as man: the nobleness of life
> Is to do thus; when such a mutual pair
> And such a twain can do't, in which I bind,
> On pain of punishment, the world to weet
> We stand up peerless.   (I, i)

The expression, considered with due care, introduces a number of ele-ments which the later action will develop. The vast spaciousness of the political background, the sense that a world order, a universal structure of society, rests as upon its keystone on the individuals whose tragedy, worthy or otherwise, is to be presented to us, is conveyed by reference to the "wide arch" of the "ranged empire"; and the very fact that Antony is prepared to turn aside from issues so vast, so endowed with univer-sality, gives weight and a presumption of value to his emotion. By con-trast to this emotion, indeed, the material nature of the outside world is stressed; kingdoms become "clay" and, in a phrase as daring as it is splendidly relevant, the earth itself is "dungy," at once contemptible and yet, when brought to life by the transforming presence of passion, potentially fertile. Against this background, both vast and petty, equally related to "beast" and "man," the presence of intense personal emotion serves to emphasize "the *nobleness* of life," a nobility which has often concerned Shakespeare in his earlier tragedies and which is here pre-sented, for exaltation and criticism, in the story of his pair of lovers. To what extent these will be able to maintain their worth, to justify the arrogant exaltation of themselves as "a mutual pair," fit each for the other and ready to assert their "peerless" quality before the world, the following action will show. At this stage it can only be said that Antony's own emotion is not left at its own estimate, that it is fol-lowed immediately by the contrasted realism of Cleopatra's comment:

> Excellent falsehood!
> Why did he marry Fulvia, and not love her?
> I'll seem the fool I am not; Antony
> Will be himself.   (I, i)

Antony's own following words confirm Cleopatra's estimate. From the high-flown expression of "nobility," of transcendent emotion, we pass at a stroke to the cloying sensuality which is equally a part of his char-acter, and which will remain with him to the end of his tragedy. He exhorts her "for the love of love and her *soft* hours" to set aside the reality of the outside world, correspondingly dismissed in terms of "conference *harsh*":

> There's not a minute of our lives should stretch
> Without some *pleasure* now. What *sport* to-night?

Sport and *pleasure*: these turn out, when we pass from the universally lyrical to concrete reality, to be the true ends of Antony's devotion. The *sport* is, characteristically, obtained by neglecting the discharge of the speaker's political duties in the hearing of the Roman ambassadors; the seizing of the *pleasure* of the moment, and the desire to endow it with

a spurious eternity by thrusting aside all other responsibilities, represent
in fact the real content of Antony's generalized expressions of emotional
nobility. The working out of the contrast so presented until, through a
fusion of poetic and dramatic resources as comprehensive and complete
as anywhere in Shakespeare, they are shown to belong to a single range
of emotion, is the true theme of *Antony and Cleopatra*.

Only a detailed analysis of the play can show Shakespeare achieving
this most ambitious aim by what is, in effect, a series of perfectly de-
finable steps. The first of these concerns his use of the political action
of the play, which is admirably adapted to a purpose that is no longer,
as it had been in *Julius Caesar* and even, though to a lesser extent, in
Coriolanus,[2] primarily political. The story of Antony and Cleopatra, as
we have already seen in considering Antony's first speech, is set against
an imperial background of far-reaching universality; and this vastness of
range is itself an important factor in the play. The story of the lovers is
influenced by events significant for the entire civilized world, and the
poetry of the play deliberately and repeatedly stresses a sense of vast
issues and tremendous dominions. Antony himself, as we have seen, is
not only an infatuated lover but "a triple pillar of the world." Even the
attendant who bears off the drunken Lepidus after the feast at which
the triumvirs meet (II, vii) carries upon his shoulders "the third part
of the world"; and Octavia again tells Antony that a quarrel between
himself and Caesar would be:

> As if the world should cleave, and that slain men
> Should solder up the rift.   (III, iv)

This emphasis on the world background of the tragedy can be related
to Antony's own behaviour in either of two ways, each of which was
anticipated in the opening scene and will assume its relevant place in
the total effect. On the one hand, as Philo from the first asserted, the
thrusting aside of responsibilities so great is at once an act of folly and
a grave repudiation of duty; on the other, if Antony, although at times
himself aware of this aspect of his conduct, is nonetheless repeatedly
moved to confirm it, then we may think that the measure of his passion
must be correspondingly universal, endowed with value in its own sight.
The first estimate will be consistently confirmed by the comments of
those who surround Antony and by the development of his own tragedy;
the second will find expression mainly in the lyricism of his own utterances and in the corresponding intensity of Cleopatra, but will loom
increasingly larger as the confirmation of his own failure in action is
brought home by the course of events.

2 Here and elsewhere in discussing the Roman plays, I am aware that *Antony and Cleopatra*
may well have been written *before Coriolanus*. Doubt on this point does not affect the
substance of the argument.

Our attitude towards this failure, indeed, is most subtly affected by the way in which Shakespeare has chosen to portray the political action of the play. For the world of the triumvirs, vast as it is and correspondingly opulent, is thoroughly mean and decayed. The presentation of it is full of touches which recall the realism of *Henry IV;* there is a good deal of the less admirable side of Prince Hal's character (though little, we must add, of Henry V's sense of the tragic burden of the royal vocation) in Caesar's controlled, ungenerous dedication to the pursuit of power; and Antony's own political folly is not exempt from a note of hard calculation, which his incapacity to calculate successfully does not make any more attractive. The expression of the play, indeed, lays continual stress upon a note of treachery mixed with corruption. Antony's account of the state of Rome near the beginning of the action is no more than typical:

> Our Italy
> Shines o'er with civil swords: Sextus Pompeius
> Makes his approaches to the port of Rome:
> Equality of two domestic powers
> Breeds scrupulous faction: the hated, grown to strength,
> Are newly grown to love: the condemn'd Pompey,
> Rich in his father's honour, creeps apace
> Into the hearts of such as have not thrived
> Upon the present state, whose numbers threaten;
> And quietness, grown sick of rest, would purge
> By any desperate change.   (I, iii)

It would be hard to find a better example of the way in which what can easily be read as no more than a straightforward piece of exposition is in fact charged with a linguistic vitality that relates it variously to the deeper issues of the play. Rome is in a dangerous state of "equality," poised between two powers which, uncertain of the future and unable to trust one another, "breed" (the verb, with its sense of organic growth, has a quality of its own) a "scrupulous," calculating "faction." Pompey, in turn, the common enemy of Caesar and Antony, is "rich" only in his father's reputation; thus speciously endowed, he "creeps" by a process of stealthy treachery into the hearts of those who have not made their fortunes, "thrived" in the "present state" of deceptive peace. These, as a result, grow (through the "breeding" process already defined, we might say) into a threatening condition, and the result of the whole development is summed up in one of those images of dislocated organic function by which Shakespeare, from *Henry IV* at least onwards, has habitually chosen to express the implications of civil strife. The discontented elements in Rome are "sick": "sick" in themselves, because domestic war is the symptom of political disorder, and "sick" too of the false state of "rest," or stagnation, by which other interests in turn prosper. The end of this sickness here, as ever, is a "purge," but one scarcely less uncertain, "desperate" in its possible consequences, than that the desire for which had inspired Northumberland and his fellow conspirators to action in the Second Part of *Henry IV*.

There are two scenes in the first, the predominantly "political" part of the play, which particularly illustrate Shakespeare's presentation of the Roman world. The first is the episode (II, ii) in which Antony and Octavius, brought together for an attempted settlement of their differences, first eye one another in mutual distrust like two hard-faced gamesters, each jealous of what he is pleased to regard as his reputation and each equally distrustful of the trick which he feels his fellow "pillar of the world" may have up his sleeve, and are finally persuaded by the calculating go-between Agrippa to build a sham agreement on the sacrifice by Caesar of his own helpless sister Octavia. The successive stages of this shameful proceeding are indeed beautifully indicated. To Caesar's frigid greeting "Welcome to Rome," Antony replies with an equally distant "Thank you," and to his further laconic invitation "Sit" with the corresponding show of wary courtesy: "Sit, sir." These preliminaries over, the true discussion is opened by Antony with a phrase that shows, in its deliberate churlishness, his determination to be the first to take offence:

> I learn, you take things ill which are not so,
> Or being, concern you not.   (II, ii)

If, after a considerable amount of mutual recrimination, in which Caesar's thin-lipped, efficient disdain and Antony's libertine carelessness display themselves to the worst possible advantage, the trend of the discussion changes, it is because of one of those sudden, theatrical changes of mood for which Antony's behaviour is notable throughout. Caesar's accusation of perjury prompts a facile gesture to "honour"—

> The honour is sacred which he talks on now—

and this in turn leads to a show of self-excuse which reflects yet another facet of Antony's shifting personality. His oath to come to Caesar's aid has been, in his view, "neglected" rather than denied; negligence, indeed, has always been an outstanding feature of his character, and the excuse is, not for the first time, that of the weak man who ascribes his own failing to the machinations of others:

> . . . when *poison'd* hours had bound me up
> From mine own knowledge.

The "poison," indeed, has worked more deeply than Antony knows. His infatuation for Cleopatra, which he is now turning with singular meanness into an excuse for his own indignity, is at least as much the product as the cause of his self-betrayal.

Having thus shifted the fault, to his own satisfaction, upon Fulvia, upon Cleopatra, upon anyone but himself, Antony's "honour" is satisfied and he is ready to come to terms. Around him are the helpless tool Lepidus, always disposed to find "nobility" in the words of the shabby cutthroats who surround him, and Agrippa, ready as a courtier should always be to whisper his supremely cynical suggestions into his master's ear:

> Thou hast a sister by the mother's side,
> Admired Octavia: great Mark Antony
> Is now a widower.

Thus seconded, and with the ground so prepared, the most dishonourable project cannot but prevail. It is, indeed, insinuated before it is openly proposed, and the jibe implied by Agrippa when he describes Antony as a "widower" is sufficient to produce in him, after Caesar's ironic reference to Cleopatra, the parody of "honour" contained in his "I am not married, Caesar": a false dignity which fittingly crowns a false situation and leads to a transaction as cynical as it is clearly destined to be impermanent. The degradation implied in Antony's relationship to the political action which surrounds him will find no expression more complete than this most specious and sordid of reconciliations.

Even more subtle, more beautifully constructed is the great drunken scene (II, vii) which celebrates this agreement, with its contrast between the witless conviviality of the triumvirs and the "quick-sands" of sober treachery represented by Menas and turned aside by Pompey less through honesty than through weakness. The opening remark of the Servant—"Some o' their plants are ill-rooted already; the least wind i' the world will blow them down"—refers as much to the farce of reconciliation now being enacted as to the business the speaker has in hand, and the further comment on the position of Lepidus—

> To be called into a huge sphere, and not to be seen to move in't, are the
> holes where eyes should be, which pitifully disaster the cheeks—   (II, vii)

adds its own contribution to the note of hollowness, at once grotesque and sinister, which the whole episode is intended to convey. The following conversation between Lepidus and Antony, taking us further at each moment from common reality, leads up to its culminating phrase in Antony's:

> These quick-sands, Lepidus,
> Keep off them, for you sink,

and thence to the return of sober calculation in Menas's blunt offer to Pompey which so effectively follows it: "Wilt thou be lord of all the world?" The offer, of course, is rejected by Pompey, though with something less than conviction; but the moral atmosphere of the episode has been established and the following descent into dissipation proceeds, as Lepidus, "the third part of the world," is carried away, in the spirit of Menas's revealing comment to Enobarbus:

> The third part then is drunk: would it were all,
> That it might go on wheels.

The construction of the whole scene, which turns upon a superb counter-pointing of the related motives of folly and treachery, is far beyond the type of political realism formerly exhibited in *Henry IV*, but the inspiration is still demonstrably related to that of the earlier play.

Shakespeare's mature experience, therefore, moves him to present his characters in a world in which imperial pretensions, themselves laden with falsity, are associated through their political expression with the presence of overripeness and luxury in individual experience. "Rest," as we have seen in Antony's account of the social significance, so to call it, of Pompey's rebellion, is the state of stagnation produced by opulence which inevitably leads to the purge of civil war. When the Messenger, in the following scene (I, iv), brings Caesar news that "flush youth revolt," he is relating imperial disorder further to bodily surfeit and its consequences; his words underline those of Octavius which immediately precede them:

> This *common* body,
> Like to a vagabond flag upon the stream,
> Goes to and back, lackeying the varying tide,
> To *rot* itself with motion.   (I, iv)

Such a speech has its own function in the play, pointing to a tightening in poetic terms of the bond which unites the political, the "Roman" action, to the fortunes of the tragic protagonists. The passion of Antony and Cleopatra, whatever may be said further of it, shares the weakness, the corruption of the world in which it grows to expression. One scarcely needs, in establishing this point, to feel the Elizabethan association of "common" with sexual promiscuity; the link which binds here the use of "rot" to the images of decay associated more than once with Cleopatra is enough to show how Shakespeare, through the continuous stressing of imagery invoking disorder and physical corruption, connects the universal situation of his play with the particular tragedy of mature love with which it is primarily concerned.

The decadence thus shown, and poetically integrated into the spirit of the play, in the Roman world is balanced by a similar effect in the expression of the love of Antony and Cleopatra; indeed, the connection between them, presented dramatically in terms of character and poetically by continuity in the use of imagery, is one of the principal keys to the total effect. Antony's advancing years are repeatedly stressed, and Caesar's exposures of his vices are too full of individuality in phrasing, too closely related to the characteristic overripeness of the play, for them to be neglected:

> . . . he fishes, drinks and wastes
> The lamps of night in revel.   (I, iv)

Nor does Shakespeare allow us to overlook the disintegration which falls upon Antony in adversity. The qualities of self-deception, and the weakness which has led him repeatedly to place responsibility for his own actions in the hands of others, are from the first evident to those who serve him; and in the hour of defeat they bear fruit in reactions which are almost invariably illogical and at times tinged with hysterical cruelty. In such a mood he finds consolation for his state in ordering the messenger of Octavius to be whipped until "he whine aloud for mercy" (III, xiii). The futile viciousness revealed by this action is an essential part of Antony's character. His relations with Cleopatra, whatever else they may be, are ruthlessly presented in terms of a weakness which the experience of disaster amply confirms. Every meeting between them, from the opening which we have already considered, is the exposure of an aging libertine and a decaying queen; though it is the peculiar triumph of this tragedy that the most important meetings, being that, are also a great deal more. Shakespeare did not write a great play by ignoring Antony's failings or the presence of a corresponding corruption in Cleopatra; rather, while giving full weight to the weaknesses, he assimilates them into a poetic mood in which other elements, positive and triumphant in their associations, contribute to the total effect. Antony's love asserts itself at the play's supreme poetic moments in spite of his continual awareness that Cleopatra is "a whore of Egypt," a stale scrap from "dead Caesar's trencher," in spite of the fact that his is the infatuation of a middle-aged soldier for a woman who has already served the pleasure of many men. It is the play's achievement to leave room for *both* estimates of the personal tragedy, the realistic as well as the lyrical; and if each has to be continually balanced against its opposite, so that the total impression can never, even at the last, rest upon one to the exclusion of the other, full understanding of what is intended rests upon an appreciation of the poetic quality so marvellously, richly present throughout the play. The gap between what is clearly, from one point of view, a sordid infatuation and the triumphant feeling which undoubtedly, though not exclusively, prevails in the final scenes is bridged by a wonderful modification of connected imagery. Rottenness becomes the ground for fertility, opulence becomes royalty, infatuation turns into transcendent passion, all by means of an *organic* process which ignores none of its own earlier stages, which, while never denying the validity of the realistic estimates of the situation which accompany it to the last, integrates these in the more ample unity of its creative purpose.

The starting point of this poetic "redemption" (if we may so call it, without unduly simplifying the complete effect) is the very rottenness we have observed in the Roman world. The overripeness of that world is variously related to the personal tragic theme; if it is a fitting background to the story of mature passion, which indeed springs from and reflects it, it also lends point to Antony's assertion of the supremacy of his personal feeling. Antony undoubtedly gambled away his dignity as "a triple pillar of the world," but the corruption and treachery of that world in part redeems his folly and justifies the contempt which at certain moments he expresses for it. To assert, however, that Shakespeare was content to make this contrast after the manner of the seeker after moral maxims (*All for love, or the World Well Lost:* axioms based indeed on a strangely indulgent morality) is vastly to underestimate his achievement. The play, as we have said, relates the rottenness of the Roman world *poetically* to the individual fortunes of the protagonists; the love imagery springs from the overripeness, sharing its decay and yet exacting from it something not entirely limited to it. The presence of this further element, incommensurate with the realistic presentation of the tragedy but not contradictory to it, is most clearly grasped, not in Antony (who may be said to receive it through participation), but in the more vital and complex poetry given, at her moments of supreme emotion, to Cleopatra.

Cleopatra, of course, is not exempted from the realistic judgement which falls, at one time or another, on all the characters in this play. We have seen already that Shakespeare insists on her ripe maturity, on her dubious past, on the corruption undoubtedly represented by her person. This, however, is not all. Cleopatra, like Antony, is to be judged not only through her own words but through the reaction of those who surround her. Even Enobarbus's famous account of her meeting with Mark Antony at Cydnus (II, ii) is at least as much an exposure as a glorification. The beauty unquestionably conveyed by his description is, like so much else in this play, deliberately overripe, artificially opulent in its effect. The poop of Cleopatra's barge was "beaten gold," the oars "silver," and she herself lay in a pavilion "cloth-of-gold of tissue"; surrounded by "pretty dimpled boys, like smiling Cupids," her own person was an elaboration, wrought less by nature than by conscious artifice, on what is already conceived as a work of art:

> O'er-picturing that Venus where we see
> The fancy outwork nature.   (II, ii)[3]

On this vessel, indeed, nature has no place, and genuine feeling correspondingly little; its sails are "purple" (the colour itself is, in a boat, unnatural) and so "perfumed" that the very winds, sharing in the prevailing tone, are "love-sick" with them. The smiling boy-Cupids and the "gentlewomen, like the Nereides," belong, as do their rhythmic motions, to a world of elaborate decoration from which Cleopatra herself was not freed until she became involved in the popular acclaim—

> The city cast
> Her people out upon her—

and until we hear of her a little later, again through Enobarbus, as able to:

> Hop forty paces through the public street;
> And having lost her breath, she spoke and panted,
> That she did make defect perfection,
> And, breathless, power breathe forth.   (II, ii)

The presence of these two contrasted elements in the description corresponds to the essential diversity of the character. Cleopatra, though the creature of the world which surrounds her, can at times emerge from it, impose upon her surroundings a vitality which is not the less astonishing for retaining to the last its connection with the environment it transcends. This combination of "nature" with artifice, vitality with corruption in a single, infinitely complex creation, is at once the essence of her personality and the key to the conflicting estimates which her relations to Antony inspire in the course of the tragedy.

The manner in which much of Cleopatra's poetry derives from the idea of Egypt, of the overflowing fertility of the Nile, is especially significant in this respect, for in Egypt, and more particularly in its sacred river, the ideas of corruption and natural growth are most closely interwoven. Her love is, in the words of Antony's promise, "the *fire* that *quickens* Nilus' slime" (I, iii), a living fertility, expressed in terms of fire, that grows by a continuous process of nature out of the corruption of "slime." The play is full of this balance between decay and fruitfulness; in her declining fortunes, Cleopatra describes herself as "the blown rose" (III, xiii), combining beauty and decline in a complex unity of sensation. So assured is Shakespeare's mastery that he can impart dig-

---

[3] The relation of "nature" to artifice is one which increasingly interested Shakespeare in his later plays. Parallels to the spirit of this description can be found in *Cymbeline*, and notably in Iachimo's description of Imogen's bedchamber (*Cymbeline*, II, ii).

nity even to Cleopatra's relations with Julius Caesar. In those days, she says, she was "a morsel for a monarch" (I, v), and the "monarch" redeems, at least in part and while the emotional spell of her utterance is maintained, the indignity of "morsel," of having been "a scrap for Caesar's trencher." But perhaps the most complete example of Cleopatra's conversion of slime into fertility is her speech to Antony immediately after the whipping and dismissal of Thyreus:

> . . . as it determines, so
> Dissolve my life! The next Caesarion smite!
> Till by degrees the memory of my womb,
> Together with my brave Egyptians all,
> By the discandying of this pelleted storm
> Lie graveless, till the flies and gnats of Nile
> Have buried them for prey.   (III, xiii)

The proper reading of this speech brings us very close to the spirit in which this tragedy is conceived. The astonishing poetic power involved is not open to question, nor is the fact that it contributes, within certain clearly laid-down limits, to a dissolution of the harshness of death into a mood of lyrical acceptance. "Discandying" imparts an intense sweetness to corruption, and "dissolve," while presenting the end of the corrupt process itself, gives it an ease and inevitability which looks forward to the final aspic scene; and the "memory of my womb" again suggests the full fertility associated with the speaker's passion, the reflection of a certain richness of life which is felt to spring from the decay so vividly implied in "the flies and gnats of Nile." Within the subtle variations of this speech, at once splendidly lyrical and ruthless in its evocation of corruption, is contained the whole range of Cleopatra's poetic development.

These complexities, indeed, have one principal aim—to evolve a certain tragic greatness for Cleopatra's passion out of its very stressed imperfections, out of the impermanence of the flesh and the corrupt world with which it is organically connected. As the story proceeds, Antony is subjected to a similar development, making him, without evading or in any way minimizing his weaknesses, fit for an end in which *value* and therefore true tragedy have a part to play. From the first, certain moments of generosity and bravery, fragments which might, under different circumstances and without the accompanying weakness, have made a complete man, are brought out in him by contrast with Caesar's calculating meanness and the treachery of the surrounding world. Even the folly and shame of his renunciation of practical affairs is to some degree compensated by the splendid assertion of his love; "kingdoms are clay" for him, as we have seen, and the only value of the clay is to be at certain moments a ground in which the fertility of love may take root. In accordance with this intention the decline of Antony's fortunes is balanced by a whole series of devices which, while they do not free him from responsibility for his fate, set him apart from the increasingly disreputable issues of the Roman world; that issues so great, so imperial in their scope can come, even if only for certain moments, to be felt as trivial is in itself a measure of the quality of his passion. The evolution of his fortunes balances a similar development in Cleopatra until, after their defeat, they are ready for the great meeting on the monument (IV, xv), in which irony and criticism are against all probability dissolved (the word is appropriate) into transcendent poetry.

It will be seen that the total effect of the tragedy is one of no small complexity. How far this is so is amply confirmed in the final scenes. Antony's death is a natural consequence of political folly and personal infatuation. We are not allowed to forget that its immediate cause is a miscarriage of Cleopatra's ingenuity, which leads her to announce falsely her own death and so drives him to despair; to the last Antony is involved in subterfuges and deceptions which spring logically from the nature of his passion. But just as "slime" was converted into the memory of fertility, just as the folly of renouncing the "ranged empire" was to some degree balanced by the rottenness of that empire, so does death, which is the consequence of Antony's prodigality, bring with it a certain liberation from triviality and an opening of the way to the poetic assertion of a truly tragic emotion. We can feel this liberation in the very movement of the blank verse, in which "labour" and its opposite are marvellously fused in what is simultaneously weakness, a renunciation of all effort in the light of admitted failure, and an intuition of peace:

> now all labour
> Mars what it does; yea, very force entangles
> Itself with strength.   (IV, xiv)

A little further on, death is explicitly associated with love:

> I will be
> A *bridegroom* in my death, and run into 't
> As to *a lover's bed*.   (IV, xiv)

In the face of death the contrary judgements which this tragedy invites are maintained and marvellously fused. Not for the first time in Shakespeare the tragic hero, as he approaches the moment of resolution, incorporates expressions that proceed from the weakness, the self-indulgence that is destroying him, into an effect that transcends them. Antony's suicide, indeed, becomes thus an integral part of the final lyrical assertion of emotional *value* and therefore, up to a point, of life.

It looks forward to its counterpart in the poetry of Cleopatra's death, in which "baser life" is finally transmuted into imagery of fire, air, and immortality.

The spirit of the great scene on Cleopatra's monument (IV, xv) is thus prepared for by what has gone before. Its poetry is marked by the extraordinary range of imagery which characterizes the play, and which implies an equally extraordinary power of fusing it into a single and continuous effect. Shakespeare himself could not have written this at any previous point in his career:

> O, see, my women,
> The crown o' the earth doth melt. My lord!
> O, withered is the garland of the war,
> The soldier's pole is fall'n; young boys and girls
> Are level now with men; the odds is gone,
> And there is nothing left remarkable
> Beneath the visiting moon.   (IV, xv)

One has only to attempt to separate a few of the images in this "knot intrinsicate" of poetry to realize the *extent* of the poet's control. "The crown o' the earth" carries on naturally enough the tone of transcendent royalty with which Cleopatra has emphasized Antony's greatness and the depth of her love and grief. The verb "melt," so repeatedly used in this play and with such a varied range of associations, from deliquescence to spiritualization, is not *factually* related to "crown"; it has been chosen because it removes the sense of harshness from Antony's death by suggesting a natural, gentle dissolution into purest air (there is a similar feeling about Cleopatra's own death—"As sweet as balm, as soft as air, as gentle") and so prepares for the sense of triumph associated with her grief. "The soldier's pole" is probably the standard of war; but "pole," taken together with "crown" and the following "boys and girls," bears a complex suggestion of May Day, when love and the renewed life of spring meet in triumph. If we set these joyful associations against the corresponding depths of desolation, we shall feel something of the tremendous emotional range covered by the episode. The final reference to the "visiting moon" lends further point to this relation of joy to death and sorrow. The fact that after Antony's death there is left nothing "remarkable" beneath the moon not only suggests the extent of Cleopatra's loss but also implies that their union, while it lasted, reduced all earthly things to a dull uniformity. The whole passage is built upon a breadth of imagery which does not yield in complexity to the greatest ambiguities of the sonnets; but, unlike them, its variety is subdued to a harmony which regards both desolation and triumph as integral parts of a complete mood. The poetry which sublimates emotion in *Antony and*

Cleopatra—and it is not suggested that the mood thus expressed is permanent or covers the whole meaning of the tragedy—no longer turns, like that of even the later tragedies, upon a cleavage between "good" and "evil" within the unity of experience. It depends rather, while it lasts, upon a perfect continuity between the "flesh," with its associations of earth and death, and the justification of passion in terms of emotional value and intensity. This continuity is in no way vague or sentimental, but is splendidly realized in a harmonious scale of related imagery; this scale is most completely expressed in Cleopatra's final speeches.

Cleopatra's death is preceded by a successive loosening of the bonds which have so far tied her to the political action. The loosening is, characteristically, gradually achieved. Her last negotiations with Caesar are marked, deliberately, by calculation and even fear; she seeks to obtain from him what she can, and is even detected in a stratagem to set aside material provision for her future purposes. The true direction of the scene, however, is set from the first deathwards; and death itself is indicated, in its very first speech, in a manner as complex as it is intensely poetical:

> . . . it is great
> To do that thing that ends all other deeds;
> Which shackles accidents and bolts up change;
> Which sleeps, and never palates more the dug,
> The beggar's nurse and Caesar's.   (V, ii)

Once more we are in the presence of the astounding breadth of reference which is typical of the imagery of this play; and once more each element in it contributes, beyond itself, to the total effect of the tragedy. That the intention of suicide is, at this moment and in the mind of this speaker (the reservation is important, for other judgements are possible and relevant), nobly conceived is beyond doubt; it is "great" precisely in that it ends Cleopatra's slavery to the world of contingencies, that—in the splendid emphasis of her own phrase—"it *shackles* accidents and *bolts up* change." The prisoner of her fate, in other words, now aims to take her own fate captive. She does so, moreover, by an act which she conceives to be gentle as "sleep," a sleep differentiated only by its eternity from that shown, in all times and conditions, by the baby at rest on its mother's breast. Only—it is essential to remember, lest the beauty of the image induce in us a mood of surrender, of unqualified acceptance which is foreign to the total intention—the baby will, in due course, turn out to be the aspic, and the sleep, though associated with images of peace and fulfilment, will be that of death.

The next stage in Cleopatra's progress lies in her exaltation, through memory, of the Antony whom she has lost in life. Once more the breadth of reference is only paralleled by the poetic power which can fuse impressions so diverse into a single, unstrained effect:

> For his bounty,
> There was no winter in't; an autumn 'twas
> That grew the more by reaping: his delights
> Were dolphin-like; they show'd his back above
> The element they lived in: in his livery
> Walk'd crowns and crownets; realms and islands were
> As plates dropp'd from his pocket.   (V, ii)

That such an apostrophe can be accepted as natural, unstrained, and that images so diversely and intensely conceived can be gathered together to produce one impression, is a sign that we are dealing with emotion of no common depth; that Dolabella explicitly denies that it corresponds to reality[4] warns us, at the same time, against making exclusive claims upon its relevance to the whole conception. Cleopatra is living in a world which is the projection of her own feelings. That world, while it lasts, is splendidly valid, vital in its projection; but only death, which is the end of vitality, can prevent an awakening from it. For that reason, if for no other, Cleopatra is resolved to die.

Her last great speech opens significantly with an assertion of "immortal longings." The reference to immortality is in full contrast to the impression of "dungy earth," from which her love sprang and in virtue of which Antony's fall and her death were both inevitable. Yet the immortality thus evoked has a content, which memory supplies; it is simply the highest assertion of her love for the dead and infinitely exalted Antony, whom she can now call for the first time in the play, precisely because he is dead, "Husband!" In the light of this association of love and immortality, death assumes a fresh poetic function. It becomes a dissolution, a purging of all the earthly elements upon which love had been based:

> I am fire and air; my other elements
> I give to baser life.

On the edge of death the sense of dissolution, already so insistently and variously conveyed, acquires a further significance; only the purest elements of feeling remain in Cleopatra—and those, by a paradox, which are most fully, most intensely alive. From a great distance, as it seems, we are reminded of the other elements of "baser life," the earth and fertile slime from which love sprang, with which its degradation was

---

[4] CLEOPATRA:
>   Think you there was, or might be, such a man
>   As this I dreamed of?
> DOLABELLA: Gentle madam, no.   (V, ii)

associated, and in virtue of which defeat and death were inevitable; but defeat and death themselves have now become subdued, at least in the speaker's exaltation, to the "immortal longings" which they themselves brought into being, and the adverse fortunes of the world are dismissed as

> The luck of Caesar, which the gods give men
> To excuse their after wrath.

In spite of this note of transcendence, however, the firm foundation on the senses of the imagery by which the speech achieves its purpose is essential to the full effect. It conveys no abstract triumph imposed upon the rest of the play. The elements of "fire and air" represent a continual refining process from the comparative earthliness of the opening, and the effect of Cleopatra's longing is reinforced by the keenly sensed reference to "the juice of Egypt's grape," suggesting all that is most alive and delicate in the activity of the senses.

This impression of continuity balanced by infinite remoteness is the key to the whole development of *Antony and Cleopatra,* in which self-indulgence and valid emotion are bound together in the death which is their common end. Shakespeare has so refined, so intensified his love poetry by a progressive distillation of sensible experience that it is able to assimilate the apparently incompatible fact of death, which is simultaneously release and the reflection, on the plane of common realism, of moral failure:

> The stroke of death is as a lover's pinch
> Which hurts and is desired.

"Hurts" and "desired," which seem so contradictory, reinforce one another in a splendid balance of sensations; the pain implied in "hurts" is so delicately, so intensely felt that it becomes fused with the keenness of the lover's desire. Thus the death which is the supreme proof of failure becomes, seen from this point of view, a mere untying of "this knot intrinsicate" of body and soul, of infinite desires hitherto subject to adverse and earthly circumstance. The whole development of the play has been tending to this point. The balancing of the generosity which Antony's folly sometimes implies against Caesar's successful meanness, the gradual ascent of the love imagery from earth and "slime" to "fire and air," are all part of one great process which now needs death to complete it. For death, which had seemed in the sonnets and early tragedies to be incontrovertible evidence of the subjection of love and human values to time, now becomes by virtue of Shakespeare's poetic achievement an instrument of release, the necessary condition of an experience which, although dependent upon time and circumstance, is by virtue of its *value* and intensity incommensurate with them—that is, "immortal." This effect, moreover, is achieved at the same time that death is seen, from another point of view, as the inevitable end of a line of conduct in which folly and self-indulgence have consistently predominated. The emotions of Antony and Cleopatra, like their weaknesses, are built upon "dungy earth," upon "Nilus' slime," and so upon time which these elements by their nature imply; but, just as earth and slime are quickened into fire and air, while retaining their sensible qualities as constituent parts of the final experience, so time itself, in which this tragedy of waste and vanity was nurtured, becomes simultaneously a necessary element in the creation of "immortality."

L. C. KNIGHTS

Antony and Cleopatra and *Coriolanus*

IN both *Antony and Cleopatra* and *Coriolanus* we are confronted with
something very different from the deliberate perversion of values that
is the subject of *Macbeth*. In each Shakespeare dramatizes modes of
experience that—for all the intensity with which they are expressed—we
recognize as coming very close indeed to the common run of human
experience. The themes of the two plays are indeed complementary in
obvious but interesting ways, sexual passion being by its nature personal
and subjective, though never merely a matter of individual feeling, the
impulse towards authority and command necessarily manifesting itself
in a wide social field, though both its origin and effects belong to the
realm of personal life. In each play, moreover, tragic failure is expressed
in terms of a failure of relationship between strongly asserted personal
values and something very much greater than those values. And lest this
should seem an intolerable moralizing of poetry so commanding I would
remind the reader of two points that, I think, necessarily become clear
in any consistent attempt to follow the course of Shakespeare's development. The first, already touched on, is that the assured judgment of the
later tragedies supervened on a long process of personal questioning.
Naturally I do not mean that Shakespeare had to make his own standards: it is obvious enough that he inherited a rich and complex tradition
of moral enquiry and evaluation. I mean that because he had questioned
experience with such urgent honesty, the only answers that would serve
were those that satisfied the personality as a whole: Shakespeare's
judgment is not the application of a rule or measure, it is the bringing
to bear of a sense of life as rich and generous as it is clear-eyed and
not to be deceived. My second point, therefore, concerns the nature of
moral judgment when this is equated with the imaginative apprehension
of life working at its highest power. There is, as I have said, no ques-

Reprinted from *Some Shakespearean Themes* by L. C. Knights, pp. 143–56 and 181–83,
with the permission of the publishers, Stanford University Press, and the author. © 1959 by
L. C. Knights.

tion of the application of a formal code. When the imagination judges it does not hold at a distance; it brings close and makes vivid, and of any mode of being it asks only one question,—Does this, when most fully realized, when allowed to speak most clearly its own name, make for life?—life being understood not as random impulse but as power proceeding from an integrated personal centre, rational, clear-sighted and deeply responsive to all human claims. We touch here on what is only at first sight a paradox. It is because, in the later plays, judgment is made from a personal centre, in the light of values to which the whole personality gives its adherence, that it combines with so wide reaching a sympathy. In the last analysis perhaps we need not say that Shakespeare judges; he simply reveals.

1

In *Macbeth* we are never in any doubt of our moral bearings. *Antony and Cleopatra,* on the other hand, embodies different and apparently irreconcilable evaluations of the central experience. There is the view, with which the play opens, of those who stand outside the charmed circle of "Egypt":

> Take but good note, and you shall see in him
> The triple pillar of the world transform'd
> Into a strumpet's fool. (ɪ. i. 11–13)

This attitude is strongly represented in the play; there are repeated references to "lascivious wassails," "the amorous surfeiter," "salt Cleopatra," "the adulterous Antony" who "gives his potent regiment to a trull," and so on. The "Roman" world of war and government—the realm of political "necessity" (ɪɪɪ. vi. 83) rather than of spontaneous human feelings—is of course itself presented critically; but although the way we take the Roman comments is partly determined by our sense of the persons making them, they do correspond to something of which we are directly aware in the Egyptian scenes. We do not need any Roman prompting to be aware of something cloying in the sexual insistence (in the opening of ɪ. ii, for example), and of something practised in (to borrow a phrase from North) the "flickering enticements of Cleopatra unto Antonius."

On the other hand, what Shakespeare infused into the love story as he found it in Plutarch was an immense energy, a sense of life so heightened that it can claim to represent an absolute value:

> Eternity was in our lips, and eyes,
> Bliss in our brows' bent; none our parts so poor,
> But was a race of heaven. (ɪ. iii. 35–7)

This energy communicates itself to all that comes within the field of force that radiates from the lovers, and within which their relationship is defined. In Enobarbus's description of the first meeting of Antony and Cleopatra (II. ii. 190 ff.) the energy counteracts the suggestion of a deliberate sensuousness; the inanimate is felt as animate; and the passage, although a set-piece, modulates easily into a racy buoyancy:

> The city cast
> Her people out upon her; and Antony,
> Enthron'd i' the market-place, did sit alone,
> Whistling to the air; which, but for vacancy,
> Had gone to gaze on Cleopatra too,
> And make a gap in nature.

Wilson Knight rightly insists on "the impregnating atmosphere of wealth, power, military strength and material magnificence," the cosmic imagery, and "the continual suggestion of earth's fruitfulness," in terms of which Antony and Cleopatra are presented to us,[1] and the suggestions of scope and grandeur are blended with continual reminders of what is common to humanity. It is the richness and energy of the poetry in which all this is conveyed that, more than any explicit comment, defines for us the vitality of the theme.

Shakespeare, in short, evokes the passion of the lovers with the greatest possible intensity, and invests it with the maximum of positive significance. But, more realist than some of his critics, he makes it impossible for us not to question the nature and conditions of that very energy that the lovers release in each other. The sequence of scenes between Actium and the final defeat of Antony opens, as Granville Barker noticed,[2] with a suggestion of dry and brittle comedy. In an apparent abeyance of feeling the lovers are more or less pushed into each other's arms by their respective followers; and there is an inert resignation in the reconciliation that follows. Here indeed the most memorable verse is not love poetry at all; it is Antony's bare and emphatic statement,

> Egypt, thou knew'st too well,
> My heart was to thy rudder tied by the strings,
> And thou shouldst tow me after. O'er my spirit
> Thy full supremacy thou knew'st, and that
> Thy beck might from the bidding of the gods
> Command me.   (III. xi. 56–61)

Feeling does not well up in Antony until he discovers Caesar's messenger kissing Cleopatra's hand. It is a perverse violence of cruelty—

---

[1] See "The Transcendental Humanism of *Antony and Cleopatra*" in *The Imperial Theme.*
[2] *Prefaces to Shakespeare, Second Series*, p. 146.

"Whip him, fellows, Till like a boy you see him cringe his face"—that goads him into a semblance of energy; and it is in the backwash of this emotion that Cleopatra can humour him until she is, as it were, again present to him. Shakespeare, however, leaves us in no doubt about the overwrought nature of Antony's feelings: the very look of him is given us by Enobarbus—"Now he'll outstare the lightning" (III. xiii. 195).

Antony, in short, is galvanized into feeling; there is no true access of life and energy. And the significance of this is that we know that what we have to do with is an emphatic variation of a familiar pattern. Looking back, we can recall how often this love has seemed to thrive on emotional stimulants. They were necessary for much the same reason as the feasts and wine. For the continued references to feasting—and it is not only Caesar and his dry Romans who emphasize the Alexandrian consumption of food and drink—are not simply a means of intensifying the imagery of tasting and savouring that is a constant accompaniment of the love theme; they serve to bring out the element of repetition and monotony in a passion which, centring on itself, is self-consuming, leading ultimately to what Antony himself, in a most pregnant phrase, names as "the heart of loss." Indeed, the speech in which this phrase occurs (IV. xii. 9–30) is one of the pivotal things in the play. In its evocation of an appalled sense of insubstantiality it ranks with Macbeth's, "My thought, whose murder yet is but fantastical . . ." With this difference: that whereas Macbeth is, as it were, reaching forward to a region "where nothing is, but what is not," Antony is driven to recognize the element of unreality and enchantment in what he had thought was solid and enduring. The speech has a superb sensuous reality that is simultaneously felt as discandying or melting, until the curious flicker of the double vision—both intensified and explained by the recurrent theme of "Egyptian" magic and gipsy-like double-dealing—is resolved in the naked vision:

> O sun, thy uprise shall I see no more,
> Fortune and Antony part here, even here
> Do we shake hands. All come to this? The hearts
> That spaniel'd me at heels, to whom I gave
> Their wishes, do discandy, melt their sweets
> On blossoming Caesar: and this pine is bark'd
> That overtopp'd them all. Betray'd I am.
> O this false soul of Egypt! this grave charm,
> Whose eye beck'd forth my wars, and call'd them home;
> Whose bosom was my crownet, my chief end,
> Like a right gipsy, hath at fast and loose
> Beguil'd me, to the very heart of loss.[3]   (IV. xii. 18–29)

[3] Shakespeare, Granville Barker rightly says, "is never the vindictive moralist, scourging a man with his sins, blind to all else about him" (*Op. cit.*, p. 196), and the play certainly

Cleopatra's lament over the dying Antony, her evocation of his greatness and bounty, have perhaps weighed too heavily in the impression
that many people have taken from the play as a whole. That these
things are great poetry goes without saying. But the almost unbearable
pathos of the last scenes is for what has not in fact been realized.[4]

> CLEOPATRA.   For his bounty,
>   There was no winter in't: an autumn 'twas
>   That grew the more by reaping: his delights
>   Were dolphin-like, they show'd his back above
>   The element they lived in: in his livery
>   Walk'd crowns and crownets: realms and islands were
>   As plates dropp'd from his pocket.
> DOLABELLA.   Cleopatra!
> CLEOPATRA. Think you there was, or might be such a man
>   As this I dreamt of?
> DOLABELLA. Gentle madam, no.
> CLEOPATRA. You lie up to the hearing of the gods.
>   But if there be, nor ever were one such,
>   It's past the size of dreaming: nature wants stuff
>   To vie strange forms with fancy, yet to imagine
>   An Antony were nature's piece 'gainst fancy,
>   Condemning shadows quite.   (v. ii. 86–100)

emphasizes Antony's admirable qualities, especially his ability to make friends with the
men he commands and his generosity. But it is in this very respect also that Shakespeare
shows himself so far from "blind." When Antony reproaches "the hearts . . . to whom I
gave their wishes," we are compelled to ask, What had he given? The answer of course is,
gifts ranging from kingdoms to mule-loads of treasure—visible and tangible symbols of
worldly power. He has "play'd" as he pleased "with half the bulk o' the world . . . making
and marring fortunes" (III. xi. 64–5); "realms and islands were As plates dropp'd from his
pocket" (v. ii. 91–2); and at his call "kings would start forth," "like boys unto a muss"
(III. xiii. 91). If all this—which forms the background of his bounty—is felt as discandying
it is, surely, not just because Antony is defeated, but because it is of the very nature of the
wealth that he deals in to betray an exclusive trust. It is certainly vain and arrogant pomp
that is insisted on in the account of the distribution of the kingdoms in Act III, scene vi:

> I' the market place, on a tribunal silver'd,
> Cleopatra and himself in chairs of gold
> Were publicly enthroned . . .
>   . . . she
> In the habiliments of the goddess Isis
> That day appear'd . . .

The resounding catalogue of proper names (ll. 14–16, 68–76) is to the same effect. I do
not think it matters that the description is made by the unsympathetic Caesar; Shakespeare
need not have dwelt on it at such length, and the fact that he does so suggests that he was
deliberately following Plutarch's lead: "it was too arrogant and insolent a part, and done
. . . in derision and contempt of the Romans" (*Shakespeare's Plutarch*, ed. C. F. Tucker
Brooke, Vol. II, p. 86).

[4] A view of the play in some ways similar to this is expressed by Professor John F. Danby
in *Poets on Fortune's Hill: Studies in Sidney, Shakespeare, Beaumont and Fletcher*, Chap.
v. "*Antony and Cleopatra*: a Shakespearean Adjustment." An excellent description of the
imaginative effect of the passage from the play next quoted in my text is given by Mr L. G.
Salingar in his essay on "The Elizabethan Literary Renaissance," in the Pelican *Guide to
English Literature, 2, The Age of Shakespeare*, pp. 106–9.

The figure that Cleopatra evokes may not be fancy—the poetry invests it with a substantial reality; but it is not the Antony that the play has given us; it is something disengaged from, or glimpsed through, that Antony. Nor should the power and beauty of Cleopatra's last great speech obscure the continued presence of something self-deceiving and unreal. She may speak of the baby at her breast that sucks the nurse asleep; but it is not, after all, a baby—new life; it is simply death.

It is, of course, one of the signs of a great writer that he can afford to evoke sympathy or even admiration for what, in his final judgment, is discarded or condemned. In *Antony and Cleopatra* the sense of potentiality in life's untutored energies is pushed to its limit, and Shakespeare gives the maximum weight to an experience that is finally "placed." It is perhaps this that makes the tragedy so sombre in its realism, so little comforting to the romantic imagination. For Shakespeare has chosen as his tragic theme the impulse that man perhaps most readily associates with a heightened sense of life and fulfilment. It has not seemed necessary here to explore the range and depth of the poetry in which the theme of vitality twinned with frustration, of force that entangles itself with strength, is expressed; but it is, of course, the range and depth of the poetry that make Antony and Cleopatra into universal figures. At the superb close, Cleopatra—both "empress" and "lass unparallel'd"—is an incarnation of sexual passion, of those primeval energies that insistently demand fulfilment in their own terms, and, by insisting on their own terms ("Thy beck might from the bidding of the gods Command me"), thwart the fulfilment that they seek. "There is no evil impulse," says Martin Buber, "till the impulse has been separated from the being."[5] It is precisely this that *The Tragedy of Antony and Cleopatra* reveals.

2

Shakespeare's earlier plays on political themes, from *Henry VI* onwards, had shown an increasing realism, a developing concern for the actuality—the specific human substance—of situations commonly seen in abstract and general terms. *Coriolanus*, in this respect, is the consummation of Shakespeare's political wisdom. But if *Coriolanus* thus links with a large group of earlier plays, it could only have been written after *King Lear* and *Macbeth*. There is now an assured grasp of those positive values that alone give significance to conflict; the play is a tragedy, not a satire. And the verse, close packed and flexible, has that power of compressed definition that we associate with the plays of Shakespeare's maturity, so that the immediate action is felt as the focus of a vision of life that is searching and profound.

[5] Martin Buber, *I and Thou* (translated by Ronald Gregor Smith), p. 48.

Caius Marcius dominates the action of the play to which he gives his name, but the protagonist is Rome, the city.[6] It is a city divided against itself, and the first scene presents the conflict in lively, dramatic terms. It also contains Menenius's fable of the belly, which is a reminder of the ideal of mutuality in a healthy social organism, but which certainly does not answer the specific complaints of the citizens—"What authority surfeits on would relieve us." Menenius himself habitually thinks in terms of a distinction between "Rome" and "her rats"; and although there is no idealization of "the people"—who are a mixed assortment of individuals—the courtesy of the patrician class among themselves is more than once placed in effective contrast to their rudeness to the plebeians.[7] A semblance of unity is restored by the granting of tribunes to the plebs and by the approach of external danger. The battle scenes show us the real bravery of Caius Marcius, as well as the less admirable characteristics of some of the commoners. They also make us vividly aware of the simplifying effect of war; but with the return of peace internal strain promptly reasserts itself. Coriolanus's behaviour in seeking the consulship brings the conflict to a head.

No summary account can do justice to the dramatic and poetic force of the third act which culminates in Coriolanus's banishment, but three points may be mentioned. The first is that in such things as Coriolanus's speech at III. i. 139–60, we are vividly aware of the social conflict as a conflict of vital energies that have become inextricably tangled in a process of mutual thwarting and stultification:

> . . . purpose so barr'd, it follows
> Nothing is done to purpose.

Secondly, a large part of the meaning is conveyed by a sharp intensification of the imagery of disease; what each side wants is health or "integrity," but each can think only in terms of surgery, of "plucking out" a tongue (III. i. 154–5), or "cutting away" a diseased limb (III. i. 292). And in the third place, when we relate this superb act to the play as a whole, it is impossible not to connect the "disease" of the body politic with the lop-sided development, the defective humanity, of the central figure.

The fact that our sense of Coriolanus is created largely by poetic

[6] Wilson Knight, in his essay on *Coriolanus* in *The Imperial Theme*, shows how city life is constantly present to us in imagery and allusion.
[7] The Tribunes are not admirable, but it is a Tribune who gives the just and necessary comment on Coriolanus's character:
> You speak o' the people
> As if you were a god to punish, not
> A man of their infirmity.   (III. i. 79–81)
John Palmer, in a valuable essay in *Shakespeare's Political Characters*, points out that it is the "conservative" Coriolanus who is only too anxious to abrogate "custom" when it doesn't suit his wishes.

means[8] should not hinder us from seeing in the play a subtle psychological probing of the springs of conduct, or a rich sociological interest. When, in the first scene of the play, Coriolanus's prowess is mentioned, we are told, "He did it to please his mother, and to be partly proud" (i. i. 37–8). Almost immediately after the first public appearance of the hero, we are given a domestic scene in which our attention is directed to the mother, and the mother as a representative of a class (the very tones of "polite" conversation are caught in the Lady Valeria). Volumnia, the Roman matron, is a perfect embodiment of what has been called "the taboo on tenderness."[9] The culture of which she is a representative stresses those "masculine" qualities that range from genuine physical courage to hardness and insensitiveness in the face of life: her laconic comment on young Marcius's "mammocking" of the butterfly—"One on's father's moods"—is worth several pages of analysis. Now in the great central scenes the patrician "honour" to which she so frequently appeals is subjected to a radical scrutiny. Act iii, scene ii, shows the patricians in council after Coriolanus's first reverse; the question is whether he shall submit himself to the people, and Volumnia urges a politic submission:

> . . . now it lies you on to speak
> To the people; not by your own instruction,
> Nor by the matter which your heart prompts you,
> But with such words that are but roted in
> Your tongue, though but bastards and syllables
> Of no allowance to your bosom's truth.
> Now, this no more dishonours you at all
> Than to take in a town with gentle words,
> Which else would put you to your fortune and
> The hazard of much blood.
> I would dissemble with my nature where
> My fortunes and my friends at stake requir'd
> I should do so in honour.   (iii. ii. 53–64)

It is to the spirit of this that Coriolanus finally responds:

> Pray, be content:
> Mother, I am going to the market-place;
> Chide me no more. I'll mountebank their loves,
> Cog their hearts from them, and come home belov'd
> Of all the trades in Rome.   (iii. ii. 130–4)

[8] See D. A. Traversi's essay on the play in *Scrutiny*, Vol. VI. No. 2.
[9] The phrase was coined by Ian D. Suttie in *The Origins of Love and Hate*, Chap. VI. The taboo on tenderness he saw as a defensive reaction—a sour-grapes attitude—to bad psychological weaning: those who embrace the taboo and hold up "toughness, aggressiveness, hardness, etc., as prime virtues" are really carrying on into adult life a form of infantile protest; they can't afford to be anything but "tough," not having reached an adequately grounded maturity that would allow them to admit gentleness and tolerance into companionship with their strength. See also D. W. Harding, *The Impulse to Dominate*, Chap. XIV.

I do not remember seeing it remarked in any commentary on the play that the "honour" in question, being divorced from the "bosom's truth," is of a very dubious quality, and that Coriolanus, in agreeing to this persuasion, shows a wanton disregard for the values that form the moral basis of any decent society, just as they are at the heart of personal relationships:

> I'll mountebank their loves,
> Cog their hearts from them . . .

Coriolanus has none of the apocalyptic quality of *Macbeth*. It is not a world where the sun refuses to rise or horses eat each other; it is a world where petty justices "wear out a good wholesome forenoon in hearing a cause between an orange-wife and a forset-seller," where people "buy and sell with groats," and "tradesmen sing in their shops" —a familiar world; yet the evil at the heart of the state—though not, as in *Macbeth,* deliberately willed—is just as firmly stated as in the earlier tragedy. In cutting himself off from a responsive relationship to his society (as he had in fact already done before his banishment) Coriolanus has diminished his own stature as a human being:[10]

> —I go alone,
> Like to a lonely dragon, that his fen
> Makes fear'd and talk'd of more than seen.
> (iv. i. 29–31)

And in the concluding acts there are constant reminders of the unnatural reversal of values in social life that springs from a personal failure to achieve integration and relationship. Thus the "comic" talk of the serving-men (IV. v) about the superiority of war to peace (peace "makes men hate one another"—"Reason: because they then less need one another") merely transposes into another key Volumnia's denial of values essential to life. The logic of that denial, which her son accepts, is worked out to its end; and the imagery of falling and burning buildings in the latter part of the play suggests the public counterpart to the angry isolation and self-destruction of one who, being a man, can only find his true life in society:

> I'll never
> Be such a gosling to obey instinct, but stand
> As if a man were author of himself,
> And knew no other kin.
> (v. iii. 34–7)

In the face of his mother's dignified and moving appeal to spare the

---

[10] In an article on *"Coriolanus,* Aristotle and Bacon" (*Review of English Studies,* **New** Series, I. 2. 1950) F. N. Lees aptly applies to the play Aristotle's remark, "He that is incapable of living in a society is a god or a beast."

city, Coriolanus finds that he has to "obey instinct," and there is tragic
dignity in his reply to Volumnia:

> O, mother, mother!
> What have you done? Behold the heavens do ope,
> The gods look down, and this unnatural scene
> They laugh at. O my mother, mother! O!
> You have won a happy victory to Rome;
> But, for your son, believe it, O, believe it,
> Most dangerously you have with him prevail'd,
> If not most mortal to him. But let it come.
>
> (v. iv. 182–9)

But there is also tragic irony; it is to his mother that he yields—the
mother who has made him what he is. He returns to Antium, "No more
infected with my country's love Than when I parted thence" (v. vi.
71–2), still unable to know, to recognize, "the other kin," who would
include even the plebeians, with their "pardons, being asked, as free As
words to little purpose" (iii. ii. 88–9). At the height of the civil com-
motion, we may recall, Cominius had attempted to intervene:

> Let me speak:
> I have been consul, and can show for Rome
> Her enemies' marks upon me. I do love
> My country's good with a respect more tender,
> More holy and profound, than mine own life,
> My dear wife's estimate, her womb's increase
> And treasure of my loins.   (iii. iii. 109–15)

There is suggested the reconciling conception of the state as an extension
of the organic bonds of the family, a conception analogous to the ideal
of creative mutuality hinted at by Menenius's fable of the belly. But a
wholehearted response to that ideal demands some personal integration
and maturity, and Coriolanus, as Wyndham Lewis remarked,[11] remains
to the end the "boy" that Aufidius taunts him with being.

Not indeed that we accept Aufidius's perverse statement of the whole
situation.

> You lords and heads o' the state, perfidiously
> He has betray'd your business, and given up,
> For certain drops of salt, your city Rome,
> I say "your city," to his wife and mother;
> Breaking his oath and resolution like
> A twist of rotten silk, never admitting
> Counsel o' the war; but at his nurse's tears
> He whin'd and roar'd away your victory,
> That pages blush'd at him, and men of heart
> Look'd wondering each at other.   (v. vi. 90–9)

11 Wyndham Lewis, *The Lion and the Fox*, pp. 202–3 and Part VII. Chapter II.

That, taken as a whole, is a lie. But as defence against it Coriolanus can only reassert those partial and over-simplified values which, accepted as absolutes, have stood between him and an adequately integrated and responsive life. That is his personal tragedy. But there is also the tragedy of the divided and mutilated city; and a fundamental insight that this play embodies is that political and social forms cannot be separated from, are in fact judged by, the human and moral qualities that shape them, and the human and moral qualities that they foster. That is Shakespeare's answer to Renaissance and modern "realism" that would resolve political questions solely to questions of power. There are wide implications here that may perhaps be suggested by the compressed and powerful lines from Blake's *Jerusalem*—

> The land is mark'd for desolation & unless we plant
> The seeds of Cities & of Villages in the Human bosom
> Albion must be a rock of blood.[12]

---

[12] *Jerusalem*, IV. 83.

SAMUEL JOHNSON

GENERAL OBSERVATION ON
Coriolanus

THE TRAGEDY of *Coriolanus* is one of the most amusing of our author's performances. The old man's merriment in Menenius; the lofty lady's dignity in Volumnia; the bridal modesty in Virginia; the patrician and military haughtiness in Coriolanus; the plebeian malignity and tribunitian insolence in Brutus and Sicinius, make a very pleasing and interesting variety; and the various revolutions of the hero's fortune fill the mind with anxious curiosity. There is, perhaps, too much bustle in the first act and too little in the last.

Reprinted from Samuel Johnson's edition of *The Plays of William Shakespeare*, London, 1765.

PAUL A. JORGENSEN

THE SOLDIER IN SOCIETY
From Casque to Cushion

MORE so than in any of his earlier works, Shakespeare seeks in *Corio-lanus* a clear demarcation between war and peace as social areas for exposing the strengths and weaknesses of his soldier hero. In plays like *Titus Andronicus* and *1 Henry IV*, an early part of the action is given to praising the recent military triumphs of the hero. In *Coriolanus,* how-ever, there is an added emphasis on this traditional aspect of the play in that the hero is not merely praised upon his return from war but is seen vividly engaged in battle. The effect of this new emphasis is not only to magnify Coriolanus as a warrior but, through the manner of his fighting, to foreshadow personality traits which will cause him trouble once he returns to the "cushion." As a soldier he proves to be a fierce, individual fighter rather than a deliberate, army-minded general. His youthful impetuosity, as we have seen, contrasts with the cautiousness of his soldier-statesman fellow, Cominius. Shakespeare also increases the dissension between Coriolanus and the common soldiers, thereby affording a parallel in war to the more serious dissension in peace when the General will be forced to sue rather than command.

Nevertheless, Coriolanus proves so successful in the Volscian cam-paign that he returns a national war hero. The tribune Brutus describes bitterly (II.i.221) the idolatry of the welcoming throngs. A herald announces the great honors that Coriolanus has won, and proclaims—in one of Shakespeare's nicest touches of dramatic irony—"Welcome, / Welcome to Rome, renowned Coriolanus!" (II. i. 182). It seems to be merely *Titus Andronicus,* highly amplified, all over again. But this time Shakespeare is prepared to use more than tragic irony. He is now to demonstrate, detail by detail, the traits in Coriolanus' nature that pro-duce his tragic incompatibility with society. The dramatist does not, as he had done in *Titus,* build all the tragedy incongruously upon a single

Reprinted from *Shakespeare's Military World*, 1956, pp. 295–314, by permission of the University of California Press and the author.

error in judgment made by the triumphant warrior at the beginning of the play.

In *Titus Andronicus*, it will be recalled, the protagonist refuses the office of dictator, due him for his military services, merely because of old age. Coriolanus also dislikes the idea of standing for consul—an honor which his mother and friends consider incumbent upon him—but he shrinks from the office because his very nature rebels against its political demands. He has, indeed, firmly held convictions about government, and his thinking is by no means limited to the battlefield. But it is only on the battlefield that he is thoroughly at ease. The consulship requires a political skill and, especially, a tactful relationship with the people of which he knows himself incapable. As he tells his mother,

> I had rather be their servant in my way
> Than sway with them in theirs.   (II.i.219)

His disinclination to become a politician represents an apprehension—which he never clearly grasps or expresses—of the Renaissance concept of degree. Professor Phillips has demonstrated how this concept pervades Shakespeare's Greek and Roman plays. In *Coriolanus* it is most notably expressed in Menenius' fable of the belly and the members. But one of the citizens names the distinct parts of the body politic in a form specially applicable to Coriolanus (I.i.119):

> The kingly crowned head, the vigilant eye,
> The counsellor heart, the arm our soldier,
> Our steed the leg, the tongue our trumpeter.

As Phillips points out, Coriolanus is "the arm our soldier," and there is no evidence that his "celebrated service to Rome was ever of anything but a military nature."[1] And the General has rightly a distrust of changing his occupation from war to politics.

The underlying formula for Coriolanus' troubles as a politician is to be found in Plutarch. Nevertheless, Shakespeare gave this formula a Renaissance interpretation not only in a new emphasis on degree but in changes made upon Plutarch's aristocratic warrior so as to bring him closer to the Elizabethan version of the socially inept soldier. The haughty, class-minded patrician is still strongly evident in Shakespeare's interpretation, but his personality and social intelligence suffer a diminution almost comparable to the shrinkage which we observed in Alcibiades.

Although Plutarch states that Coriolanus "lacked the gravity and affability that is gotten with judgment of learning and reason,"[2] the historian

---

[1] James E. Phillips, *The State in Shakespeare's Greek and Roman Plays* (New York, 1940), p. 162.
[2] *Shakespeare's Plutarch*, ed. C. F. Tucker Brooke (London, 1909), II, 162.

does not ascribe this lack of learning to a military background, nor does he show the hero suffering from the conventional soldierly disabilities. Plutarch's Coriolanus is a clever and eloquent, though not a wise or disciplined, character. He is capable, as has been seen, of craft in war on at least two occasions. And he is conspicuously an orator. Addressing Volscian lords, he "spake so excellently in the presence of them all, that he was thought no less eloquent in tongue, than warlike in show: and declared himself both expert in wars, and wise with valiantness."[3] To most Renaissance readers, Plutarch's characterization would suggest the well-rounded-gentleman ideal, blemished only by passion and a lack of affability.

Shakespeare rejected this interpretation in favor of a more clearly defined distinction between warrior and politician. He accepted quite literally Plutarch's statement that Coriolanus lacked education, and he assumed that the lack was due to the limited type of experience which he had described in *Othello*. A man who had spent his "dearest action in the tented field" would be "rude" in speech, "little bless'd with the soft phrase of peace," and unable to speak more of "this great world" than "pertains to feats of broils and battle." The military reason for Coriolanus' uncouth speech is amply commented upon later in the play, but it is first adumbrated in an interesting hint which is generally overlooked. Volumnia says of Coriolanus' young son, "He had rather see the swords and hear a drum than look upon his schoolmaster." Her old family friend, Valeria, adds enthusiastically, "O' my word, the father's son" (I.iii.59–61). The audience would have recognized here the old conflict between scholar and soldier, alluded to in *Othello* in Cassio's comment on Iago, "You may relish him more in the soldier than in the scholar" (II. i. 166). In Breton's *The Scholler and the Souldiour*, the soldier acknowledges a childhood similar to that of young Marcius (and of Coriolanus himself): "What shall I say, I loved a Drumme and a Fyfe, better than all the fidling Musicke in the worlde: and growing to some yeeres, I woulde practise now and then a little of warlike exercises, till in the ende, the delight therein, drewe me quite from my Booke."[4] Shakespeare's hero, who presumably had preferred drum to schoolmaster, vividly demonstrates, as Plutarch's Coriolanus does not, his limited ability in speech.

Shakespeare exposes this limitation most effectively in the two crucial episodes of the candidacy for the consulship and the resultant trial for treason. The first of these episodes is of Shakespeare's own devising. Whereas, as MacCallum observes, Plutarch stresses the political background for the circumstances resulting in Coriolanus' banishment, Shake-

---

[3] *Ibid.*, p. 184.
[4] In *The Wil of Wit* (1597), sig. I I[v].

speare traces the exile almost exclusively to the hero's inept behavior as a candidate, "and this behaviour . . . is altogether a fabrication on Shakespeare's part."[5] In Plutarch, the returning General exhibits no reluctance toward becoming a candidate for consul. He goes unprotestingly to sue for the people's "voices." And he does not demur at the Roman custom of showing his wounds to the people; nor does he address them uncivilly. Although the citizens ultimately revoke their approval of his candidacy, they do so not because of his rude speech but because they see him proceeding proudly to the market place, accompanied by the nobility, and recognize that they can never look to him for justice. In contrast, Shakespeare's hero ruins his fortunes by his surly, reluctant address to the citizens in a scene to which Shakespeare has given full and grim dramatization.

But despite Coriolanus' crude manners, he does not guide himself to ruin. Shakespeare has brought his hero still more closely into the familiar Elizabethan scene by supplying the equivalents of the courtier vilifier. These equivalents, the two tribunes of the people, are, of course, present in Plutarch's story. There, however, although mean-spirited demagogues, they have little of the crafty scheming found in Shakespeare's tribunes. They are directly opposed to Coriolanus the patrician rather than to Coriolanus the soldier, and the contrast in social intelligence is accordingly not so great. In Shakespeare they succeed in producing their enemy's downfall because they understand so thoroughly his soldierly traits and, like Iago in *Othello,* lead the noble warrior into situations impossible for him.

Shakespeare's tribunes are not courtiers; but that he may have had certain traits of the courtier in the back of his mind is suggested by the contrast drawn by an officer of the Capitol. In discussing Coriolanus' qualifications for the consulship, he observes (II.ii.27):

> He hath deserved worthily of his country; and his ascent is not by such easy degrees as those who, having been supple and courteous to the people, bonneted, without any further deed to have them at all into their estimation and report; but he hath so planted his honours in their eyes and his actions in their hearts that for their tongues to be silent and not confess so much were a kind of ingrateful injury; to report otherwise were a malice that, giving itself the lie, would pluck reproof and rebuke from every ear that heard it.

It is the tribunes, obviously, who have "been supple and courteous to the people," and it is these politic creatures also who "report otherwise" than the truth about Coriolanus and who therefore show a "malice" suggestive of the conventional invidious antagonist of the soldier.

5 M. W. MacCallum, *Shakespeare's Roman Plays and Their Background* (London, 1925), p. 510.

That these demagogues succeed in public affairs, whereas Coriolanus fails, is due in part to their ability to talk. The contrast between artful speech and heroic action is emphasized in a bitter exchange between the tribune Brutus and the General. Having struck home with a malicious comment, Brutus notices that Coriolanus is preparing to leave. He inquires, with mock concern (II.ii.74):

> Sir, I hope
> My words disbench'd you not?

Coriolanus replies:

> No, sir. Yet oft,
> When blows have made me stay, I fled from words.

Although the retort is complacently made, the trait of which Coriolanus is proud proves less successful in peace than it had in war. But Coriolanus' lack of appropriate "words" is not, of course, an endorsement of the opposite characteristic, embodied in the tribunes. Volumnia supplies the proper scorn for these talkers when she berates them after her son has been banished (IV.ii.18):

> Hadst thou foxship
> To banish him that struck more blows for Rome
> Than thou hast spoken words?

In Shakespeare's version of the story, it is the "foxship" of these men that leads the people to renounce Coriolanus, whereas in Plutarch the people had done so on their own initiative. It is also Shakespeare's innovation to make the tribunes responsible by their provocative words for Coriolanus' furious outburst against the people. And it is this outburst, together with his resistance of lawful authority, that results in the General's arraignment for treason.

In the tumult which follows Coriolanus' ill-fated candidacy, the conflict between warrior and civil law is revealingly depicted. The tribune Sicinius is at first unwilling to honor Coriolanus with a lawful trial (III.i.266):

> He shall be thrown down the Tarpeian Rock
> With rigorous hands. He hath resisted law,
> And therefore law shall scorn him further trial
> Than the severity of the public power,
> Which he so sets at naught.

Whereupon Menenius, Coriolanus' "humourous" old friend, defends the General by strategy similar to the formal defenses of the military profession (III.i.298):

What has he done to Rome that's worthy death?
Killing our enemies, the blood he hath lost
(Which I dare vouch, is more than that he hath,
By many an ounce) he dropp'd it for his country;
And what is left, to lose it by his country
Were to us all that do't and suffer it
A brand to th' end o' th' world.

But, like the senators in *Timon*, the tribunes refuse to shift the issue from peace to war. "This is clean kam," they protest. "Merely awry. When he did love his country, / It honour'd him." Menenius, more skillful as an advocate than Alcibiades had been, shows the relevance of his argument by an expert analogy (III.i.305):

The service of the foot,
Being once gangren'd, is not then respected
For what before it was.

The body imagery reminds one of "the arm our soldier." The tribunes, however, are no more cognizant of the whole body politic than is Coriolanus, and they threaten to refuse all further discussion of the matter.

Menenius is thereupon forced to resort to the standard apology for the rude soldier (III.i.320):

Consider this: he has been bred i' th' wars
Since 'a could draw a sword, and is ill-school'd
In bolted language; meal and bran together
He throws without distinction.

"Give me leave," he continues,

I'll go to him and undertake to bring him
Where he shall answer by a lawful form
(In peace) to his utmost peril.

The tribunes consent. Perhaps they are willing to condone Coriolanus' rude conduct in the light of the defense that Elizabethans had long been asked to accept. But it is more likely that they recognize the difficulty of dealing effectually with Coriolanus by force—his element—and prefer to have him brought by his friends into their own arena, that of words and politics. They further recognize that the General has not the slightest chance of answering them successfully "by a lawful form / (In peace)." Their sinister understanding of their enemy's limitations appears in the advice which Brutus gives his fellow tribune concerning how to disable Coriolanus at the trial (III.iii.25):

> Put him to choler straight. He hath been us'd
> Ever to conquer, and to have his worth
> Of contradiction. Being once chaf'd, he cannot
> Be rein'd again to temperance; then he speaks
> What's in his heart, and that is there which looks
> With us to break his neck.

All that will be necessary is to "chafe" the warrior. Having been accustomed to victory and command in battle, he will be unable to endure contradiction in peace.

Indeed, it proves almost impossible for Coriolanus' friends to induce him even to present himself for trial, let alone do so in a "lawful form." In this respect again Shakespeare has markedly altered his source in the interest of greater friction between warrior and society. Plutarch's hero goes without protest to answer the accusations against him. In fact, it is his patrician friends who demur, and Coriolanus, because he wishes to help them, who insists upon going. In the play, the efforts of the patricians and his mother to make him go to the Forum produce one of the most dramatic episodes. Although there is no single precedent for this scene in earlier literature on soldiers, most of its important details are clearly reminiscent of this literature.

Persuasions by Menenius and the senators, arguing the welfare of Rome, have no discernible effect on the stubborn General. It is his mother, who knows his temperament even better than the tribunes do, who prevails upon him. Sensing his deep feeling of wounded honor, she refrains from asking him to abandon revenge, and merely insists that he direct his anger "to better vantage" (III.ii.29–31). What she must persuade him to do is to use "policy," a quality distasteful to him. With a strategy worthy of the tribunes, she phrases her argument in the form of a military analogy (III.ii.41):

> I have heard you say,
> Honour and policy, like unsever'd friends,
> I' th' war do grow together. Grant that, and tell me,
> In peace what each of them by th' other lose,
> That they combine not there.

Hearing his own military pronouncement thus strangely translated into the language of peace, Coriolanus can answer only, "Tush, tush!" Menenius expresses the approval of the bystanders, "A good demand." She then proceeds to apply the military parallel specifically to her son's present situation (III.ii.52):

> now it lies you on to speak
> To th' people, not by your own instruction,
> Nor by th' matter which your heart prompts you,

> But with such words that are but roted in
> Your tongue, though but bastards and syllables
> Of no allowance to your bosom's truth.
> Now, this no more dishonours you at all
> Than to take in a town with gentle words
> Which else would put you to your fortune and
> The hazard of much blood.

Coriolanus is significantly silent. Perhaps he is trying, as his mother instructs him, to think of this incredible situation in terms of a military campaign. Perhaps he is perplexed by her reasoning—though recognizing its military soundness—because he has never, at least in the play, been known to use policy or to "take in a town with gentle words." But Menenius recognizes jubilantly that the shaft has found a mark. "Noble lady!" he exclaims. Volumnia is wise enough not to stop here. She knows that her son must be thoroughly briefed not merely in the need for policy but in all details of the necessary strategy (III.ii.72):

> I prithee now, my son,
> Go to them, with this bonnet in thy hand;
> And thus far having stretch'd it (here be with them),
> Thy knee bussing the stones (for in such business
> Action is eloquence, and the eyes of th' ignorant
> More learned than the ears), waving thy head,
> Which often, thus, correcting thy stout heart,
> Now humble as the ripest mulberry
> That will not hold the handling—say to them
> Thou art their soldier, and, being bred in broils,
> Hast not the soft way which, thou dost confess,
> Were fit for thee to use, as they to claim,
> In asking their good loves.

Still he is silent. What she asks of him, except the plea based on having been "bred in broils" and lacking the appropriate "soft way," is utterly repugnant to him. That he considers acquiescing at all may be not merely because of her strong hold over him but also because the soldierly apology had acquired, in Elizabethan times, a manly sort of dignity. The playwright surely recognizes this fact when he has her stress it in her detailed directions. In the same line of strategy is Volumnia's next plea, for it penetrates understandingly to Coriolanus' fundamental incompatibility with peacetime tactics (III.ii.89):

> Prithee now,
> Go, and be rul'd; although I know thou hadst rather
> Follow thine enemy in a fiery gulf
> Than flatter him in a bower.

Although Coriolanus is not asked to become, strictly speaking, a courtier, Volumnia's imagery shows that Shakespeare had in mind the convential antithesis of court and wars. Volumnia further acknowledges the sharp antithesis when she pleads with him that, as her "praises make thee first a soldier," so

> To have my praise for this, perform a part
> Thou hast not done before. (III.ii.108)

In consenting, Coriolanus painfully pictures to himself "a part which never / I shall discharge to th' life." "Well, I must do't," he announces miserably.

> Away, my disposition, and possess me
> Some harlot's spirit! My throat of war be turn'd,
> Which quier'd with my drum, into a pipe
> Small as an eunuch or the virgin voice
> That babies lulls asleep!
> . . . .
>   A beggar's tongue
> Make motion through my lips, and my arm'd knees,
> Who bow'd but in my stirrup, bend like his
> That hath receiv'd an alms! (III.ii.111)

One of his most intense utterances, this speech derives its power ultimately from the same source as Othello's great "Farewell." It is consciously a farewell to his occupation, but unlike Othello's speech it expresses not only the glorious aspects of war that he is renouncing but the meaner, courtier-like arts of peace that he must try to "discharge to th' life." As it turns out, his farewell to the military profession is of short duration. In fact, it scarcely lasts through the trial scene which follows.

This scene is one of the three great episodes toward which Shakespeare is building in this play. In Plutarch's version it is scarcely a scene at all, but merely a summary statement. That Shakespeare built toward a trial scene as the first great crisis in the play is evidence of the strong convention governing the construction of stories and plays dealing with the misplaced soldier.

Coriolanus proceeds stoically to the Forum, the "words that are but roted in" held resolutely in mind. In response to Menenius' "Calmly, I do beseech you," he promises to take insults meekly. He seems almost to be rehearsing his "bastard" words as he makes a grim prayer for peace (III.iii.33):

> Th' honour'd gods
> Keep Rome in safety, and the chairs of justice

> Supplied with worthy men! plant love among's!
> Throng our large temples with the shows of peace
> And not our streets with war!

The mechanical tone of the prayer is amplified in the meaningless repetition of the word "peace" throughout the scene. It is harshly echoed by an Aedile's cry, "Peace, I say"; by the tribunes' clamorous "Peace, ho!"; and, after the people begin to riot, by Sicinius' command, "Peace!" Repetition of this inappropriate word, in a scene leading from civil trial to war, is an ironic accompaniment to Coriolanus' inability to "answer by a lawful form / (In peace) to his utmost peril."

Upon Menenius and Cominius falls the task of guiding their difficult charge through the trial. They wait uneasily for him to recite the soldier's apology that his mother had taught him. As the scene progresses, and Coriolanus begins to show the effect of being "chaf'd," the two patricians recognize with dismay that the apology is not forthcoming. Anxiously Menenius attempts to make it for him, taking advantage of Coriolanus' single agreeable utterance, that he is "content" to stand for trial. "Lo, citizens, he says he is content"; Menenius relays the curt statement to the throng, elaborating it in his own manner (III.iii.49):

> The warlike service he has done, consider.
>   Think
> Upon the wounds his body bears, which show
> Like graves i' th' holy churchyard.

But possibly Menenius senses the unpleasant truth that the citizens can only "think" of these wounds, since the General has refused to show them. Nor is his plea helped by Coriolanus' sardonic attempt at humility (reminiscent of his behavior as a candidate):

> Scratches with briers,
> Scars to move laughter only.

Menenius hastens to the agreed-upon apology for Coriolanus' soldierly speech (III.iii.52):

> Consider further,
> That when he speaks not like a citizen,
> You find him like a soldier. Do not take
> His rougher accents for malicious sounds,
> But, as I say, such as become a soldier
> Rather than envy you.

Menenius' apology is not helped by Coriolanus' prompt illustration of the need for it. Forgetting that it is he who is on trial, he turns angrily upon the people and tries to make them the defendants in the scene. It now requires only Sicinius' pointedly worded charge of treason to move Coriolanus "to choler straight," and the rest of the scene is mainly his mighty vituperation against citizens and tribunes.

Although he fails in this scene to utilize any of the humble aspects of the soldier's traditional apology, Coriolanus takes advantage of its more assertive features by denouncing the people's ingratitude toward the military profession. Upon being banished, he cries out, much in the manner of Alcibiades (III.iii.123):

> I banish you!
> And here remain with your uncertainty.
> Let every feeble rumour shake your hearts!
> Your enemies with nodding of their plumes
> Fan you into despair! Have the power still
> To banish your defenders, till at length
> Your ignorance (which finds not till it feels,
> Making not reservation of yourselves,
> Still your own foes) deliver you, as most
> Abated captives, to some nation
> That won you without blows!

Coriolanus is thus untutored by his failure to live harmoniously in a peaceful Rome. His instinctive solution to his personal problem is not to correct himself but to correct Rome, and to do so by blows rather than words. The composure that he exhibits in the next scene is not so strange as readers have occasionally felt it to be. It is merely the result of his returning to his occupation after a miserable attempt to measure up to the code of civil government. Already he has made up his mind to offer his services to the enemy. There is, accordingly, an appropriateness, which he alone recognizes, in his parting assurance to his friends (IV.i.51):

> While I remain above the ground, you shall
> Hear from me still, and never of me aught
> But what is like me formerly.

In giving up Rome for Antium, Coriolanus is not, therefore, giving up the fatal limitations that Menenius had recently acknowledged:

> Consider further,
> That when he speaks not like a citizen,
> You find him like a soldier.

It is as a soldier that he approaches Antium. To him, the city is a military area (IV.iv.1):

> A goodly city is this Antium. City,
> 'Tis I that made thy widows. Many an heir
> Of these fair edifices fore my wars
> Have I heard groan and drop.

And it is only as a soldier that he can serve this city, just as he had been of use to Rome only during war.

As a prospective military savior of Antium, he is idolized by his former enemies (IV.v.202): "Why he is so made on here within as if he were son and heir to Mars; set at upper end o' th' table; no question ask'd him by any of the senators but they stand bald before him." And his triumphant reëntry parallels his earlier reception in Rome. He "returns splitting the air with noise,"

> And patient fools,
> Whose children he hath slain, their base throats tear
> With giving him glory. (V.vi.50)

But once again it is his misfortune that the end of the war will leave him not only useless but vulnerable in his new country. He seems to be aware of this fact, and his awareness of it gives an added poignancy to his sacrifice in obeying his mother. When Volumnia prevails upon him to give up his attack on Rome, he speaks what are probably his most connotative lines in the play (V.iii.185):

> O my mother, mother! O!
> You have won a happy victory to Rome;
> But for your son—believe it, O believe it!—
> Most dangerously you have with him prevail'd,
> If not most mortal to him. But let it come.

Then he turns to Aufidius (V.iii.190):

> Aufidius, though I cannot make true wars,
> I'll frame convenient peace.

Of all men, he is the least capable of exchanging "true wars" for "convenient peace." This fact Aufidius thoroughly understands. It was he who had made the analysis of Coriolanus' tragic flaw that was quoted early in this chapter: that Coriolanus' nature could be only one thing,

> not moving
> From th' casque to th' cushion, but commanding peace
> Even with the same austerity and garb
> As he controll'd the war.

But in the Volscian situation, as in the Roman, Coriolanus does not go unescorted to disaster. Aufidius himself serves now as the cunning adversary who will misrepresent the Roman's actions to the populace and move him "to choler straight." It is partially to achieve this end that Shakespeare debases Aufidius in the final episode almost to the level of the Roman tribunes.

This final episode is clearly designed as a restatement of the theme expressed in Coriolanus' Roman ordeal. Here, once more, he returns from wars to brief acclaim at home. Once more, when charges are brought against him, he is compelled to justify himself to the people, and he again fails because he thinks in terms of blows rather than words. He reminds the people how "like an eagle in a dovecoat," he had "flutter'd your Volscians in Corioles." "Alone I did it," he roars, just before he is killed, longing in this crisis again for a chance to use his "lawful sword."

These parallels with the first trial scene are not accidental. In achieving this reiteration of theme, Shakespeare was forced not only to debase Aufidius but also to contradict Plutarch's express interpretation of the tragedy. In the historian's version, Aufidius so respects the Roman's command of oratory that he does not give Coriolanus a chance to speak in his own defense, but has him cut down instantly.[6] For Plutarch, the crisis in Coriolanus' career was the episode in which he allows his mother to dissuade him from "true wars." In Shakespeare, the scene is still supremely moving—in fact, it is transcribed almost verbatim from North's language—but in the context of the play it is not in itself disastrous. Consistent in a way that Plutarch seldom is, and rare even for himself, Shakespeare carries to the play's end his distinctive reason for Coriolanus' failure. Twice the Roman has tried to move from the casque to the cushion, and twice he has failed.

In *Timon of Athens*, we recall, Shakespeare prevented a clear-cut judgment upon Alcibiades as a rude warrior by failing to keep the same warrior and the same society to the end of the play. Coriolanus, on the other hand, is the same person at the finish as at the start; and although the social scene shifts from Rome to Antium, there is no substantial difference in Shakespeare's depiction of the two cities. But the dramatist, while repeatedly stressing the fact of his hero's failure, again finds ways of baffling any attempt to assess the exact extent of his blame.

Changes from Plutarch's version indicate that Shakespeare intended both to worsen certain of Coriolanus' unsocial traits and to find new ways to defend them. By lessening the warrior's social intelligence and by utilizing the historian's hint about meager education, he created a citizen more convincingly troublesome and vulnerable than the original. But these changes also tended to diminish those flaws in Plutarch's hero that derived from his greater cleverness. Plutarch's Coriolanus, having more of a brain to guide his actions, comes closer to being a villain. In Shakespeare's interpretation of the story, much of the villainy is transferred from the character of the protagonist to external agents, notably the tribunes and Aufidius. Had the dramatist's primary intention been to censure Coriolanus' character, he would not have highlighted the criminal cunning of his adversaries.

Shakespeare's reasons for giving a greater simplicity to Coriolanus seem to have been friendly ones on the whole, for the transformation permitted him to bring the harsh Roman aristocrat into a context wherein the Elizabethan audience would understand, if not fully condone, his difficulties. In this context—that of the noble soldier who fails as a citizen—the soldier still commanded much of the respect as a tragic hero that Rich had once given him. Jacobean pacifism and the reaction to Essex's rebellion had indeed made the soldier's place in the story a less comfortable one. But, as Chapman's Byron and Daniel's Philotas had proved, the position was by no means indefensible and certainly not ignoble. Soldier citizens of this caliber could no longer claim a political endorsement, but they still exhibited an integrity and largeness of spirit that lifted them above their meaner adversaries as subjects for tragic drama.

WILLARD FARNHAM

Coriolanus

III

SHAKESPEARE is so far from being blind to the faults of Coriolanus that
he makes them as pernicious as any moralist of his age makes them.
He gives them, with regard to their effects in this world, the destructive
powers of deadly sins, and he allows them to wear the aspects of deadly
sins. Outwardly the Coriolanus of Shakespeare is much like the haughty
and angrily impatient Coriolanus of Plutarch, but inwardly he is a very
different man; for as Coriolanus passes through the hands of Shakespeare, the overlying haughtiness, the "hawtie obstinate minde," given
him by Plutarch becomes an underlying pride, a spiritual flaw reaching
to the depth of his being, and this deep-going pride has deep-going
wrath in its train instead of mere angry impatience. Moreover, the wrath
of Shakespeare's Coriolanus is much more clearly subsidiary to pride
than the angry impatience of Plutarch's Coriolanus is subsidiary to
haughtiness. Shakespeare's Coriolanus is often a wrathful man, but
always and before all else he is a proud man. Whenever we see his
wrath, we know that it is fed by pride.

The tragedy made by Shakespeare out of Plutarch's story of Coriolanus is not that of a noble spirit ruined by lack of education, which is
the tragedy that Plutarch outlines. It is the tragedy of a noble spirit
ruined by something in itself which education cannot touch, or at least
does not touch. We do not hear anything in Shakespeare's play about
the hero's lacking instruction because of his father's death and thus
acquiring a faulty character. On the contrary, we learn that Volumnia,
the strong-willed mother of the hero, has been both father and mother
to him, has devoted herself, according to her lights, to the education of
his character, and has certainly not failed to teach him how to be manly.

Reprinted from *Shakespeare's Tragic Frontier*, 1950, by permission of the University of
California Press and the author. The selection printed here represents sections iii, v (in
part), vi, and vii of chapter V of the original work.

By her precepts and her praises she has stimulated his valor. We have her own word for it that she does not approve of his unbending pride, and presumably she has done what she could to check it when she saw it standing in the way of his advancement. She is not the best of teachers to show him how to overcome his pride, but at least she can condemn it as something not drawn from her:

> Thy valiantness was mine, thou suck'dst it from me,
> But owe thy pride thyself.   (III, ii, 129–130)

The pride she condemns is what she says it is, a thing of his own, fixed in his nature. It is in the original substance of his character and is not an untutored churlishness acquired through the accident of his father's death.

But there is that about the pride of her son which Volumnia is quite incapable of understanding. Though she sees clearly that it can keep him from gaining the highest honors in Rome, she does not see that it can also keep him from base timeserving. It is more worthy of condemnation than she knows, but at the same time it is worthy of praise in a way that she does not even suspect. Her pupil shows reaches of nobility for which she is not responsible, and he shows them even in his valor, which is not a virtue of her creation, as she seems to think, but a virtue grounded in his natural pride. This valor has been developed but not called into being by her instruction.

The pride of Coriolanus has two very contradictory faculties. It is the tragic flaw in his character and therefore has the well-known power of pride the preëminent deadly sin to produce other faults and destroy good in the spirit of its possessor; but it is at the same time the basis of self-respect in his character and thus has power to produce good in his spirit. Whether destructive of good or productive of good, it is a fierce pride, accompanied by a wrath that makes it work at white heat. The wrath is like the pride it accompanies in not always having the qualities of a deadly sin; it can at times be righteous wrath, directed against human baseness. Hence both the pride and the wrath of Coriolanus can be admirable as well as detestable. Just as taints and honors "wage equal" with the sensualistic Antony, so do they with the proud Coriolanus.

Shakespeare lets us know in the first scene of the play that even among the worst enemies of Coriolanus his honors ask to be balanced against his taints. It is with praise alone that Shakespeare surrounds a deeply flawed but noble hero at the opening of *Macbeth,* and it is with scorn alone that he surrounds such a hero at the opening of *Antony and Cleopatra;* but it is with praise and scorn together, set one against the other, that he surrounds such a hero at the opening of *Coriolanus,* and if the praise does not receive so much dramatic emphasis as the scorn, it is nevertheless honest praise and weighs all the more when we consider that it is offered in defense of Coriolanus by a fair-minded man who has no reason to love him.

When the mob of citizens riot for bread in the beginning lines of the play, First Citizen, who is the leader, makes a case against Coriolanus, and Second Citizen, at some disadvantage because of his secondness, makes a case for him. First Citizen maintains that Coriolanus is the chief enemy of the people among the patricians and that if the people kill him they will have corn enough at their own price. All the citizens except Second Citizen agree that Coriolanus should be killed, for he is "a very dog to the commonalty." Second Citizen shows courage when he asks his starving fellows to think of the patriotic services rendered by Coriolanus to his country. First Citizen argues somewhat subtly that Coriolanus deserves no "good report" as a reward for what he has done to benefit his country because for "what he hath done famously" he pays himself well enough: he pays himself "with being proud" and with pleasing his mother. Coriolanus is proud, declares First Citizen, "even to the altitude of his virtue." The implication is that the pride Coriolanus takes in his ability to fight for his country and the happiness he takes in pleasing his mother with his exploits make his patriotic valor into something so completely selfish that it does not really deserve the name of virtue.

Second Citizen thinks this is speaking "maliciously" about Coriolanus and excuses him by saying, "What he cannot help in his nature, you account a vice in him." It is to be remembered that exactly the same defense of a deeply flawed tragic hero is made in *Antony and Cleopatra* by the tender-minded Lepidus when the tough-minded Octavius passes judgment upon Antony with extreme severity. Lepidus, like Second Citizen, implies that great faults possessed by a great spirit are simply to be accepted when they are so much a part of his essential nature that the great spirit cannot remove them. Lepidus says that the faults of Antony are

> hereditary
> Rather than purchas'd; what he cannot change
> Than what he chooses;   (I, iv, 13–15)

and he thinks that in Antony one cannot find

> Evils enow to darken all his goodness.   (I, iv, 11)

Second Citizen does not defend Coriolanus so enthusiastically as Lepidus defends Antony, but he defends him stoutly. He urges in conclusion that though Coriolanus can be accused of pride, he must in no way be accused of covetousness. First Citizen replies tartly that nevertheless plenty of accusations can be made, for Coriolanus "hath faults, with surplus, to tire in repetition." We are reminded that the Antony in whom Lepidus finds much undarkened goodness is seen by Octavius as

> the abstract of all faults
> That all men follow.   (I, iv, 9–10)

As the action of the opening scene progresses, we find that First Citizen is not a man to back down when he comes up against more formidable opposition than that provided by Second Citizen.[1] He stands up to Menenius when that affable patrician justifies the Senate in characteristic fashion by telling the "pretty tale" of the good belly and the rebellious members of the body. What is even more to his credit, he stands up to Coriolanus when that patrician the reverse of affable justifies the Senate in equally characteristic fashion by pouring vilification upon the common people. First Citizen argues with Menenius. He does not have an opportunity to argue with Coriolanus, but he is briefly ironic when Coriolanus begins his tirade by calling the citizens "dissentious rogues." "We have ever your good word," says First Citizen in reply to this name calling. It is the last we hear from him. He has served his purpose, and not the least of the things he has done is the making of this last remark.

The phrase "good word," spoken by First Citizen in scorn, is a spur to Coriolanus that sets him off upon a most revealing course of argument. His good word for the citizens! Why, begins Coriolanus,

> He that will give good words to thee will flatter
> Beneath abhorring.   (I, i, 173–174)

There is no virtue whatever in the citizens, he declares, and any man who tells them they have virtue is a base, flattering politician. This, as we shall learn, is not mere sound and fury, pumped up by Coriolanus as a means of cowing the mob. It is honest passion. The idea that to flatter the common people is a supremely detestable thing is fixed in his mind and insistently appears in his speeches throughout the first half of the play. Here, in what he says to the rioters, he is expressing the idea for the first time. The words "flatter" and "beneath abhorring" look forward to the soul struggle he is to experience as he becomes convinced that to get the consulship he must somehow canvass for votes from the populace.

Under one aspect *Coriolanus* is the tragedy of a great spirit who can-

---

[1] I accept a change in the Folio text which is usually made by editors. The change puts First Citizen in the place of Second Citizen as the maker of replies to Menenius and Coriolanus. These replies should obviously be given to the leader of the rebellion, who, of course, is First Citizen.

not stoop to flattery in the way of the world. But the nobility of Coriolanus is never simple or outright; one may be led to qualify, or even
reject, the praise of his nature offered by the loquacious Menenius in
these well-known lines:

> His nature is too noble for the world:
> He would not flatter Neptune for his trident,
> Or Jove for 's power to thunder.   (III, i, 254–256)[2]

It is of course Coriolanus' pride with all its viciousness, the same pride
that First Citizen sees as the impelling force behind his valorous patriotism, which makes him "too noble" to stoop to flattery. Yet this pride,
which can paradoxically be good as well as evil, makes him react not
only with anger but also with horror to that ironic remark of First
Citizen, "We have ever your good word." Coriolanus, it would seem,
has had the shocking thought before the play opens that he might some-
time be tempted to flatter the populace, and thus be completely false to
his "own truth," in order to win the consulship.

That Coriolanus has thoroughly honest principles and thoroughly
honest reasons for detesting the citizens, it may be hard for us of a
democratic age to believe; but we are certainly meant to understand
that he does have them and that they are well based according to his
view of things. They are put before us clearly in the speech with which
he answers the ironic remark of First Citizen. The citizens, says Coriolanus, are good for nothing, either in war or peace, since war "affrights"
them and peace makes them "proud." It is entirely characteristic of
Coriolanus to divide all life into war and peace and to judge any man
by asking first whether he is a true man of war. The true men of war
are of course the warrior aristocrats, who are bred through generations
to bear arms, to strive for honor, and never to show cowardice. Coriolanus thinks that these have an absolute right to rule the state because
without them to defend it the state could not exist at all in a world where
dog-eat-dog conflict is recurrent. The common people, who are not true
men of war, could be true men of peace if they were not corrupted by
peace into thinking that they should have power in the state. It is
abundantly plain that they are thus corrupted, says Coriolanus, and thus
that they are proud. It is ironic that he should make this statement so
soon after he himself has been accused by First Citizen of being proud.

If Coriolanus had heard First Citizen accuse him of pride, he might
have said in reply that trustworthy patricians have a right to be proud.
What he says as he accuses the citizens of pride is that mere plebeians

---

2 O. J. Campbell makes a thought-provoking argument for the rejection of this praise of
Coriolanus as coming from a buffoonish commentator in a tragical satire (*Shakespeare's
Satire*, New York, 1943, p. 209).

are never under any circumstances trustworthy and therefore, by implication, do not have any right to be proud. One who trusts them to show
courage finds them hares instead of lions, and one who trusts them to
show intelligence finds them geese instead of foxes. They discover
worthiness in the offender condemned by justice and curse the justice
that condemns him. The man who deserves greatness deserves their
hate, and the man who would achieve greatness by depending upon
their favor "swims with fins of lead." They are so fickle that with every
minute they change their minds, now swinging from hatred to adoration, and now from adoration to hatred. And these untrustworthy commoners are crying out against the trustworthy noble Senate, against an
aristocracy who may be counted upon in time of war to save the state
from destruction by forces without and in time of peace from destruction by forces within. For in peace as in war there is dog-eat-dog conflict which can ruin the state; freed from the control of the Senate, the
commoners, "curs" that they are, would devour each other. "What's the
matter," he asks them,

> That in these several places of the city
> You cry against the noble senate, who,
> Under the gods, keep you in awe, which else
> Would feed on one another?   (I, i, 191–194)

Coriolanus does not offer the citizens a picture of the patrician Senate
gathering up the goods of life and distributing them to the commoners,
a picture such as Menenius offers when he tells the fable of the belly
and the members. The amiable food-loving and wine-loving Menenius
very naturally sees the good commonwealth as a body in which there
is plenty of nourishment flowing out to all its parts, though of course
as a patrician he believes that the Senate should control according to
its wisdom the distribution of good things. Coriolanus, on the other
hand, just as naturally sees the good commonwealth as something aus-
terely negative rather than something gratifyingly positive. We may be
sure that Coriolanus is no more subject to the deadly sin of gluttony
than to the deadly sin of covetousness, and that his thoughts are always
above sensual delights as much as they are above material rewards. He
has reached spiritual heights of which Menenius, the amiable feeder
and drinker, knows nothing. But his spirit is so bleak that he can only
picture the good commonwealth as one in which the many who are
brutish are properly restrained from eating each other up by the few
who are their betters. And he tells the citizens that under the beneficent
restraint of the Senate they are fortunate brutish members of a well-
ordered commonwealth.

We understand from these lines which Coriolanus speaks thus early in the play, in justification of all he stands for, that for him the virtue of all virtues is trustworthiness. The good man is the trustworthy man, and the trustworthy man is the complete aristocrat, who not only is born with blue blood but also lives in accordance with inherited principles and thus by rules of conduct well established. Such a man, thinks Coriolanus, runs true to form. You know what he will admire and what he will detest, and you know that he will not change his mind except for solid cause. Naturally, a part of the trustworthiness acquired from aristocratic warrior ancestors is his courage. He can be counted upon in battle to do credit to his noble blood. Since he is not a coward, he does not tell lies, for the liar is a coward afraid to tell the truth; and since he does not tell lies, he flatters no man. Flattery is the weakling's way of gaining favor and advantage in the world, and the trustworthy man will not stoop to it. Especially will the noble trustworthy man, the aristocrat, not stoop to flattery when he deals with the base, untrustworthy man, the commoner. Commoners are

> no surer, no
> Than is the coal of fire upon the ice,
> Or hailstone in the sun.   (I, i, 178–180)

To say good words to them is to "flatter beneath abhorring," and to give them tribunes who will "defend their vulgar wisdoms," as has just been done, is to "break the heart of generosity." By this condemnation of the citizens for their lack of trustworthiness and by the attendant revelation of his faith in an aristocratic ideal of trustworthiness Coriolanus asks to be judged according to the measure of his own trustworthiness. That measure, as we shall see, is in one direction admirably large and in another pitifully small.

V

When we see Coriolanus in battle against the Volscians, we are able to judge for ourselves the quality of service which he renders his country with his sword. As he goes to make preparation for the Volscian campaign, the tribunes analyze his character and decide that in pride he has no equal. From them we hear once more what we have already heard from First Citizen, that Coriolanus is a self-centered seeker after fame, driven by excessive pride to show outstanding valor. From them we hear further that his pride is a scheming pride which makes him willing to serve under Cominius in the Volscian campaign in order that he may have the opportunity of winning fame as a warrior without any risk of losing fame as an unlucky commander-in-chief. As Coriolanus sweeps all before him in the campaign, moving with the ease and surety of genius in an element seemingly made for him, we see that he is indeed a man driven by inordinate pride, but not so ignobly driven, by any means, as the tribunes think.

In making out that Coriolanus is a schemer as he prepares to serve under Cominius against the Volscians, and in attributing to him the deviousness of a politician, the tribunes only betray that they themselves are schemers and that political deviousness is to them second nature. They believe that any man with the pride of Coriolanus will of course desire the highest position of power in any undertaking of which he is a part unless he finds that by accepting a lower position he stands to profit later. Coriolanus never at any time shows the political sense and the ability to calculate advantage for himself that the tribunes credit to him. This, quite obviously, is one reason for his tragic fall. Also, Coriolanus never at any time shows a desire for power as power. This it is most important to realize if we are to understand the nature of the ambition engendered by his pride.

For Coriolanus is not a Julius Caesar or an Augustus, with an intelligent craving for supreme executive power, and neither is he a Tamburlaine, with a blind lust for supreme conquering power. What he yearns for ambitiously is recognition in Rome of his supreme worth as a valorous and entirely trustworthy patrician warrior, and he wants power only as it stands for that recognition. In short, he wants power only so far as it is honor. This is seen clearly when he becomes a candidate for the consulship. Moreover, he is completely scrupulous according to his lights and does not want to be dishonorable in gaining the power that for him is honor. By turning traitor to Rome he shows a tragic blind spot in his aristocratic perception of the honorable, but as he fights against the Volscians, and as he lets himself be put forward for election to the consulship, his eye for the honorable is that of a thoroughly upstanding Roman patrician; his vision is limited by the traditions of his class, but within limits it is admirable.

When Coriolanus agrees to serve under Cominius, he is keeping a promise which as a man of honor he cannot break. "It is your former promise," Cominius reminds him. Coriolanus replies: "Sir, it is; / And I am constant" (I, i, 244–245). His service under Cominius proves that he is a great soldier, not that he is a great general. In warfare he is an invincible champion, an inspiring example of what one brave man can do with a sword, rather than a wise and skillful leader of men. On the battlefield, pride leads him to show the very finest of his noble qualities, but, as one might expect, it tends to cut him off from those around him even while it makes him win their praises. In Shakespeare's eyes, Coriolanus is the complete opposite of that happy warrior Henry V in his attitude toward the mass of common soldiers. He can curse them effectively and shame them effectively; for he never commands them to do anything that he himself cannot and will not do better than they, but never in the least does he make himself one with them, as Henry does when he says to his men before the Battle of Agincourt:

> For he today that sheds his blood with me
> Shall be my brother; be he n'er so vile
> This day shall gentle his condition.
>
> *(Henry V, IV, iii, 61–63)*

Gentle the condition of the common file? It is flattery, demagogic flattery, for a general to use such words, Coriolanus would say. His faith is firm that only "our gentlemen" are brave and that common soldiers are always ready to run "from rascals worse than they" (I, vi, 42–44). It is typical of him that he performs prodigies of valor to enter the gates of Corioli and then, because he is not followed by his men, who of course have no love for him and think him foolhardy, has to perform more prodigies of valor to get out of the city again and shame the Romans into making a victorious assault upon it. "Mark me, and do the like," he cries as he storms the gates.

In the main, Shakespeare follows Plutarch closely as he shows the nobility of Coriolanus on the Volscian battlefield. Like Plutarch he presents a superbly valorous hero who is above any desire for material reward and who scorns to take a share of the Volscian spoils but is quite willing to accept—in the way of honor—such gifts as a war horse and the commemorative name of Coriolanus. But because Shakespeare is giving a paradoxical side to the nature of Coriolanus, something of which Plutarch has no conception, he makes a notable change in one of Plutarch's incidents. This incident, offered to show magnanimity in the conqueror of Corioli, is given the following form by the biographer. Coriolanus, after rejecting mercenary reward for what he has done in the battle, begs to be granted one boon. He requests freedom for a Volscian, "an olde friende and hoste" of his, "an honest wealthie man, and now a prisoner, who liuing before in great wealth in his own countrie, liueth now a poore prisoner in the hands of his enemies" and is about to be "solde as a slaue." In Shakespeare's hands this Volscian host of Coriolanus's changes from a rich man to a poor man, and Coriolanus is given an extra measure of magnanimity when he is made to plead not only for an enemy but for an enemy who stands far down in the social scale. Yet along with this extra measure of virtue goes an extra measure of defect, and the virtue seems inseparable from the defect. When Coriolanus is asked for the name of the poor Volscian whom he wants to benefit, he cannot remember it!

Nor does he seem concerned that he cannot remember the man's name. After all, we are to infer, this was a lowly Volscian and hence one of no importance, even though he once put Coriolanus in debt to him for friendly services. Who could expect that his name would be remembered? Because Coriolanus is spurred by pride to stand out among men as the most virtuous of great-spirited soldiers, he is also spurred by pride to be magnanimous to an enemy, even a plebeian enemy. But his pride is always a passion which cuts him off from true sympathy with, and true interest in, any other human being.

The pride of Coriolanus leads him to be gratified by praise given to his prowess and magnanimity, but—to complete the paradox of his nature —it also leads him to have contempt for such praise. Mr. John Palmer makes the just remark that the qualities in Coriolanus which "claim our admiration in these battle scenes are inherent in his defects," and hence that we think "his contempt of praise is rooted less in modesty than in pride."[3] The pride of Coriolanus makes him impatient when he is praised because it makes him think himself greater than any praise can indicate, and for this his pride is certainly not commendable. But just as certainly it is commendable because it makes its immodest possessor strive honestly to be more and more worthy of praise—even, be it noted, of praise for modesty.

Coriolanus is morbid upon the subject of flattery, whether flattery expected from him or flattery offered to him. When he is honored on the battlefield with a flourish of drums and trumpets and with cheers, he replies to his generous companions in a speech that should be regarded by them as insulting, though they are good enough not to take it that way. The acclamations are "hyperbolical," he says, and imply the existence in him of a base yearning that his "little should be dieted / In praises sauc'd with lies" (I, ix, 52–53). It is the next thing, of course, to calling his praisers liars. Matters are brought to such a pass, says Coriolanus to his kind friends, that drums and trumpets, noble instruments of war, must "i' the field prove flatterers" and be guilty of the "false-fac'd soothing" found in courts and cities. In any situation, Coriolanus is a most difficult person for his associates to bear with, but Cominius deserves special credit for showing restraint in his answer to this wild talk about lying flattery. His reply is merely that the "too modest" Coriolanus is more cruel to his good report than grateful for it. . . .

The test of integrity forced upon Coriolanus when he becomes a candidate for the consulship does not at first seem to him a very serious matter. Indeed, he thinks he can avoid it. After he is approved by the Senate for the consulship, he is told that he must speak to the people and ask them for their voices in the usual manner. He requests that

[3] *Political Characters of Shakespeare* (London, Macmillan, 1945), p. 265.

he be excused from following the custom, but he does not make an issue of his request. When the tribune Sicinius declares bluntly and provocatively that the people will not bate one jot of ceremony, and Menenius urges him to conform to the custom, Coriolanus surprises us by going in without a struggle, albeit ungraciously. He lets it be known that he will act the part of a pleader for votes before the people, though he will blush to do it. He seems to have yielded ignominiously to a temptation to buy the consulship with flattery and to have yielded with indecent haste, as soon as the temptation was presented.

But it turns out that he has not yielded at all, according to his view of the matter. Though he acts the part of a flatterer of the people, he does so in a supercilious way and thus serves notice as he performs his role that he really is not a flatterer. He makes no attempt to deceive the citizens. On the contrary, by insulting them he takes pains to keep them from being deceived. Says he to one of them: "I will, sir, flatter my sworn brother the people, to earn a dearer estimation of them; 'tis a condition they account gentle: and since the wisdom of their choice is rather to have my hat than my heart, I will practice the insinuating nod, and be off to them most counterfeitly" (II, iii, 101–106). Though there is irony here, the speech is plain-spoken enough in all conscience. Coriolanus has the feeling that even as he "begs" votes he remains openly and honestly himself, every inch a scorner of the people, and that because he hides none of his scorn he suffers no damage to his inner man.

The trouble is that the slow-witted citizens are deceived even while Coriolanus is scornfully warning them not to be deceived. They have a sense of justice and want to give him the consulship as a reward for his victories. They have some doubts that what he has been saying to them as he has solicited their votes is exactly as it should be, but they do not understand it fully and they promise him the consulship. When they change their minds, after being prompted to do so by the tribunes, Coriolanus finds himself faced anew with a problem which he thought he had put aside. In his anger that the people should change their minds, he berates the "mutable, rank-scented many" who cannot rule and will not suffer themselves to be ruled. Let them, he says,

> Regard me as I do not flatter, and
> Therein behold themselves.   (III, i, 66–67)

No voice in public affairs, he lets it be known, should ever have been given them. When Sicinius calls him a traitor, his passion becomes blind rage. As an aristocrat who believes proudly that aristocracy justifies itself by defending the state from all harm, and who thinks of himself as the foremost of state defenders, Coriolanus takes the word "traitor" as a fighting word. As we shall see, this is not the only time

he does so. Both as a potential traitor and as an actual one he is painfully sensitive to the accusation of treason.

The riot precipitated by Coriolanus when Sicinius calls him traitor
leaves his problem clearly defined and makes it urgent. Coriolanus now
sees that he cannot avoid a test which he once thought he could avoid
easily. As soon as he sees that the test must really be met, his instinct
is to adopt a course of complete honesty by defying the people and
declaring with all the scorn he has for them that even though they seize
him to cast him from the Tarpeian Rock he will still "be thus to them."
Since he is truly brave, he does not fear to follow this instinct. But his
mother, assuming a role of which there is no hint in Plutarch, plays the
tempter and succeeds so well in confusing his judgment that he decides
to go contrary to all his principles. On this occasion, as always, the
principles of the individualistic Coriolanus are nothing more than his
instinct. To do right seems to him only a matter of being his natural
self. He is amazed that his mother does not approve of his honest
desire to defy the upstart "woollen vassals" and he demands of her:

> Would you have me
> False to my nature? Rather say I play
> The man I am.   (III, ii, 14–16)

The honesty of Coriolanus, which has regard for nothing but this pre-
cious "nature" of his, is thus a selfish honesty; but it is just as insistent
in the demands it makes upon him as any unselfish honesty could be,
and just as uncompromising in its conception of truth. It is never a
doubtful or halfway virtue. This is more than can be said, certainly, of
his mother's honesty. When she explains her disapproval of his plan for
honest defiance of the people, Volumnia shows herself perfectly capable
of juggling with truth according to expediency and of letting the de-
spised commoners force her to play fast and loose with the concept of
honor.

Thus Volumnia proves a very different patrician from her son, despite
the spiritual bond between them. She is a political-minded patrician
with something of the Machiavellian in her character. One may say
that she is a most necessary kind of person for the aristocrats to have
in their number when the common people begin to acquire power and
become a threat to aristocracy, but, to use a word of her own, she is
not "absolute" in her aristocratic pride. At a certain point she will
compromise with the nonaristocratic part of the world and do so even
at the cost of being ignoble, in the belief that nobility must at times
save itself by ignoble means. The aristocratic nature of Coriolanus which
leads him to be arrogantly truthful wins high praise from her, but when

he asks whether she would have him be false to that nature, her answer is an unhesitating yes:

> You are too absolute;
> Though therein you can never be too noble,
> But when extremities speak.   (III, ii, 39–41)

In other words, to be fearlessly honest would now, she thinks, be for Coriolanus a noble luxury that he could not afford. She tells him that he should dissemble.

> I would dissemble with my nature where
> My fortunes and my friends at stake requir'd
> I should do so in honour.   (III, ii, 62–64)

This dissembling "in honour" is not like plain dissembling. It is "policy." There is a kind of sharp practice which, as he very well knows, can be used honorably to deceive an enemy in time of war. Why can it not be used honorably to deceive an enemy in time of peace, especially when the fortunes of himself and his friends, of the whole aristocratic class, are at stake?

Coriolanus goes down before his mother's assault, which is supported by Menenius and Cominius, but he yields only after a struggle. As his mother very well says, he would rather follow his enemy in a fiery gulf than flatter him in a bower. He promises to go back to the people and flatter them, not superciliously as he has done before, but with real intent to deceive.

Coriolanus yields to Volumnia and yet is not fully corrupted by her. He retains his conscience. He cannot answer her argument and cannot keep his judgment from being confused by it, but in his heart he knows perfectly well that flattering the people in downright fashion will for him be heinous wrongdoing. It will mean letting himself be possessed by "some harlot's spirit." For his mother the end will justify the means, but not for him. He has no sooner yielded to his mother than he changes his mind and says that he cannot and will not go through with what is wanted of him, because to do so might make him go so completely against his inner sense of truth that he would convert his inherent nobility into inherent baseness.

> I will not do 't,
> Lest I surcease to honour mine own truth
> And by my body's action teach my mind
> A most inherent baseness.   (III, ii, 120–123)

Volumnia finally prevails over Coriolanus by using tactics which, as we shall see later when she stops him from burning Rome, are not to be resisted under any circumstances. What Volumnia does as a last resort to make sure that her son will placate the people is simply to tell him that he must flatter them *for her sake*. She has asked him to flatter them in order that general ruin may be avoided—not, she would have him know, because she has a heart less stout than his and therefore fears them. He finds dishonor in flattering them and begging the consulship from them. Very well, she counters:

> At thy choice then:
> To beg of thee it is my more dishonour
> Than thou of them.   (III, ii, 123–125)

Volumnia is as shrewd as her son is lacking in shrewdness, and she is never more shrewd than when in desperation she appeals to him thus, by demanding that he dishonor himself in order that he may not dishonor her. She does not base her appeal upon his love for her, though this love is greater than that he has for his wife, or his son, or anyone else. She bases her appeal upon his loyalty to her. Coriolanus the self-centered individualist is not capable of sacrificing himself for any other human being—even his mother—in the way of love. But Coriolanus the self-centered worshiper of honor is capable of sacrificing himself for one other human being—his mother—in the way of loyalty. The loyalty felt by him for his mother is the only true loyalty he has, and only where she is concerned can he place the honor of another above his own honor. Coriolanus knows well enough that the honor among his fellows which he proudly wants to maintain for himself demands that he have loyalty to others. He counts himself a good patrician and a good Roman, two things which in his mind amount to the same thing, and he knows that he is called upon to be loyal to his class and to Rome. Yet though he *knows* the need of such loyalty, he does not *feel* it. His loyalty to his mother is his only true loyalty because it is the only one whose need is for him an emotional reality.

We see in the proudly self-centered Coriolanus a man who has almost but not quite achieved spiritual isolation and has been saved from it largely because he honors his mother. He has almost but not quite come to the point of finding no compulsion outside himself and holding nothing sacred outside himself. To be a good Roman patrician he must have reverence for his class and its traditions and have veneration for Rome itself as a body politic created and supported by his class, but for him everything sacred about his class and about Rome, everything in the way of tradition and substance that must absolutely remain inviolate, is gathered in his mother. She is the one holy vessel in his Roman temple. She prevails over him not by making him accept her version of truth, but merely by making him feel the sheer weight of her matriarchal dominion. One may say that she treats him as a bad boy and scolds or browbeats him until he surrenders, but one must go farther to explain her power over him.

Thus, because Coriolanus agrees with Volumnia that it is more dishonor for her to beg of him than for him to beg of the people, he finally agrees to "mountebank" the loves of the people, though he continues to feel, as she does not feel, that to dissemble in this way is inherently base. The result is a very unstable solution of his difficulties. Try as he will, he cannot be a fulsome political mountebank, but he really steels himself to placate the citizens by telling them an untruth. He appears before them and announces, without giving any sign of having mental reservations, that he is "content" to submit himself to the people and their officers and to suffer lawful censure for faults proved upon him. This is as far as he can go with his flattery. By this simple statement he acknowledges, though his heart denies each word of what he says, that the people are entitled to their tribunes and have the right to pass judgment upon him. It is only momentarily that he is able thus to dishonor his own truth. As soon as the tribune Sicinius, knowing very well what the effect will be, charges that Coriolanus has contrived to gain tyrannical power and has become a "traitor to the people," Volumnia's work is all undone. Pride and wrath surge up in Coriolanus to overwhelm the respect he has for his mother, and make him throw the lie in the tribune's teeth. The accusation that he has schemed to win tyrannical power is of course utterly unfounded, but what really stirs his wrath is the word "traitor." He has had trouble enough over a loyalty to his class which his mother has urged him to recognize, and now he must be told that he owes loyalty to the people and has betrayed them —the people, who are so detestable that they can make no call upon anyone's loyalty, his least of all. From the dishonesty of flattery he turns to the honesty of curses and finds relief for his spirit as he cries:

> The fires i' the lowest hell fold-in the people!
> Call me their traitor!   (III, iii, 67–68)

This is the turning point of the tragedy. Coriolanus has reached the pinnacle of his fortune and as he leaves Rome to go into banishment he begins his descent to destruction. Because we can see very well that he brings misfortune on himself by his pride, and because we can see equally well that his pride is a vicious defect, we may feel that when misfortune comes to him he thoroughly deserves it. Nevertheless, there is irony in the fact that he is banished and started on his way to ruin because his pride keeps him from being false to the truth. One of his heroic aspects is that of a martyr to honesty.

VI

As Coriolanus says farewell to his family and friends and goes into exile, he makes this promise:

> While I remain above the ground you shall
> Hear from me still; and never of me aught
> But what is like me formerly. (IV, i, 51–53)

There is unconscious irony in his words, for it fortunes that he lives up to them in a way he does not think of when he utters them. He does not continue to make his mark in the world by continuing to be the honorable man he has been formerly, which is what he means to say he will do. He continues to make his mark in the world only by becoming a traitor. And yet when he follows the course of treason there is nothing in him which is essentially not like him formerly, because with his inordinate love of self and his total lack of any loyalty except that to his mother he has always been potentially a traitor.

Only after a severe soul struggle has Coriolanus undertaken to be a dissembling politician and flatter the people. He undergoes no soul struggle at all as he prepares to become a traitor to his country. His pride gives him a conscience to support in him the virtue of plainspoken honesty, but it does not even intimate to him that for the kind of patrician he has taken himself to be, namely, a trustworthy man born to rule and defend his country, treason is an unforgivable sin. Suddenly, quite without warning, we find him saying in a soliloquy that he hates Rome and will turn to Corioli to do it what service he can. He has the idea that his change of allegiance is entirely natural in a world of "slippery turns," where fast friends can in a moment become bitter enemies. Later he shows no sign of compunction as he tells Aufidius that he is offering his sword to the Volscians "in mere spite," to be revenged upon his banishers. He implies by what he says to Aufidius that he owes no more consideration to his own class, the "dastard nobles" who have not been able to keep him from being banished, than to the Roman plebeians, the "slaves" who have decreed his banishment.

Once Coriolanus has perpetrated treason, there is really nothing new to be learned about him, since the remainder of his tragedy is a second perpetration of treason brought about by the same deficiency in his nature that is responsible for the first. Everything that happens when he betrays the Volscians has a completely familiar quality. It is true that he does not betray them as he has betrayed the Romans, to get revenge for an insult to his ego; but he betrays them for a purpose sufficiently characteristic—to please his mother. When Coriolanus appears before Rome with his army of Volscians, he seems so fiercely bent upon taking the city and reducing it to fire-blackened ruins that he cannot possibly be turned from his destructive course, and yet his mother, pleading successfully after he has proved deaf to other Roman suppliants, saves the city. She does so by making him feel once more the full power of that authority which to him is her matriarchal sacredness.

At the beginning of her plea Volumnia shocks him by kneeling to him. "What is this?" he asks:

> Your knees to me! to your corrected son!
> Then let the pebbles on the hungry beach
> Fillip the stars.   (V, iii, 57–59)

The deep respect he shows her promises well for her efforts, but as she proceeds with her plea she finds it useless to search for patriotism in him or to confront him with his wife and child and appeal to his love for them. She also finds it useless to argue deviously, in a manner of which she has once before shown herself a master, that he is too inflexible in his conception of honor. Her argument is extremely plausible. He should realize, she says, that though it would be "poisonous" to his honor to save the Romans by destroying the Volscians, it would greatly increase his honor to make a peace in which the Volscians and the Romans could enjoy reconciliation and in which the Volscians could acquire merit by showing mercy to the Romans. The truth is that, no matter how good it might be for all concerned if the Volscians could show mercy, Coriolanus has got himself into a position where the decision to grant mercy or withhold it is simply not his to make. Indeed, where there is any question of foregoing a part of the Volscian victory over the Romans, he needs, if he is to be honorable, to lean backward. Coriolanus himself is quite aware that this is the way things stand. He has told Menenius that his affairs are now "servanted to others" and that any "remission" for the Romans must come from "Volscian breasts." Again we see that Coriolanus has a sense of honesty far more surely grounded than his mother's.

Volumnia finally has success by bringing against Coriolanus the accusation that he is not being honorable so far as *she* is concerned, since he is restraining from her "the duty which / To a mother's part belongs" (V, iii, 167–168). There is no man "more bound to's mother" than he, she would have him know. It is not of any bond of love between her son and herself that she speaks, but only of a bond of duty. Once more she kneels before him, together with the ladies who accompany her. "Let us shame him with our knees," she cries. As he remains obdurate, she rises to lead her fellow petitioners back to Rome, but turning to leave she lets him understand that when the city is afire he must be put to further shame by his dishonored mother, for at that time she will yet again "speak a little." It is only after this parting shot is delivered that Coriolanus at last gives way.

Thus Volumnia demands that Coriolanus spare Rome at the cost of dishonoring himself, just as she has demanded that he win the Roman consulship at the cost of dishonoring himself. Both times, she gets him to dishonor himself by asking him to honor her. It is true, of course, that in bringing upon him the dishonor of betraying the Volscians she saves him from the dishonor of destroying his native city and keeps him from proceeding to the ultimate violation of the allegiance to which he was born. But the good she does for her son comes far short of balancing the ill, because, though she brings him to the point of saving his native Rome, she cannot bring him to the point of saving his soul as a Roman. She cannot make him reaccept the old allegiance after she has made him turn false to the new, and she cannot even make him feel repentance—not the smallest—for having betrayed Rome in the first place. Hence the result for Coriolanus spiritually is that he is left unmitigatedly guilty of compound treason.

This time, Coriolanus yields to his mother without any sense of losing his integrity. Breaking faith with the Volscians is to him a very different matter from flattering the Roman plebeians, for it leaves his inner being quite untouched. He knows that such faith-breaking is wrong, but his knowledge of its wrongness is so superficial and so unimportant that it is not what keeps him so long from granting his mother's petition. The struggle within him is between his desire for revenge against Rome and his respect for Volumnia as the "honour'd mould" wherein he has been formed. Once he has decided to put his respect for his mother ahead of his desire for revenge, his spirit is at rest. As for the wrongness of his breaking faith with the Volscians, he feels that he must acknowledge it but not brood over it; and acknowledge it he does, to Aufidius:

> Aufidius, though I cannot make true wars,
> I'll frame convenient peace.   (V, iii, 190–191)

His mother, as we have seen, has tried to make him think that by neglecting to press home the Volscian victory he would be working not against the Volscians, but for them, since he would be allowing them to show mercy and thus act nobly. This specious reasoning makes no impression on him. Bluntly he lays his sparing of Rome to his inability to "make true wars" for the Volscians, and calls the peace he is about to procure nothing more than "convenient." To the very end of his career the pride of Coriolanus gives him brave hatred for all paltering, and this virtue his mother is never able to corrupt, however hard she tries. But to do Volumnia justice, she is by no means villainous when she works to corrupt her son. She is a person of strong character who has succeeded in bending truth to her will and has succeeded so well that she has deceived herself about the nature of truth.

When Coriolanus says to his mother that she has won a happy victory for Rome, but that for him her success is most dangerous, "if not most mortal," he is looking at the oncoming shadow of his catastrophe. The Volscians are to exact his life in payment for his offense against them, after Aufidius has played out his role of villain. Aufidius is not without generous instincts. Though he can hate Coriolanus as an enemy, he can respect him as a glorious opponent and, when Coriolanus joins the Volscians, can embrace him as a "noble thing" that he can truly love. Even when Aufidius begins to grow jealous of his too successful associate, he can say, after talking about the pride of Coriolanus and his defects in general, "But he has a merit / To choke it in the utterance" (IV, vii, 48–49). Yet when Aufidius is confirmed in his jealousy and feels that the time has come to ruin Coriolanus, he stops at nothing, either to justify his aim or accomplish it. To justify his aim he goes so far as to make the accusation that Coriolanus has worked against him underhandedly among the Volscians by the seductive use of flattery. This, of course, is simply not to be believed. No such use of flattery is shown in the play, and everything we see of Coriolanus early or late in his career makes him seem incapable of it. Moreover, there is the admission by Aufidius that he is putting "a good construction" on his "pretext to strike" at Coriolanus. To accomplish his aim Aufidius forms a conspiracy and traps Coriolanus to his destruction. The scheme of entrapment is exactly the same as that used by the Roman tribunes, namely, to call Coriolanus traitor and thereby make him so angry that he must throw all caution to the winds and expose nakedly whatever is most offensive in his pride.

Upon his return to Corioli from his victory against Rome, Coriolanus appears before the Volscians with the declaration that he is still their soldier and that he is "no more infected" with love of his country than when he set forth to fight against it. This is quite true, and to him it seems to be all that really matters, but it is also true that (to use the words of Aufidius) he has sold the blood and labor of the Volscians and has denied them the full measure of victory which was rightfully theirs. By admitting his inability to "make true wars" for the Volscians, Coriolanus has acknowledged the wrong he has done them, and yet he has never seen the true quality of that wrong. He has never been infected with patriotism and has betrayed his own country without compunction; one would not expect him to acquire among the Volscians a sure understanding of treason. He knows that he has not kept faith with the Volscians, but, because of his pride and his consciousness that he is still ready to serve them heroically in any way short of delivering Rome into

their hands, he cannot abase himself to the point of thinking himself
their traitor. Traitors are scorned as ignoble. How can he, the noble
Coriolanus, be scorned as ignoble by the Volscians, upon whom he
once proved his nobility with his sword? Moreover, he has done the
Volscians a great favor by fighting for them, even if he has done them
wrong by not giving them Rome to loot and burn. What he has done
for them and is still willing to do for them weighs much more, he thinks,
than anything he has promised to do and not done.

Thus, when Aufidius brings out the word "traitor" in accusing him
before the assembled Volscians, Coriolanus is like a man struck in the
face by an unexpected blow. He is ludicrously unprepared to meet the
attack and is ludicrously thrown off balance. He can only bluster:
"Traitor! How now!" When Aufidius presses the attack and loads him
with calculated insults, Coriolanus is toppled into the pit dug for him.
Raging against the Volscians and boasting of his singlehanded conquest
of their city of Corioli, he turns the Volscian common people against
him and falls under the conspirators' swords.

But even as the Volscian people call for his blood a Volscian lord
tries to save him from "outrage" and pays tribute to his nobility in these
exalted words:

> The man is noble and his fame folds in
> This orb o' the earth.   (V, v, 126–127)

There is another Volscian lord who calls the dead hero the "most noble
corse" that herald ever followed to his urn. And Aufidius himself ends
the play with a speech declaring that Coriolanus, despite the injuries
he has done to the Volscians, "shall have a noble memory."

VII

Coriolanus, then, can be thought of as greatly noble, and a chorus of
Volscians urges us at the end of the tragedy to remember him thus. He
is probably the last of the paradoxically noble heroes of Shakespeare's
last tragic world. It is likely that few of us would call him the best of
those "rare spirits" and that many would call him the worst. He is
monstrously deficient as a human being, and his deficiency is the more
unfortunate because it tends not to foster pity for him but to destroy
any that we might give him. As a tragic hero he therefore has a marked
disadvantage which is not shared by Timon, Macbeth, or Antony. Each
of these others asks for our pity in a manner not to be denied—even
Macbeth, who himself is pitiless but comes to know pitifully that by
being pitiless he has lost "honour, love, obedience, troops of friends."
Coriolanus, the fanatical lover of himself who never knows disillusion-

ment, whose pride is so great that his spiritual self-sufficiency is never shaken, repels pity at any time, and when he does not inspire admiration, he is apt to inspire such detestation as to leave no room for pity.

As Shakespeare gives form to his last tragic world, he is always daring in his efforts to make the paradox of the deeply flawed noble hero yield subtle truth. In *Coriolanus* he pushes this paradox to its limit of tragic validity, and sometimes even beyond, with the result that he makes it more acceptable to the mind than to the heart. The deeply flawed Coriolanus who repels pity is too deeply flawed for Shakespeare's tragic purposes. Most of us who perceive nobility of spirit in him would doubtless rather praise it than associate with it.

In *Coriolanus* the problem of evil, once terribly urgent for Shakespeare, is almost completely absorbed within the dramatic hypothesis of a man who is supremely guilty of pride the vice and at the same time supremely noble in pride the virtue. Shakespeare constructs the hypothesis with mathematical precision. He uses the very greatest care to strike a balance between the repellent Coriolanus and the admirable Coriolanus, and he keeps the balance in a spirit both ironically superior and dispassionately just. The achievement, though delicately beautiful, has a quality that can only be called forbidding. About the play as a whole there is a lack of essential warmth amounting even to bleakness, and it is not for nothing that the verse is often eloquent but seldom deeply moving, often impressive but seldom sublime. *Coriolanus* is a magnificent failure in which Shakespeare seems to have brought his tragic inspiration to an end by taking tragedy into an area of paradox beyond the effective reach of merely human pity.

D. J. ENRIGHT

CORIOLANUS
Tragedy or Debate?

CAN *Coriolanus* really be called a tragedy? Or, since there is no point
in haggling over literary categories, let us ask instead: What is the
status of the play within the canon of Shakespearean tragedy?

The simplest theory of all has it that the tragedy in question consists
in the fatal clash between a noble individual and an ignoble people,
between personality and society. If we accept Menenius's word—"His
nature is too noble for the world"—then the theory must stand. But
there seems little reason to suppose that Menenius is as impartial or as
wise as his famous set-piece, the fable of the belly and the members,
might at first sight suggest. The mutiny of the members, as he describes
it, is apparently without cause:

> There was a time when all the body's members
> Rebell'd against the belly . . .

The members were not complaining of hunger, as are the citizens of
Rome; and the fable, though it is indeed "a pretty tale," will not allevi-
ate social indigestion. And when Menenius ends his story with a well-
turned gibe at one of his audience—"you, the great toe of this assembly"
—we must realize that if (as the Second Citizen says) he is "one that
hath always loved the people," then the sickness of Rome is too deep-
seated to be "fobbed off" with urbanity and wit.

The attitude of somewhat sophisticated contempt which the patricians
commonly display towards the plebeians in the play—it is of course
much more pronounced in Coriolanus than in Menenius—is not likely to
operate favourably towards the creation of a great tragic hero. Whatever one's politics, the scene in which Coriolanus shows himself in the
market-place, dressed in "a gown of humility," is distasteful. It is bad
enough when Menenius rehearses him, and he visualizes himself as
saying,

Reprinted by permission of Secker & Warburg, Basil Blackwell, and the author. This essay was
first published by Basil Blackwell in *Essays in Criticism*, IV (1954), 1–19, then revised and
incorporated in *The Apothecary's Shop*, published by Secker & Warburg in 1957, pp. 32–53.

> Look sir, my wounds!
> I got them in my country's service, when
> Some certain of your brethren roar'd and ran
> From the noise of our own drums . . .

In addition to the patrician's dislike for this vulgar formality and his very self-conscious attitude towards his standing as military hero, this outburst indicates a notable lack of human understanding and compassion. (And the first, at least, of these qualities would seem appropriate to a candidate for consulship.) But what actually happens is worse; and we are hard put to it to laugh at Coriolanus's witty ironies:

> CORIOLANUS: You know the cause, sir, of my standing here.
> THIRD CITIZEN: We do, sir; tell us what hath brought you to't.
> CORIO.: Mine own desert.
> SECOND CIT.: Your own desert!
> CORIO.: Ay, but not mine own desire.
> THIRD CIT.: How! not your own desire!
> CORIO.: No, sir; 'twas never my desire yet to trouble the poor with begging.
> THIRD CIT.: You must think, if we give you any thing, we hope to gain by you.
> CORIO.: Well, then, I pray, your price o' the consulship?
> FIRST CIT.: The price is, to ask it kindly.

The First Citizen has certainly scored a point there; and with a quite patrician urbanity. At the end of this painful, exquisitely made scene, our sympathies are more with the deluded citizens than with the proud, tormented candidate—and to such an extent that we feel relieved when the tribunes (utter scoundrels though they are)[1] direct the attention of their followers to what has really happened.

But if this were the whole story we should not be discussing the status of *Coriolanus* in the body of tragic drama which includes *King Lear* and *Macbeth*. The commons are obviously gullible, illogical and cowardly; "the beast with many heads" is not something that can stand up against the soldier who enters the gates of Corioles alone, against the national hero who begins his banishment with the denunciation,

---

[1] Professor Kenneth Muir has objected to this description as being "the Patrician view . . . also the orthodox view." He admits that the tribunes are cunning and unscrupulous in their actions, but excuses them on the grounds that "their position and the cause of the people are at stake." Surely, though, if we are to judge Coriolanus by normally decent standards, we cannot very well apply the standards of political expediency to his opponents? In any case, the conversations of the tribunes reveal a plain jealousy of Coriolanus as a man which has nothing to do with their jealous concern for the people's rights. At least, we feel, he is more of a man than they are. We should take into account, too, the fact that they incite the mob (which by now *is* a mob) to jeer the banished Coriolanus out of Rome's gates—which does not seem a useful political manœuvre. And as for their political ideals, "the kitchen malkin pins/Her richest lockram 'bout her reechy neck" is not Coriolanus's way of putting it, but Brutus the tribune's. Professor Muir is correct, though, in saying that Shakespeare "saw both sides more clearly than some of his critics" (*Essays in Criticism*, Vol. IV, No. 3, July 1954).

> You common cry of curs! whose breath I hate
> As reek o' the rotten fens, whose loves I prize
> As the dead carcasses of unburied men
> That do corrupt my air, I banish you . . .

or against the cornered alien who makes that magnificent and magnificently tactless speech in Antium (or, better, in Corioles itself):

> If you have writ your annals true, 'tis there,
> That like an eagle in a dove-cote, I
> Flutter'd your Volscians in Corioles:
> Alone I did it.

But neither is *that* the whole story. Coriolanus in a tight corner is an awe-inspiring spectacle: there, while it lasts, he is really alive: a hero is the thing he is best at being. Even without the exacerbating influence of the tribunes, however, we cannot believe that he would make a suitable consul, for in the play we see no talent, no gift of character, relevant to any position other than that of wartime general. And when he is not actually officiating as that, then he still keeps up the role in his imagination. His outburst after Volumnia's advocacy of an ordinary piece of vote-catching strategy is not simply the indignation of a noble and outraged mind. He is being asked to lend himself to a political compromise when he would rather lead a military *putsch:*

> Away, my disposition, and possess me
> Some harlot's spirit! my throat of war be turn'd,
> Which quired with my drum, into a pipe
> Small as a eunuch, or the virgin voice
> That babies lulls asleep! the smiles of knaves
> Tent in my cheeks, and schoolboys' tears take up
> The glasses of my sight! a beggar's tongue
> Make motion through my lips, and my arm'd knees,
> Who bow'd but in my stirrup, bend like his
> That hath receiv'd an alms!

In the face of his mother's unexpected attack on his susceptibilities, the hero invokes in rapid succession the harlot, eunuch, virgin, knave, schoolboy and beggar, and through these contraries he reaffirms and reinforces his humiliated self-image. This is excellently done, but we may detect an element of cool caricature at the heart of the torrent which prevents us from taking it altogether seriously. The verse of this play has strength and sinewiness, and a keen eye for the spot where its sword is to fall, but its range of tone and feeling is unusually narrow for mature Shakespeare. The commons do have good reason to reject the candidature—"if he would incline to the people, there was never a worthier man"—even though Sicinius and Brutus are bad reasons. And Brutus is not at all unfair when he remarks,

> You speak o' the people
> As if you were a god to punish, not
> A man of their infirmity,

for, as I shall suggest later, Coriolanus's infirmity—though at first sight it seems very different—is closely akin to the infirmity of the people.

While we expect a certain amount of comment by one character on another, the fact remains that this play contains a curiously large number of explicit judgments so made. "Shakespeare treats Marcius himself detachedly, as a judge might, without creative warmth," Harley Granville-Barker says, "both sides of his case are to be heard. . . . Finally, something like justice is done."[2] My own feeling is that, from the point of view of our present concern, justice is finally done too accurately and too coldly.

A little quotation would show that what Granville-Barker says about the treatment of Coriolanus can also be applied to other leading figures in the play. But Coriolanus claims our attention: and the first thing we notice is that the witnesses in this judgment are many—as if Shakespeare felt little confidence in his character's ability to emerge from his own words (he is, indeed, so little introspective) in the way that Macbeth or Othello emerges; as if Coriolanus can only display himself in active battle, and even in ancient Rome there cannot be perpetual war.

The play opens with some brief, forcible comments from the citizens: "he's a very dog to the commonalty," and, we are told, what he has done for his country "he did it to please his mother, and to be partly proud." These comments are backed up by the conversation between the tribunes: "Was ever man so proud as is this Marcius?" And then from the opposite camp comes Volumnia's account of her son's youth and of his military prowess:

> His bloody brow
> With his mail'd hand then wiping, forth he goes,
> Like to a harvest-man that's task'd to mow
> Or all or lose his hire

—a description whose effect is qualified by the unmistakable rant which follows it:

> the breasts of Hecuba,
> When she did suckle Hector, look'd not lovelier
> Than Hector's forehead when it spit forth blood
> At Grecian sword, contemning.

[2] *Prefaces to Shakespeare, Fifth Series: Coriolanus,* 1947.

After this *grandguignolesque* collocation of mother's milk, blood and spittle, we are not surprised that his young son's ugly treatment of a butterfly should be adduced to further the account of Coriolanus's martial fury: "One on's father's moods."

Coriolanus's disappearance behind the closed gates of Corioles draws this premature obituary from Titus Lartius:

> Thou wast a soldier
> Even to Cato's wish, not fierce and terrible
> Only in strokes; but, with thy grim looks and
> The thunder-like percussion of thy sounds,
> Thou mad'st thine enemies shake, as if the world
> Were feverous and did tremble.

But victory is achieved, and then follows the crowning of the hero in the field, his entry into Rome, the jealous but often accurate comments of the tribunes, and the conversation of the officers while laying cushions in the Capitol. Granville-Barker remarks of the latter, "here is—to modernise it somewhat—the permanent official's detached view of the politician, with its somewhat cynically critical discrimination":

> That's a brave fellow; but he's vengeance proud, and loves not the common people,

says the First Officer; indeed,

> he seeks their hate with greater devotion than they can render it him, and leaves nothing undone that may fully discover him their opposite.

Yet, "he's a worthy man," and the Second Officer draws our attention again to the services he has rendered Rome. If this is "cynically critical," then the cynicism pervades the play, for these "permanent officials" with nothing at stake one way or the other are the most reliable witnesses it affords. But "cold" is rather the adjective we should apply to this scene: for it has a coldness about it which is hardly expected in the neighbourhood of a tragic hero.

During the election by the senate, Cominius makes another formal speech in commendation of Coriolanus:

> At sixteen years,
> When Tarquin made a head for Rome, he fought
> Beyond the mark of others . . .

and so forth, until he reaches the present, in this grim picture of Coriolanus in Corioles:

> his sword, death's stamp,
> Where it did mark, it took; from face to foot
> He was a thing of blood, whose every motion

> Was tim'd with dying cries: alone he enter'd
> The mortal gate of the city, which he painted
> With shunless destiny; aidless came off,
> And with a sudden reinforcement struck
> Corioles like a planet.

As comment on the military hero, the passage is ambivalent. "Struck Corioles like a planet" is vital and splendid, but it clashes with—and cannot eradicate—the suggestion of a mechanical Juggernaut conveyed in the earlier image:

> from face to foot
> He was a thing of blood, whose every motion
> Was tim'd with dying cries . . .

and the shocking actuality of the later reference:

> he did
> Run reeking o'er the lives of men, as if
> 'Twere a perpetual spoil.[3]

Coriolanus is far from being a happy, romantic warrior; he is certainly heroic, but his heroism requires a grim theatre, and the widows of Corioles are allowed to have their short say. The military hero is not necessarily the same kind of thing as the tragic hero: if only, we may feel, he could be rather more introspective—in the way that Macbeth is —rather more conscious of the cries of his lawful victims! If only we were persuaded that there is more to him than is reflected in his armour.

Next comes the debate on Coriolanus's behaviour among the citizens, led by Sicinius and Brutus; their change of mind; and the fracas between patricians and plebeians. The latter are put to flight, but one of the former remarks of Coriolanus, "This man hath marr'd his fortune." The rabble reappears and Menenius resumes the debate over his friend's character with them; he begins tactlessly, with a significant assumption:

> Hear me speak:
> As I do know the consul's worthiness,
> So can I name his faults,

and once again Coriolanus's military record is rehearsed. Then, a little later, Volumnia makes her contribution:

> You might have been enough the man you are
> With striving less to be so . . .
>   You are too absolute . . .

---

[3] "He is almost an automaton in fight, a slaying-machine of mechanic excellence" ("The Royal Occupation: An Essay on *Coriolanus*," *The Imperial Theme*, G. Wilson Knight, 1931).

which is echoed immediately afterwards by Brutus:

> He hath been us'd
> Ever to conquer, and to have his worth
> Of contradiction: being once chaf'd, he cannot
> Be rein'd again to temperance; then he speaks
> What's in his heart . . .

After Coriolanus has joined Aufidius in Antium his bearing is described cogently—more convincingly than Volumnia could have done it —by the Third Servant, in a fine piece of dramatic prose:

> Why, he is so made on here within, as if he were son and heir to Mars; set at upper end o' the table; no question asked him by any of the senators, but they stand bald before him. Our general himself makes a mistress of him; sanctifies himself with's hand, and turns up the whites o' the eye to his discourse. . . . He'll go, he says, and sowl the porter of Rome gates by the ears. He will mow all down before him, and leave his passage poll'd.

Coriolanus's pride very soon proves too much for his ally:

> He bears himself more proudlier,
> Even to my person, than I thought he would
> When first I did embrace him; yet his nature
> In that's no changeling . . .

And this is followed by a more sustained character study, quite a formal piece of portraiture:

> First he was
> A noble servant to them, but he could not
> Carry his honours even; whether 'twas pride,
> Which out of daily fortune ever taints
> The happy man; whether defect of judgment,
> To fail in the disposing of those chances
> Which he was lord of; or whether nature,
> Not to be other than one thing, not moving
> From the casque to the cushion, but commanding peace
> Even with the same austerity and garb
> As he controll'd the war; but one of these,
> As he hath spices of them all, not all,
> For I dare so far free him, made him fear'd,
> So hated, and so banish'd . . .

Coriolanus in exile is described from a different viewpoint by Menenius, who is smarting from the failure of his embassy, and out to curdle Sicinius's blood:

> The tartness of his face sours ripe grapes: when he walks, he moves like an engine, and the ground shrinks before his treading: he is able to pierce

a corslet with his eye; talks like a knell, and his hum is a battery. He sits in his state, as a thing made for Alexander. . . .

Another account of him, after he has given in to Volumnia, is obviously coloured, since it comes from Aufidius: "thou boy of tears," "this unholy braggart." Then, having made his valediction (which reminds us of Othello's, though it is more violent, less complex, and less of "a superb *coup de théâtre*"),[4] he is put to death.

Though Coriolanus must be the most talked-about character in Shakespeare, it cannot be said that all this talk evokes for us a rich personality or a creature who is truly human or truly alive, except in a narrow and equivocal sense. For much of it is repetition, and what Sicinius says about his enemy is essentially what Menenius says about his friend, though naturally the tone and the implications are different. And the sum of what is said about him comes to little more than he has told us himself, bluntly and effectively enough, in two scenes—the scene of battle outside Corioles, and the scene of election in the market-place. He is a most successful soldier, and a most unsuccessful politician.

"We are left detached observers of Coriolanus," Granville-Barker says. And one may add that the particular treatment of the central figure which I have noted—its use, so to speak, as a subject for argument among parties who are fundamentally in agreement on the matter—extends to the common people of Rome, though it is there less developed, and less repetitive. The play has certain qualities of an intellectual debate; the metaphor is perhaps a little drastic, but my impression is that the implications which the theme could carry for us, for ordinary humanity, are left tacitly aside—as is the convention in debating—to a degree unparalleled in any comparable work. In this sense, *Coriolanus* is certainly the "purest" of Shakespeare's tragedies; and it would be unjust to ascribe the general public's lack of enthusiasm for it to any subtle peculiarity beyond their reach or experience. Coriolanus is described so heavily from outside that, despite his grandeur in battle and his final defiance of his enemies, the man we actually see and hear is something of a disappointment to us. After all this talk we find it easy to sympathize with him—he is obviously less reprehensible than Macbeth and, equally obviously, more *deserving*—but what we feel for him is a sympathy which exists only in the head: a very conscious sympathy, perhaps not unmixed with a little pitying contempt, which is altogether different from that disturbing "sympathy" we feel towards Macbeth. Coriolanus—the character and the play—can be shaken off too easily; too easily, that is, for great tragedy; the implications do not stick.

The critics have provided various sign-posts to the right reading of

[4] "Diabolic Intellect and the Noble Hero," *The Common Pursuit*, F. R. Leavis, 1952, *q.v.*

the play. Thus John Palmer writes,

> our hero . . . is essentially the splendid oaf who has never come to maturity.
> His vanity in the field, his insolence to persons outside his own particular
> set, his intolerance of anything outside his special code of honour are more
> characteristic of an adolescent than a grown man. It is this, in fact, that
> makes his conduct, which would be intolerable in a responsible adult, so
> far acceptable as to qualify him for the part of a tragic hero.[5]

Surely, if we had to remind ourselves that Lear was an old man (and
old men are apt to do strange things) in order to see him as a tragic
hero, then he simply would not be a tragic hero? Yet Palmer's remark
on "the adolescent" in Coriolanus seems to support what I have suggested: it is a "point" to be made in debate and, such is the low tension of the play as a whole, we are not prohibited from making it ourselves. But even then, having made a conscious effort, do we really
forgive Coriolanus for his vanity, insolence and intolerance, on the
grounds of immaturity? It seems to me that neither forgiveness nor its
opposite is demanded of us by the play; and that we are given to understand, in a quite business-like fashion, that the hero got what was
coming to him. And in that sense it is true that the play is a remarkable
piece of workmanship, though what is exercised is our intellectual
"curiosity" (I borrow the word from Johnson), whereas *Macbeth* and
Lear exercise a good deal more.

I have submitted that the figure of Coriolanus strikes us as thin: in
spite of the documentation, it remains shadowy. The description "military hero," as applied to Coriolanus, is remarkably exclusive. The way
in which it excludes the consul, the statesman, we have seen plainly
enough, and it might prove interesting to glance at what we are offered
in Coriolanus as a private person among other persons. The Coriolanus
whom we meet in North's *Plutarch* is an even simpler figure: on the
one hand his "natural wit," "great heart," "stoutness and temperance"
are listed, but on the other hand, "for lack of education, he was so
choleric and impatient, that he would yield to no living creature: which
made him churlish, uncivil, and altogether unfit for any man's conversation." These are stronger words than we could use of Shakespeare's
hero, though we must note that Plutarch's Coriolanus does display himself in the market-place without any fuss. The corresponding scene in
Shakespeare stresses his hero's self-esteem, his stark consciousness of self,
and his unhuman attitude—an attitude which implies a remarkable self-
complacency—towards his social and military inferiors. We are bound
to think of another captain, who won the love of his men, although he
eventually forfeited some of their respect; and Antony raises the whole

question of Coriolanus's relationship with his immediate circle of friends, and particularly with his wife.

Love appears in this play primarily in the aspect of metaphor—metaphors applied to war and warriors. Thus in the excitement of battle Coriolanus addresses his comrade-general, Cominius,

> O, let me clip ye
> In arms as sound as when I woo'd; in heart
> As merry as when our nuptial day was done,
> And tapers burn'd to bedward,

and the response, appropriate and business-like, is

> Flower of warriors,
> How is't with Titus Lartius?

Similarly, Aufidius receives his banished enemy with an almost bridal welcome:

> Let me twine
> Mine arms about that body, where against
> My grained ash an hundred times hath broke,
> And scarr'd the moon with splinters: here I clip
> The anvil of my sword, and do contest
> As hotly and as nobly with thy love
> As ever in ambitious strength I did
> Contend against thy valour. Know thou first,
> I lov'd the maid I married; never man
> Sigh'd truer breath; but that I see thee here,
> Thou noble thing, more dances my rapt heart
> Than when I first my wedded mistress saw
> Bestride my threshold.

This is confirmed by the Third Servant's report, which I have already quoted: "Our general himself makes a mistress of him; sanctifies himself with's hand, and turns up the white o' the eye to his discourse. . . ." The imagery of love is also invoked by Volumnia:

> If my son were my husband, I should freelier rejoice in that absence wherein he won honour than in the embracements of his bed where he would show most love,

and to the same end—that it may at once yield pride of place to war and the honour that war brings. (This play badly needs a Falstaff!) Under the circumstances it is an unkind cut, and we at once begin to pity Virgilia: "His bloody brow! O Jupiter, no blood." The powerful characters of the play all throw in their weight against life—against the kind of love which Virgilia dares to stand up for, against the common pleasures of living which the citizens themselves point to. Virgilia, we feel, is lost in the household of Coriolanus. "Ah! my dear," he says to her in his tenderest moment, returning victorious from the wars,

> Such eyes the widows in Corioles wear,
> And mothers that lack sons.

But we sympathize with her tears: they are just, for there is something of the widow about her right from the start. The most moving moment of the play, and the most moving line, is generally held to be that in which Coriolanus addresses her, "My gracious silence, hail!" Yet it may be felt that her silence, at this moment, does little to enrich her husband's civilian character; at any rate, it seems a less unambiguous silence than that between Hermione and Leontes at the end of *The Winter's Tale*. "Her husband"—the inappropriateness of the term is suggestive; though the fact that "son" seems so much more to the point needs no labouring: psycho-analytical commentators tell us rather less about the relationship between the hero and his mother than the play makes abundantly clear. It is true that Coriolanus greets Virgilia with tenderness when she comes to plead for Rome:

> Best of my flesh,
> Forgive my tyranny . . .

But in what follows—

> O, a kiss
> Long as my exile, sweet as my revenge!

—we may feel that the exile and the revenge, and the bitterness of his humiliation, loom larger than the kiss . . . and immediately afterwards, with the words "You gods! I prate" (unless we reject Theobald's emendation), he turns to his mother, and the rest of the scene is hers.

It may be held that Coriolanus's friendship with Menenius is all that it can be. That he should rebuff his old friend when he intercedes for Rome is as it must be, of course, and he draws Aufidius's attention to the significance of what he has done:

> This man, Aufidius,
> Was my belov'd in Rome: yet thou behold'st!

Later, however, he says,

> This last old man,
> Whom with a crack'd heart I have sent to Rome,
> Lov'd me above the measure of a father;
> Nay, godded me indeed . . .

And here he stresses, not his own feeling towards Menenius, but Menenius's love (and more, or less, than love) for him. Moreover, as Palmer observes, what he says is not quite accurate: "there is no sign of a cracked heart": for when we next meet Menenius he is busy, with a good deal of relish, putting the fear of God into Sicinius—

> there is no more mercy in him than there is milk in a male tiger; that shall our poor city find: and all this is long of you.

Rome, as we see it in this play, is a hard city. "The present civilization is clearly a hard one," Professor Wilson Knight puts it, "a matter of brick and mortar, metals and stones." Its inhabitants form parties rather than relationships either as individuals or as members of a community, and under no circumstances could the world be well lost for them. Their first question is, "What is in it for us?" And the answer, if it is to satisfy, must be in terms of power, of status or of corn. The voice of Virgilia has no place in the debates which are held there: she must remain a "gracious silence." And in this sense it may certainly be said to be a "political play," for its final impression of aridness and waste might well be considered a warning against the petrifaction of humanity which occurs when people think exclusively in terms of parties and movements and manifestos. Patricians and plebeians: they remain very consciously and very rigidly either one or the other; and this is especially true of Menenius, apparently the intermediary between the two sides.

Perhaps this consideration points to an aspect of the play which is worth a little investigation. Commentators have variously claimed that Shakespeare throws his weight on the side of the patricians against "the beast with many heads"; that the play (when we consider the hero's end and his mother's seeming callousness) is a warning against totalitarian ambitions; and—more cautiously—that a careful balance in sympathy is preserved between the two factions. In every case, an opposition is predicated. The nature of that opposition is clear enough, but I wonder whether sufficient attention has been paid to an essential, deeper identity between the citizens and Coriolanus himself. For it seems to me that, finally, the behaviour of the one underlines, by its similarity, the behaviour of the other. The tragedy is the tragedy of Rome: its sickness is traced to a pronounced lack of self-understanding both in its people and in Coriolanus, the most determined of "the right-hand file."[6]

In each case this weakness—an ignorance of self which makes its victims both dangerous and vulnerable to danger from without—is presented with something of a comic effect. It is obvious enough in the people. First they promise Coriolanus their votes—"God save thee, noble consul!"—and then, with a little prompting, "almost all / Repent in their election." But when the rejected candidate returns at the head of a Volscian army, they exclaim with hurt indignation,

6 "The failure of Coriolanus, contrasted with the triumphant life of Antony, is a failure in sensitivity, a failure in living; and it represents a failure on the part of a whole society" ("Coriolanus," D. A. Traversi, *Scrutiny*, June 1937).

That we did we did for the best; and, though we willingly consented to his banishment, yet it was against our will.

The situation is much the same in Antium, for when Aufidius's servants discover that the "marvellous poor gentleman" whom they have attempted to eject is the famous Roman general, they at once change their tune:

> *Second Servant.* Nay, I knew by his face that there was something in him: he had, sir, a kind of face, methought,—I cannot tell how to term it.
> *First Servant.* He had so; looking as it were,—would I were hanged, but I thought there was more in him than I could think.
> *Second Servant.* So did I, I'll be sworn . . .

The masters only echo, in their deeper voices, the vacillations and contradictions of their men. There is no need to discuss Aufidius's failure to live up to his welcome of Coriolanus, but some examination of the latter's case will be very much to the point. His force and single-minded determination as a soldier in the field cannot blind us to his lack of these qualities elsewhere—where the situation is not so straightforward as the killing of a prescribed enemy. We observe that those whom he addresses as "my friends of noble touch" in Act IV Scene ii have become, when he reveals himself to Aufidius in Scene v, "our dastard nobles, who / Have all forsook me"; and we should pay some attention to that strange speech between these two episodes in which for once he soliloquizes: "O world, thy slippery turns!" Just as sworn friends grow enemies "on a dissension of a doit," he says,

> so, fellest foes
> Whose passions and whose plots have broke their sleep
> To take the one the other, by some chance,
> Some trick not worth an egg, shall grow dear friends
> And interjoin their issues. So with me:
> My birthplace hate I, and my love's upon
> This enemy town.

What seems so strange about this speech is that, coming at the turn of the play, at the very hinge of the tragic action, it should refer us to "some trick not worth an egg." And the possibility that Coriolanus is merely generalizing seems to be precluded by the repeated allusion to broken sleep directly afterwards in Aufidius's speech:

> . . . I have nightly since
> Dreamt of encounters 'twixt thyself and me;
> We have been down together in my sleep,
> Unbuckling helms, fisting each other's throat . . .

No, he is talking about himself—"So with me"—and the implication is that Rome must burn for "some chance, / Some trick not worth an egg."

When we think of Macbeth's utterances at a comparable juncture, or even of Othello's (though he too is a soldier, and "self-knowledge . . . is a virtue which Othello . . . hasn't had much need of"),[7] we feel that Coriolanus is quite determined not to be a tragic hero on their scale.

In case this account should seem unfair, let me refer to three instances where, with an effect of irony, he is made to point clearly to the disastrous unreality of his conception of himself. Firstly when, speaking of Aufidius, he tells Cominius,

> Were half to half the world by the ears, and he
> Upon my party, I'd revolt, to make
> Only my wars with him: he is a lion
> That I am proud to hunt

—he does revolt later, but for exactly the opposite reason. The effect is underlined just before the tribunes enter to announce their followers' change of mind, when Coriolanus enquires after Aufidius:

> At Antium lives he? . . .
> I wish I had a cause to seek him there,
> To oppose his hatred fully.

And then, at the crisis, his ignorance of self (the corollary of his stark, limited self-consciousness) and the absence of any sense of relationship with other people emerge with an almost farcical effect, in close proximity to his last magnificent cry of self-assertion:

> Measureless liar, thou hast made my heart
> Too great for what contains it. Boy! O slave!
> Pardon me, lords, 'tis the first time that ever
> I was forc'd to scold.

The play has been full of scolding: either by Coriolanus or of him.

The "theme" of the play, growing out of the kind of debate which we have followed, seems to me one that is proclaimed in Coriolanus and confirmed in his apparent opposite, the mob: the dangers that are often implied in the word "political"—the dangers of a situation in which each opposing side understands the other (in the way that Coriolanus is right about the plebeians, and the plebeians are right about Coriolanus), but neither side understands itself. The theme is announced and sustained in an admirably workmanlike fashion, and it is provided with copious illustration. Yet the tension remains noticeably lower than in *Othello*, a play which we might otherwise adduce for its similarity of situation. The theme is not pursued to the point at which a truly tragic conflict occurs, for there is no real conflict present in the play other than that of the "adventure story," of sword against sword. The constriction and

[7] "Diabolic Intellect and the Noble Hero," F. R. Leavis.

brutality of the predominant imagery is repeated in the curt, efficient disposal of the hero among the Volscians, while in Rome the "tribes" "unshout the noise that banish'd Marcius."

Yet Professor Wilson Knight speaks in his essay of "the victory of love" as Volumnia prevails over her son: "Love, after all, rules this metallic world." While we are undeniably moved by Coriolanus's outburst,

> O mother, mother!
> What have you done? Behold, the heavens do ope,
> The gods look down, and this unnatural scene
> They laugh at . . .

we may not find ourselves agreeing with Professor Wilson Knight's statement that "Coriolanus now, as never before, enlists our total sympathy." He enlists *more* sympathy than ever before, but we should think of Macbeth as he fights with Macduff in full knowledge of the "juggling fiends"—and of all that crowds behind that moment—before we talk of "total" sympathy. There simply is not enough behind Coriolanus for him to blossom out in the way suggested here. And do we really feel, during the subsequent rejoicing in Rome, that "we are in a new world— the world of *Antony and Cleopatra*"? For such a very new world could not arise out of the brief glimpses we have of the "triumphant fires" lit by senators and citizens alike, nor from the civic welcome which greets the victorious, unfeeling Volumnia. The drums and trumpets sound ironically in our ears: an explosion of relieved feelings on the part of those who for a time feared they would have to pay the price of their own actions. Do we not rather feel that it is a victory less of love than of Volumnia's prestige and of her hardness (a Hecuba who sees no need for "bisson rheum"); that the mother has had what is really the last word, and the debate is soon to come to an end, with yet another balanced comment on its topic?—

> Though in this city he
> Hath widow'd and unchilded many a one,
> Which to this hour bewail the injury,
> Yet he shall have a noble memory.

The effort to do full justice to what the play offers should not, I think, lead to the large claim which, after some acute analysis of selected passages, Mr. Traversi makes for it. "*Coriolanus* is a very great play," he writes, "an artistic success as assured as that of *Macbeth*." Its success is assured—the play is remarkable for its neatness and impetus, for the precision with which it achieves itself, as was demonstrated by the production at Stratford-upon-Avon in 1952—but it is surely a success of an altogether lower order than that of *Macbeth*.